That Type of Girl

That Type of Girl

Notes on Takako Shimura's *Sweet Blue Flowers*

Frank Hecker

Self-published

That Type of Girl: Notes on Takako Shimura's *Sweet Blue Flowers*
Frank Hecker, Ellicott City, MD 21042
Published 2022-03-12, last revised 2022-03-14

ISBN (paperback : KDP): 979-8-9858113-3-9

Cover illustration by Ola Tarakanova.

Contents

Preface

Between 2004 and 2013 the Japanese comic artist Takako Shimura published her manga *Aoi hana* ("Blue Flower[s]") in the (now defunct) magazine *Manga Erotics F. Aoi hana*, a work in the "yuri" genre featuring romantic relationships between girls or women, depicted the high school years of two Japanese teenaged girls, Fumi and Akira, their renewal of a friendship forged in their childhood, Fumi's coming out as a lesbian, her desire to be more than a friend to Akira, and Akira's uncertain and halting response to that desire. *Aoi hana* was collected in a Japanese edition of eight volumes[1] and eventually released in English in a four-volume omnibus edition as *Sweet Blue Flowers*.[2]

As a relatively recent manga fan, I enjoyed reading *Sweet Blue Flowers* and found myself intrigued by it. It seemed to me that Shimura set out to create a work that was not just another simple tale of schoolgirls in love, but that—albeit often messily and imperfectly—was trying to say something about the yuri genre itself and about the Japanese society in which that genre arose and was popularized. This book is my own messy and imperfect attempt to explore what that something might be—or, at least, what I imagine it might be.

In writing these notes, I encountered three significant obstacles. First, I do not know Japanese and must rely on the English version. Any nuances that are "lost in translation" are lost on me.

Second, I am not young, not a woman, not queer, and not Japanese—in other words, I'm about as far away from directly identifying with the characters of this manga and their life experiences as it's possible to be. I write as an outsider, with all the limitations that an outsider has in trying to interpret dialogue, events, and cultural and social contexts.

Finally, as mentioned above, I am a relatively recent reader of manga, and I have no education or experience as a critic of literature in general or manga in particular.

Therefore this book is best thought of as a collection of tentative and personal answers to idiosyncratic questions that came to me based on my limited perspective. I welcome comments and corrections that might improve my understanding and possible future editions of this book. (See the colophon for details.)

The plan of the book

In case anyone reading this book is at the same time reading through the four volumes of *Sweet Blue Flowers*, I've divided the book as follows:

The initial chapters contain minimal spoilers and are intended as background reading for the series. The chapters in the following four sections discuss the events of each volume and (with minor exceptions) contain spoilers for the series only through the end of that volume. Finally, the concluding chapters contain my final thoughts on the yuri genre and the place of *Sweet Blue Flowers* within it.

I have also included other material that may be of interest, including an index of characters, errata for the VIZ Media edition, a summary of previously-published reviews, and suggestions for further reading.

I discuss the official English release of *Sweet Blue Flowers* as published by VIZ Media in print and e-book form; all page references are to that edition. I do not discuss the anime adaptation except to compare it with the manga. When I do so, I assume that readers have seen all eleven episodes of the anime. There were also two previous authorized English e-book releases of volume 1 of the Japanese edition, one of which I discuss briefly concerning translation choices. Occasionally I go back to the Japanese edition to puzzle out the exact terms that Shimura used.

In discussing the characters, I follow the conventions used in the VIZ English release: Western order for given name and family name (Akira Okudaira, not Okudaira Akira) and simplified romanization (Manjome, not Manjoume or Manjōme). I follow Wikipedia's conventions for Japanese names and terms outside the context of *Sweet Blue Flowers*.

I've included notes and a bibliography for those wishing to further explore works that I cite. However, in general I have not included citations for works available only in Japanese or for information that can be easily found in Wikipedia or similar online sources.

Finally, some parts of *Sweet Blue Flowers* touch on issues meriting a content note. I have included such notes when I discuss those issues.

Resources and inspirations

At this point most authors would acknowledge the contributions of those who helped them in the writing of their books. However, this book is a solo effort that I created as a private spare-time project. I can thus say more truly than most that any faults in it are mine and mine alone.

But although I cannot include a conventional list of acknowledgments, I would be remiss in not mentioning those without whom this book would not exist or would be a more amateurish affair than it already is.

First and foremost, I owe thanks to Takako Shimura, without whom there would be no *Aoi hana* or *Sweet Blue Flowers* for the world to read and for me to write about. Thanks also go to the team at VIZ Media who brought *Aoi hana* to us in English in complete and definitive form as *Sweet Blue Flowers*: translator John Werry, editor Pancha Diaz, Monalisa De Asis, who did touch-up art and lettering, and Yukiko Whitley, who did the design.

To try to remedy my complete lack of knowledge about gender and sexuality in the context of Japanese history, culture, and society, and how these are reflected in manga, anime, and other works, I took advantage of the extensive academic literature produced by scholars in these fields. Those whose books, papers, and other works I found particularly useful include (in alphabetical order) Sharon Chalmers, Hiromi Tsuchiya Dollase, Sarah Frederick, Mark McLelland, Verena Maser, Gregory Pflugfelder, Jennifer Robertson, Deborah Shamoon, Michiko Suzuki, and James Welker.

In writing at length about *Sweet Blue Flowers* I am following in the footsteps of the many Western fans writing online about manga and anime, especially those who review and critically analyze works in depth. I particularly single out those whose work I read early in my time as a manga and anime fan, and continue to read with pleasure today: the writers and editors of the Anime Feminist website ("Japanese pop culture through a feminist lens"),[3] and Erica Friedman, creator and editor of the *Okazu* blog and Yuricon website covering and promoting all things yuri.[4]

Finally, in writing down my idiosyncratic views regarding *Sweet Blue Flowers* I took inspiration from Adam Mars-Jones and his book *Noriko Smiling*.[5] Mars-Jones set himself against previous Western interpreters of the films of Yasujirō Ozu and proposed a different take on Ozu's film *Late Spring*, analyzing its story of a woman in postwar Japan who did not want to get married and speculating freely as to why she might have felt that way. Whether his conclusions are objectively "correct" or not, I can't help but admire his ambition and approach.

Takako Shimura is not as great an artist as Ozu, and I am not as good a writer as Mars-Jones. Nonetheless, I've tried to do something similar in this book, speculating at length about what to my mind Shimura might be saying in her own story of two twenty-first-century Japanese schoolgirls.

1. Takako Shimura, *Aoi hana*, 8 vols. (Tokyo: Ohta Books, 2006–13).
2. Takako Shimura, *Sweet Blue Flowers*, trans. John Werry, 4 vols. (San Francisco: VIZ Media, 2017–18). Unless otherwise noted, all citations to *Sweet Blue Flowers* are to this edition, hereafter cited in the text as *SBF*.
3. "About Us," Anime Feminist, https://www.animefeminist.com/about.
4. Erica Friedman, ed., *Okazu* (blog), http://okazu.yuricon.com.
5. Adam Mars-Jones, *Noriko Smiling* (London: Notting Hill Editions, 2011).

Before Reading

Introduction

I begin my consideration of *Sweet Blue Flowers* by looking at its author, her manga in general, and what I consider to be the main themes of *Sweet Blue Flowers* in particular.

Very little has been published about Takako Shimura in English. Her English Wikipedia entry has a scant seven sentences apart from the listing of her works. The Japanese Wikipedia entry is a bit longer but does not appear to have much more information about Shimura herself.

According to Wikipedia, Shimura was born on October 23, 1973, in Kanagawa prefecture. I could find no indication of where exactly in the prefecture Shimura was born. However, Kanagawa prefecture includes both the port of Yokohama and the popular tourist destination Kamakura, in which *Sweet Blue Flowers* is set.

Shimura's first published work under that name was in February 1997, when she was twenty-three years old. Since then, she has published about two dozen works, depending on how you count them; some of these were one-shots, while others were serialized comics later published in book form.

Relatively few of Shimura's works are available in licensed English translations. Of her works listed on Wikipedia, only four have had official releases in English at the time of writing: *Sweet Blue Flowers* (*Aoi hana*), *Happy-Go-Lucky Days*[1] (*Dōnika naru hibi*), *Wandering Son*[2] (*Hōrō musuko*), and her more recent effort, *Even Though We're Adults* (*Otona ni natte mo*).[3]

Of the three earlier works previously published, only *Sweet Blue Flowers* is still readily available in complete form. Even that occurred after multiple false starts: volume 1 of *Aoi hana* was translated into English and published as *Sweet Blue Flowers* by JManga and then by Digital Manga,[4] but neither publisher released any further volumes. The manga was also adapted into an anime series of eleven episodes, subsequently released in a subtitled English version.[5] (Plans for a second season were abandoned, apparently due to poor sales of the anime's DVDs in Japan.)

Happy-Go-Lucky Days was published complete in two volumes (digital only), but is no longer available for sale in the US. However, an anime film featuring selected stories from the manga was released in 2020, including a version with English subtitles.[6]

Publication of *Wandering Son*, Shimura's most well-known work, was halted after the release of eight hardcover volumes (of a total of fifteen). It is now out of print and is not available in digital format. It, too, received an incomplete anime adaptation, subsequently released with English subtitles for online streaming in the US and other countries.[7]

At least two long interviews of Shimura have been published but both remain untranslated into English. The afterwords in the various volumes of *Sweet Blue Flowers* and *Wandering Son* contain Shimura's comments on various aspects of her life. However, these are mostly trivial and don't shed much light on how she approaches her work in terms of favorite themes, opinions on social and cultural issues, and so on.[8]

To know more about Shimura as an artist, we need to therefore look at the works themselves, starting with where they were published.

Many of Shimura's manga, including *Wandering Son*, were serialized in *Comic Beam* magazine. Both *Happy-Go-Lucky Days* and (as previously noted) *Sweet Blue Flowers* were serialized in *Manga Erotics F* magazine. Both of these magazines are (or were, in the case of *Manga Erotics F*) part of what's been referred to as a "fifth column" of Japanese manga magazines: existing outside of the four main demographic-based categories of magazines (for boys, girls, men, and women) and featuring a wide variety of stories in various genres.[9]

Thus the first thing we can discern about Shimura is that although her manga, like *Sweet Blue Flowers*, may feature children from elementary to high school age, for the most part they were written for an all-genders adult audience, with all that implies in terms of both content (including sexual content) and the knowledge that she assumes on the part of her readers.

As far as I can tell, most if not all of Shimura's manga are set in contemporary Japan: no historical fiction, and no fantasies set in other worlds—although supernatural elements are sometimes present, as in some of the stories in *Happy-Go-Lucky Days*. Shimura is also known for her focus on issues of sex and gender, and in particular for her stories

about LGBTQ characters, including the transgender youth of *Wandering Son* and the lesbians of *Sweet Blue Flowers*. These are also set in present-day Japan and offer commentary (albeit often indirect) on contemporary Japanese society.

Keeping the above in mind, here are my tentative thoughts as to what *Sweet Blue Flowers* is about:

First, *Sweet Blue Flowers* pays homage to past works in Japanese dealing with romance between girls or women, including in particular the early twentieth-century "Class S" genre set in all-girls schools. Shimura assumes that readers are familiar with the tropes of this genre and makes mention of and alludes to the most well-known Class S author, Nobuko Yoshiya, and her most famous work, the *Hana monogatari* (*Flower Tales*) series of short stories (*SBF*, 1:6, 1:190).[10]

I believe that *Sweet Blue Flowers* is at the same time a consciously-intended critique of the Class S genre and (by implication) subsequent works in the genre that came to be known as "yuri." This critique is directed not only at particular yuri tropes, such as the "girl prince," but also at the assumptions embedded in many if not most yuri works, including in particular the idea of relationships between women structured according to a hierarchy of age and status.

In contrast, I see *Sweet Blue Flowers* as highlighting relationships between women who are equal to each other and meet each other as individuals, relationships that are (by implication) opposed to and (to the extent possible) exist outside of the hierarchically-structured patriarchal society of Japan. Although the manga does not fully engage with what such an opposition and existence would entail in practice, it is far more grounded in reality than yuri works that posit a "yuritopia" in which men do not exist.

The themes of *Sweet Blue Flowers* are embodied in its two main characters, Fumi Manjome and Akira Okudaira, and in their friend, Kyoko Ikumi, whose presence in the story is so large as to almost make her a third main character. The three girls together can be thought of as representing three different "eras" of yuri: Kyoko the Class S past of ephemeral relationships between schoolgirls ultimately destined for arranged marriages, Akira the "pure yuri" present of sexual innocence and shy and tentative romance, and Fumi the LGBTQ future of women who come to self-consciously identify as lesbians.

I believe that Takako Shimura would have expected her adult audience to bring to their reading of *Sweet Blue Flowers* at least a general familiarity with the history of the Class S and yuri genres and with key works in those genres. The following chapters discuss various aspects of that history that I think are useful for a deeper understanding of *Sweet Blue Flowers* and its place in the yuri genre.

1. Takako Shimura, *Happy-Go-Lucky Days*, trans. RReese, 2 vols. (Gardena, CA: Digital Manga Guild, 2013). Kindle.
2. Takako Shimura, *Wandering Son*, trans. Rachel Thorn, 8 vols. (Seattle: Fantagraphics Books, 2011–).
3. Takako Shimura, *Even Though We're Adults*, trans. Jocelyne Allen, 3 vols. (Los Angeles: Seven Seas Entertainment, 2021–).
4. Takako Shimura, *Sweet Blue Flowers*, trans. Jeffrey Steven LeCroy, vol. 1 (Gardena, CA: Digital Manga, 2014), Kindle.
5. *Sweet Blue Flowers*, directed by Kenichi Kasai (2009; Grimes, IA: Lucky Penny Entertainment, 2013), DVD.
6. *Happy-Go-Lucky Days*, directed by Takuya Satō (2020; Houston: Sentai Filmworks, 2021), 55 min., Blu-ray Disc, 1080p HD.
7. *Wandering Son*, directed by Ei Aoki (Aniplex, 2011), https://www.crunchyroll.com /hourou-musuko-wandering-son.
8. However, as a fan of the film director Yasujirō Ozu I was amused to learn that Shimura was once so entranced by an old television drama featuring Chishū Ryū, who portrayed older men in many of Ozu's most famous films, that she bought a book of photographs of Ryū, titled *Grandpa*. Shimura, *Wandering Son*, 5:222.
9. Erica Friedman, "Overthinking Things 03/02/2011," *The Hooded Utilitarian* (blog), March 2, 2011, https://www.hoodedutilitarian.com/2011/03/overthinking-things-03022011.
10. Nobuko Yoshiya, *Hana monogatari*, 2 vols. (Tokyo: Kawade Shobō Shinsha, 2009). With the exception of one story ("Yellow Rose"), the *Hana monogatari* series is not available in an official English translation.

Class S in Context

As previously noted, *Sweet Blue Flowers* is generally considered to fall within the genre of "yuri," that is, manga, anime, and related works with lesbian themes and content. Before yuri as we know it today were Class S works, an early twentieth-century literary genre featuring intense emotional relationships between adolescent girls—"passionate friendships," to use Deborah Shamoon's phrase.[1]

Sweet Blue Flowers harks back to these earlier works, paying homage to, interrogating, and sometimes parodying their tropes. If we wish to understand the manga better, it helps to take a closer look at Class S relationships and literature and their genesis in the late Meiji and early Taishō eras (roughly 1900–20).

Erica Friedman has referred to yuri works as "lesbian content without lesbian identity."[2] However, in the case of Class S works there are conflicting views on whether the content itself is even lesbian in nature, especially in the context of the time and how S relationships were treated by the girls who participated in them and by society at large.[3]

This is a controversy I leave to be debated by those more knowledgeable than I.[4] Instead, I turn my attention to a different question, namely the social circumstances by which there came to be a Class S genre in the first place. Other people have investigated this topic in depth; besides Deborah Shamoon, see, for example, the work of Hiromi Tsuchiya Dollase,[5] Gregory Pflugfelder,[6] and Michiko Suzuki.[7]

In this chapter, I focus on four aspects of Class S relevant to *Sweet Blue Flowers*, beginning with the origin of the all-girls schools that became a staple of Class S and (later) yuri works. These schools appear in *Sweet Blue Flowers* in the form of Matsuoka Girls' High School (Fumi's school) and (especially) Fujigaya Women's Academy (which Akira attends).

After the restoration of imperial rule in 1868 that marked the beginning of the Meiji era, the leaders of the Japanese government began a frantic effort to modernize Japan. A critical element of that modernization was mass education, seen as the key to the success of the Western powers in creating industrialized societies rich and powerful enough to dominate the world, including Japan.

Thus as early as 1872 the government attempted to set out a national plan to create a new Japanese education system. Its goal was that "education ... shall be so diffused that there may not be a village with an ignorant family, nor a family with an ignorant member." Such an education was not to exclude women: "Learning ... is to be equally the inheritance of nobles and gentry, farmers and artisans, males and females." By the end of the 1870s almost a quarter of girls eligible for elementary school were attending school, compared to over half of eligible boys.[8]

This period also saw the establishment in Japan of "mission schools" (founded and run by Christian missionaries) that offered education through high school—especially important for girls since state-sponsored schools did not provide them any education past elementary school. In 1872, Catholic nuns established the first school for girls (and perhaps one of the inspirations for Fujigaya Women's Academy) in Yokohama, less than twenty kilometers northwest of Kamakura, in which *Sweet Blue Flowers* is set.[9]

The mission schools proved very popular with Japan's emerging upper-middle class and could command fees for tuition and board as high as sixty dollars a year.[10] For comparison, a contemporary American visitor to Japan found that "three or four dollars will cover the cost of food for a month for one person, and women servants expect only a few dollars in wages for that time."[11] Sending a girl to a mission school was thus about as expensive as feeding her or paying the salary of a family servant—no wonder it was seen as a luxury affordable mainly by affluent households.

In part because of the cost, the total number of girls educated in mission schools was relatively low. As of 1909, the total number of Japanese girls in Catholic mission schools was not quite six thousand, in twenty-six schools.[12] The number of girls in other Christian mission schools was even smaller: as of 1914, about four thousand high school girls in total, spread across fifty schools.[13]

Although the mission schools originally had a monopoly on girls' education beyond elementary school, this was no longer true by the end of the Meiji era. In 1899 the Japanese government passed a new order extending girls' education beyond the previously mandated six years of elementary school. This led to a rapid increase in the number of girls in high school, from less than ten thousand at the turn of the century to almost fifty-six thousand in 1910, including girls in mission schools and other private schools.[14] By 1920 there were over one hundred twenty-five thousand women in higher girls' schools.[15]

The number of girls graduating from high school remained a relatively small fraction of the overall population, around five percent of all girls near the turn of the century, rising only to twenty-five percent by the end of World War II. Nevertheless, they formed a large enough group to evolve a distinct culture of their own, a culture that reflected their middle- and upper-class background and predominantly urban environment. As an elite group within what was already a relatively elite population, the mission school girls, in particular, helped popularize Western notions of individuality and romantic love, Christian ideals of spiritual love, and the use of Christian symbols such as the white lily.[16]

This brings me to the second topic I want to discuss, one that is also relevant to *Sweet Blue Flowers*, namely marriage customs in general and arranged marriages in particular. In the Taishō era, four out of five marriages were arranged; in two out of five marriages, the couple had never even met before their wedding. Only three percent of marriages were considered to be "love marriages."[17]

This contrast between Western and Christian ideals absorbed in school and traditional Japanese marriage arrangements was bound to be a source of conflict, as vividly described by Alice Mabel Bacon, an American observer writing in 1891:

> Another difficulty, in fitting the new school system into the customs of the people, lies in the early age at which marriages are contracted. Before the girl has finished her school course, her parents begin to wonder whether there is not danger of her being left on their hands altogether, if they do not hand her over to the first eligible young man who presents himself. Sometimes the girl makes a brave fight, and remains in school until her course is finished; more often she

succumbs and is married off, bids a weeping farewell to her teachers and schoolmates, and leaves the school, to become a wife at sixteen, a mother at eighteen, and an old woman at thirty.[18]

To me this offers a key to the prevalence of Class S relationships and the literature that popularized them: as Yukari Fujimoto claims, it's possible that such relationships were attractive to girls in large part because they were relationships in which they could exercise almost entirely free choice in selecting their partners—perhaps the only opportunity in their lives to do so.[19] (Where girls were free to exercise choice in their marriage partners to some extent, this presumably amounted only to being allowed to reject some candidates out of those presented to them by their family.)

This may explain the importance in both Class S relationships and literature of courtship rituals by which one girl approaches another girl as a potential partner and the other girl decides whether to accept her affections, for example, as portrayed in the 1937 novel *Otome no minato* (*The Girls' Harbor*).[20] These rituals most notably include letters sent by one girl to another to propose an S relationship and an exchange of gifts to signify their entering into the relationship.

Unlike gifts like dowry and bride price in traditional marriage customs, which are predominantly exchanges between families, here gifts are exchanged between the girls themselves acting as free individuals. And while the practice of sending letters to prospective partners has deep roots in Japanese culture, here such letters are sent by girls to girls, taking the role that in traditional works like *The Tale of Genji* was performed by men.

The agency girls showed in pursuing their own choice of partners in an S relationship is mirrored in the agency they showed in writing their own stories about such relationships, a third aspect of Class S culture and literature relevant to *Sweet Blue Flowers*.

As noted above, in the early twentieth century, girls attending high school were predominantly from the middle and upper class. Their relative affluence combined with a high degree of literacy made them an attractive market for literary works targeted at the emerging demographic of adolescent girls (*shōjo*). These included foreign works translated and localized for a Japanese audience, most notably Louisa May Alcott's *Little Women*.[21]

However the more significant development was the establishment and growth of home-grown Japanese magazines featuring stories and articles of interest to girls. These magazines were edited by men and featured articles written by men, especially those of a didactic nature that sought to promote the ideal of girls' education as preparation for marriage and motherhood. However, they also become forums to which girls themselves contributed, in the form of both readers' comments and submitted stories, and training grounds for women writers.[22]

Finally, let me return to the question with which I started, namely the extent to which Class S relationships could be considered lesbian in nature. Whatever position one might take on this matter in general, there can be no question that some of the girls in these relationships were, in fact, lesbians by any reasonable definition, whether they explicitly identified themselves as such or not (another point we'll see echoed in *Sweet Blue Flowers*). As I discuss in the next chapter, one of those lesbians became the most famous author of Class S stories.

1. Deborah Shamoon, *Passionate Friendship: The Aesthetics of Girl's Culture in Japan* (Honolulu HI: University of Hawai'i Press, 2012).

2. Erica Friedman, "Is Yuri Queer?," Anime Feminist, June 7, 2019, https://www .animefeminist.com/feature-is-yuri-queer.

3. See, for example, Deborah Shamoon's claim that "terms like 'lesbian,' 'homosexual,' or *dōseiai* [same-sex love] are fraught with political, social, and clinical meanings that do not reflect how the girls themselves talked about their relationships." Shamoon, *Passionate Friendship*, 35.

4. See, for example, Sarah Frederick's and Erica Friedman's separate responses to Shamoon. Sarah Frederick, review of *Passionate Friendship: The Aesthetics of Girls' Culture in Japan*, by Deborah Shamoon, *Mechademia*, October 7, 2013, https://www.mechademia.net/2013/10 /07/book-review-passionate-friendship. Erica Friedman, review of *Passionate Friendship: The Aesthetics of Girls' Culture in Japan*, by Deborah Shamoon, *Okazu* (blog), February 6, 2014, http://okazu.yuricon.com/2014/02/06/passionate-friendship-the-aesthetics-of -girls-culture-in-japan.

5. Hiromi Tsuchiya Dollase, *Age of Shōjo: The Emergence, Evolution, and Power of Japanese Girls' Magazine Fiction* (Albany: SUNY Press, 2019).

6. Gregory M. Pflugfelder, "'S' Is for Sister: School Girl Intimacy and 'Same-Sex Love' in Early Twentieth-Century Japan," in *Gendering Modern Japanese History*, ed. Barbara

Monoly and Kathleen Uno, 133–90 (Cambridge, MA: Harvard University Asia Center, 2005), https://doi.org/10.1163/9781684174171_006.

7. Michiko Suzuki, *Becoming Modern Women: Love and Female Identity in Prewar Japanese Literature and Culture* (Palo Alto: Stanford University Press, 2009).

8. Benjamin Duke, *The History of Japanese Education: Constructing the National School System, 1872–1890* (New Brunswick NJ: Rutgers University Press, 2009), 71–76, 73, 281.

9. Joseph L. Van Hecken, *The Catholic Church in Japan Since 1859*, trans. John Van Hoydonck (Tokyo: Herder Agency, 1960), 156–57, https://archive.org/details/catholicchurchin0000 heck. This school still exists, as the Saint Maur International School, although it is now coeducational.

10. Margaret E. Burton, *The Education of Women in Japan* (New York: Fleming H. Revell, 1914), 56–58, https://archive.org/details/educationwomenja00burtuoft.

11. Alice Mabel Bacon, *Japanese Girls and Women*, rev. ed. (Boston: Houghton Mifflin, 1919), 311, https://archive.org/details/japanesegirlswom00baco_2.

12. Van Hecken, *Catholic Church in Japan*, 181.

13. Burton, *Education of Women*, 254–55.

14. Jason G. Karlin, *Gender and Nation in Meiji Japan: Modernity, Loss, and the Doing of History* (Honolulu: University of Hawai'i Press, 2014), chap. 4 n49, EPUB, https://www.academia .edu/42197271/Gender_and_Nation_in_Meiji_Japan_Modernity_Loss_and_the_Doing_of _History.

15. Suzuki, *Becoming Modern Women*, 170n31.

16. Shamoon, *Passionate Friendship*, 30–33.

17. Suzuki, *Becoming Modern Women*, 67–68.

18. Bacon, *Japanese Girls and Women*, 55.

19. Yukari Fujimoto, "Where Is My Place in the World? Early Shōjo Manga Portrayals of Lesbianism," trans. Lucy Frazier, *Mechademia* 9 (2014), 26, https://doi.org/10.5749/mech .9.2014.0025. However, I take issue with Fujimoto's description of Class S relationships as a "fantasy of love between girls," a characterization that could be interpreted as trivializing the reality of these relationships and what they might have meant to the girls themselves.

20. Shamoon, *Passionate Friendship*, 38–45. At the time, *Otome no minato* was credited to the Japanese modernist writer (and future Nobel Prize for Literature winner) Yasunari Kawabata, but in fact it was written by Kawabata's female disciple Tsuneko Nakazato. Deborah Shamoon, "Class S: Appropriation of 'Lesbian' Subculture in Modern Japanese Literature and New Wave Cinema," *Cultural Studies* 35, no. 1, 32–34 https://doi.org/10 .1080/09502386.2020.1844259.

21. Dollase, *Age of Shōjo*, chap. 1.

22. Dollase, *Age of Shōjo*, 19–30; Shamoon, *Passionate Friendship*, 48–57.

Homage to Yoshiya

In the introduction, I noted that *Sweet Blue Flowers* builds and comments on previous works in the yuri genre. That begins even before the start of the story proper: chapter 1 is titled "Flower Story" in homage to *Hana monogatari* (*Flower Tales*), a series of Class S fictions written in the early twentieth century by author Nobuko Yoshiya (*SBF*, 1:4).

There are at least four keys to understanding Yoshiya's life and work: she was a lesbian living in the patriarchal society of early twentieth-century Japan, a literary prodigy, a child of relative privilege and affluence, and the sole sister to three brothers.[1]

Her family belonged to the middle class (her father was the police chief of a provincial city), so Yoshiya escaped being sent by her family to work in a factory or brothel, the fate of many a girl in Meiji-era Japan. Instead, she was able to attend school, where her literary gifts were recognized by her teachers early on. Despite her showing promise as a writer, she felt neglected by her mother, who held very traditional views on men's and women's roles and showed favoritism towards her brothers. After graduating from high school, she was able to leave her home at the age of nineteen and move to Tokyo to live in relative independence.[2]

As a lesbian Yoshiya was better equipped than most to spin compelling tales of girls in Class S relationships, although the nature of Japanese society in the early twentieth century placed certain limits on the forms those tales could take, and the strategies she could pursue as an author and as a woman who loved women. On the one hand, the emerging magazines for girls popularized the idea of same-sex relationships of affection within all-girls schools, influenced by Western and Christian notions of romantic love and individualism. Yoshiya was at the heart of this trend.

At the same time Christian morality and the scientific aura around writings by Western sexologists promoted a view of same-sex relationships as "diseased" or "abnormal" if taken beyond certain bounds—thus, for example, the public scandal over the 1911 double suicide of two twenty-year-old women who were former schoolmates.[3]

Such incidents were not uncommon for the time, and sensational stories about them were a perennial feature in the popular press during the period in which Yoshiya achieved fame and financial success as a writer. Given that a persistent theme of these stories was the potential danger of schoolgirl romances, exactly the sort of topics Yoshiya was writing about, Yoshiya was forced to navigate these issues in her art and her other writings, and in her own life. In doing this, she can be seen as following three different strategies, depending on the time and situation.

First, in *Hana monogatari* Yoshiya depicted schoolgirl romances (or similar relationships between students and teachers) as inherently limited in time and place, fated to bloom for a season and then to wither and die under the harsh blasts of Japanese social norms, as the girls entered adulthood and the responsibilities of marriage. The alternative was, if not unthinkable, at least unspeakable.

For example, in "Yellow Rose" the teacher who spoke of the life and loves of Sappho to her student companion finds herself powerless to argue against the girl's parents' plans for an arranged marriage, and instead instantly agrees to help persuade her into it: "She had a whole array of arguments why it was not a good idea for parents to decide whom their children married. But now, standing before these particular parents, none of those arguments seemed the least convincing."[4]

Yoshiya also took pains in her nonfiction writing to reassure the Japanese public that schoolgirl relationships were proper and even beneficial for the students involved, drawing on the work of the English socialist Edward Carpenter to lend support to her argument.[5]

Carpenter had in turn been influenced by the English poet and literary critic John Addington Symonds. In the tradition of many Western writers since the Renaissance, Symonds sought in the classical world an alternative to Christian morality, privately publishing in 1883 the innocuously titled *A Problem in Greek Ethics*.[6] Symonds claimed that the "boy love" of classical Greece—"a passionate and enthusiastic attachment subsisting between man and youth, recognised by society and protected by opinion"—at its best embodied a noble ideal of masculine friendship: "The lover taught, the [beloved] learned; and so from man to man was handed down the tradition of heroism."[7]

Carpenter maintained a correspondence with Symonds and was sent a copy of *A Problem in Greek Ethics* in 1892 or 1893[8]. He applied a similar model to contemporary British society and in particular to education in his essay "Affection in Education," written in the 1890s, first published in 1899, and later included in his book *The Intermediate Sex*.[9] Carpenter decried "the confusion in the public mind ... which so often persists in setting down any attachment between two boys, or between a boy and his teacher, to nothing but sensuality": "Who so fit ([teachers] sometimes feel) to enlighten a young boy and guide his growing mind as one of themselves, when the bond of attachment exists between the two?"[10]

The primary focus of both Symonds and Carpenter was on male homosexuality, with relationships between women either ignored or implied to be inferior to those between men. When turning his attention to schoolgirl relationships, Carpenter wrote that "they are for the most part friendships of a weak and sentimental turn, and not very healthy either in themselves or in the habits they lead to."[11]

Thus after the translation of *The Intermediate Sex* into Japanese (in 1914 and again in 1919) it was "quite surprising and unexpected that in Japan this work was used to defend schoolgirl same-sex intimacy." In two essays published in 1921 and 1923 respectively, Nobuko Yoshiya "ignored Carpenter's negative presentation of female-female intimacy and instead adopted his positive arguments for male-male attachments" to justify relationships between an older girl and a younger one, or between a teacher and one of her students.[12]

However, Yoshiya was not content with simply portraying intimacy between women according to the template set by *Hana monogatari*, and essayed a second strategy to address this topic. During the same period that Yoshiya was publishing the stories of *Hana monogatari* in girls' magazines she also published what Erica Friedman has called "the source material for much of what we consider to be 'Yuri,'" the novel *Yaneura no nishojo* (*Two Virgins in the Attic*).[13]

Although it also features a relationship between young women, *Yaneura no nishojo* has some significant differences from the stories of *Hana monogatari*. First, it is a novel (Yoshiya's first), not a short story.

15

Yoshiya apparently wrote it as a personal work rather than a commercial endeavor, an outlet for topics and themes that she wanted to write about but could not in girls' magazines. Like many first novels, it is semi-autobiographical, based on her time attending a teacher's school after graduating from high school.

The most important setting in the novel (the "attic" of the title) is not a girls' school but a women's dormitory run by the "Young Women's Association," a thinly-veiled reference to the Young Women's Christian Association of Japan.[14] Although it was originally founded in 1905 as one element in the many overseas Christian missionary initiatives, the YWCA of Japan had less emphasis on evangelism and more on outreach to middle-class women, especially those in postsecondary education. One of the principal activities of the Tokyo YWCA was to establish hostels to house the young women who were coming to Tokyo to attend school, with the first two hostels opening in 1908 and admitting both Christian and non-Christian residents.[15]

Yoshiya stayed in one of these hostels (or another one built subsequently) while studying to become a kindergarten teacher and it became the model for the dormitory in *Yaneura no nishojo*. She further distanced the setting from a Christian one by dropping the "C" from YWCA, and having the two main characters (Akiko and Akitsu) reject Christianity. Michiko Suzuki suggests that *Yaneura no nishojo* sets same-sex love in direct opposition to this religion: "Akiko must overcome Christian teachings and its practice in the dormitory in order to acknowledge her true self."[16] If so, this is reminiscent of Symonds's and Carpenter's attempts to do an end run around the Christian proscription of homosexuality and justify its practice in terms of an alternative morality.[17]

The pairing in *Yaneura no nishojo* is also reminiscent of Carpenter's writing promoting relationships between younger boys and older boys or men, and Yoshiya's own gloss on that work. In real life Yoshiya was already an adult when she moved into the YWCA dorm and began a relationship with Yukie Kikuchi. However, Akiko, the character in *Yaneura no nishojo* modeled on herself, is depicted as being of indeterminate age and relatively childish compared to Akitsu, the character modeled on

Kikuchi: "an immature character, constantly in tears, melancholic, and nostalgic for the past. ... [Akiko] is the classic figure of the younger girl who adores her older lover from afar."[18]

The comparison with earlier stories only goes so far: unlike the characters in *Hana monogatari*, Akiko and Akitsu continue their relationship past the end of the story, with at least the possibility raised that they will share their life from then on.[19] Yoshiya herself broke off her relationship with Kikuchi, but found her own life partner only a few years later when she met Chiyo Monma.

Yoshiya and Monma's life together was in some ways characterized by the same age dynamic found in *Yaneura no nishojo* and *Hana monogatari*: Yoshiya was three years older than Monma, and in their letters to each other Monma addressed Yoshiya as "elder sister." Yoshiya also famously formalized their relationship by adopting Monma, in effect making Monma her daughter in the eyes of the law. But this did not necessarily mean that the two did not conceive of each other as equal partners in love: their expressed desire to each other was to enter into a marriage, and Yoshiya apparently adopted the scheme of adoption only after it became clear in the postwar period that there was no possibility of Japanese law being changed to allow them to marry.[20]

After she met Monma, Yoshiya had one final burst of writing on the subject of same-sex love, in the magazine *Kuroshōbi* (*Black Rose*) that she independently published from January to August 1925. In particular, the story "Aru orokashiki mono no hanashi" ("A Tale of a Certain Foolish Person") seems to be a dark companion of *Yaneura no nishojo*, as a relationship between two women ends with one of them killed by a man in a shocking act of violence, implied to be the result of her turning away from her partner to pursue a conventional marriage.[21]

The next year Yoshiya and Monma established a household together. Yoshiya began writing for women's magazines "to establish a literary niche (apart from girls' fiction) and to secure a solid, broad readership amid the shifting political and social landscape of the late 1920s and 1930s." Her new strategy was to deemphasize the idea of romantic relationships between girls or women in favor of "[representing] adult same-sex love not as an *alternative* to heterosexuality but as a kind of sisterhood, an integral part of female identity that *complements* heterosexuality." This allowed her characters to avoid the fate of the typical Class S protagonist, instead experiencing "female same-sex love ... as an intense friendship that endures despite (or because of) experiences of marriage and motherhood."[22]

Yoshiya lived the last of years of her life with Monma in the coastal city of Kamakura—the city in which the main action of *Sweet Blue Flowers* is set. In an afterword, Takako Shimura describes a trip she and her editor took to Kamakura to get reference photographs on which to model various buildings portrayed in the manga. They try to visit Yoshiya's house, now a museum, but unfortunately find it closed (*SBF*, 1:190).

Nobuko Yoshiya died on July 11, 1973, with Chiyo Monma at her side—coincidentally, only three months before Takako Shimura was born. The Class S literature that she had helped pioneer over half a century earlier had by that time been succeeded by a new type of literature for girls, as discussed in the next chapter.

1. Jennifer Robertson, "Yoshiya Nobuko: Out and Outspoken in Practice and Prose," in *Same-Sex Cultures and Sexualities: An Anthropological Reader*, ed. Jennifer Robertson (Malden, MA: Blackwell, 2005), 196–97, https://doi.org/10.1002/9780470775981.ch11.

2. Hiromi Tsuchiya Dollase, "Yoshiya Nobuko's 'Yaneura no nishōjo': In Search of Literary Possibilities in 'Shōjo' Narratives," English supplement, *U.S.-Japan Women's Journal*, no. 20/21 (2001), 153, https://www.jstor.org/stable/42772176.

3. Pflugfelder, "'S' is for Sister," 153–55.

4. Nobuko Yoshiya, *Yellow Rose*, trans. Sarah Frederick, 2nd ed. (Los Angeles: Expanded Editions, 2016), chap. 4, Kindle.

5. Michiko Suzuki, "The Translation of Edward Carpenter's *Intermediate Sex* in Early Twentieth-Century Japan," in *Sexology and Translation: Cultural and Scientific Encounters Across the Modern World*, ed. Heike Bauer (Philadelphia: Temple University Press, 2015), 205–9.

6. Shane Butler, "A Problem in Greek Ethics, 1867–2019: A History," John Addington Symonds Project, accessed February 13, 2022, https://symondsproject.org/greek-ethics-history.

7. John Addington Symonds, *A Problem in Greek Ethics, being an Inquiry into the Phenomenon of Sexual Inversion, addressed especially to medical psychologists and jurists* (London: privately-pub., 1901), 8, 13, https://archive.org/details/cu31924021844950.

8. Symonds to Carpenter, 29 January 1893, in *Letters of John Addington Symonds*, ed. Herbert M. Schueller and Robert L. Peters, vol. 3, *1885–1893* (Detroit MI: Wayne State University Press, 1969), 810–811, https://archive.org/details/lettersofjohnadd0003symo.

9. Josephine Crawley Quinn and Christopher Brooke, "'Affection in Education': Edward Carpenter, John Addington Symonds, and the Politics of Greek Love," in *Ideas of Education: Philosophy and Politics from Plato to Dewey*, ed. Christopher Brooke and Elizabeth Frazer (London: Routledge, 2013), 255.

10. Edward Carpenter, "Affection in Education," in *The Intermediate Sex: A Study of Some Transitional Types of Men and Women* (London: Swan Sonnenschein, 1908), 103, https://archive.org/details/B20442178.

11. Carpenter, "Affection in Education," 105. Symonds was even more severe on the subject of lesbianism: after nodding toward the early example of Sappho, he claimed that "later Greeks, while tolerating, regarded it rather as an eccentricity of nature or a vice, than as an honourable and socially useful emotion. ... Consequently, while the Greeks utilised and ennobled boy-love, they left Lesbian love to follow the same course of degeneracy as it pursues in modern times." Symonds, *A Problem in Greek Ethics*, 71.

12. Suzuki, "The Translation of Edward Carpenter's *Intermediate Sex*," 206–8.

13. Erica Friedman, review of *Yaneura no nishojo*, by Nobuko Yoshiya, *Okazu* (blog), May 10, 2010, https://okazu.yuricon.com/2010/05/09/yuri-novel-yaneura-no-nishojo. Nobuko Yoshiya, *Yaneura no nishojo* (Tokyo: Kokusho Kankōkai, 2003). Like *Hana monogatari*, *Yaneura no nishojo* has never had an official English translation.

14. Suzuki, *Becoming Modern Women*, 43.

15. Margaret Prang, *A Heart at Leisure from Itself: Caroline Macdonald of Japan* (Vancouver: UBC Press, 1995), 41–42, 61.

16. Suzuki, *Becoming Modern Women*, 46.

17. In this regard it's worth noting that, unlike some of their contemporaries, both Symonds and Carpenter promoted a vision of homosexuality as encompassing not only spiritual but also physical relationships. Quinn and Brooke, "'Affection in Education': Edward Carpenter," 259–60.

18. Suzuki, *Becoming Modern Women*, 44–45.

19. Again, this has parallels in Symonds and especially Carpenter, who "sought to present male love as 'unswerving devotion and life-long union,'" in contrast to the Greek model in which such relationships were, like Class S relationships, inherently time-limited. Quinn and Brooke, "'Affection in Education': Edward Carpenter," 260.

20. Robertson, "Yoshiya Nobuko: Out and Outspoken," 201–3.

21. Suzuki, *Becoming Modern Women*, 54–59.

22. Suzuki, *Becoming Modern Women*, 60. Italics in the original.

The Decline of S

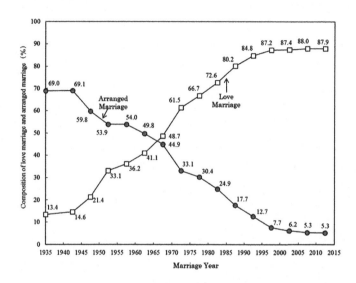

As mentioned in the introduction, *Sweet Blue Flowers* can be seen as both homage to and critique of the early twentieth-century Class S genre. What was the process by which a manga created in the early twenty-first century would ring changes on short stories and novels written almost a century before? In other words, how did we get from Class S to the genre we now know as yuri?

I do not have the time, space, or expertise to present a complete "history of yuri." Erica Friedman has provided a concise introduction[1] with a more comprehensive history to follow later this year.[2] Verena Maser's doctoral dissertation is the most in-depth academic treatment.[3]

My interest is in two specific questions. This chapter discusses the first one: why did Class S culture and literature decline (pretty much to extinction) after World War II? (The next chapter discusses the re-emergence of Class S tropes near the end of the twentieth century.)

That Class S culture and literature did suffer a precipitous decline in the postwar period is evident. Although publishers attempted to revive them after the war, the magazines that previously carried Class S stories and formed a nexus for Class S culture either shut down or shifted their focus.[4]

Recall the hypothesis in a previous chapter that the popularity of Class S relationships, and Class S literature depicting such relationships, was a function of the lack of choices open to Japanese schoolgirls: for girls destined for marriages arranged by their families, S relationships were an area in which the girls could freely choose their partners and enact rituals of courtship related to those choices.

Suppose that this hypothesis is true to at least some degree. If that is the case, a hypothesis for the postwar decline of Class S relationships and literature immediately suggests itself: that the nature of relationships between girls and boys and women and men changed significantly under the postwar American occupation, and that these changes taken together destroyed the social context within which Class S relationships had originally flourished.[5]

The first such change was public schools (and some private) moving to a coeducational model in which girls and boys attended the same schools and received equivalent elementary and secondary educations. Before the war, girls were educated separately from boys and received fewer years of schooling. Under the occupation, the American authorities encouraged the adoption of coeducation, apparently in part due to the concerns of American women staff members that this was the only way to ensure that girls received an equivalent education to boys.[6]

The second change was in Japanese attitudes and behaviors relating to relationships between men and women, particularly dating and courtship. Beginning in the Meiji era, the Japanese government attempted to exert stricter control over family life, with women expected to serve (only) as wives and (especially) mothers, and men expected to remain monogamous—albeit with the freedom to engage in sex outside of marriage.

The government redoubled these efforts in the Shōwa era after Japan invaded Manchuria in 1931, with "women being cast as mothers whose sole purpose was to breed sons for the empire, and men being regarded as fighting machines." Particular measures included a National Eugenic Law, prohibition of abortions, and restrictions on contraceptives (including censorship of discussions of the use of condoms for family planning as opposed to disease prevention).[7]

After World War II ended in Japan's defeat, many people in Japan were presumably sick of these wartime restrictions. As it happened, the American occupation authority had an explicit goal of promoting American cultural norms around love, courtship, and marriage, up to and including encouraging Japanese moviemakers to include scenes of kissing in their movies.[8] The result was not a wholesale repudiation of traditional Japanese social norms, but it did mark a fairly decisive change from prewar behaviors.

Taken together, coeducation and the rise of American-influenced dating and courtship behaviors eventually led to the (effective) end of arranged marriages, at least as an unquestioned cultural norm. This change can be seen quantitatively in statistics published by the Japanese government and qualitatively in the postwar "home dramas" of director Yasujirō Ozu, which were made for a middle-class audience and reflected middle-class concerns and aspirations.

The quantitative data are from the 2015 "Fifteenth Japanese National Fertility Survey" conducted by the Japanese government.[9] The survey queried respondents about the years in which they got married and how they happened to have met their spouse. It defined arranged marriages as marriages occurring "through an arranged introduction" or "through a marriage match-making agency." The survey defined love marriages as marriages in which the couple met in other ways, for example, at school, at work, through friends or family, or while pursuing a hobby.[10]

The graph included in the survey report features a classic S-curve showing the rise of love marriages from a low base to almost complete saturation in the population, with an early high-growth phase from World War II through the late 1960s. The decline of arranged marriages is visible in a corresponding S-curve, with the percentage of arranged marriages dropping below 50 percent around 1960 and ending up in single digits by the late 1990s.

We can match points on the curve to Ozu films made over the course of a decade. First is the 1949 film *Late Spring*, the first film in the so-called "Noriko trilogy," featuring (unrelated) characters named Noriko.[11] In the late 1940s, arranged marriages were still the dominant norm, and love marriages were the province of a small minority. Thus it's no surprise that the first Noriko feels she has no choice but to defer to her father and marry a man suggested to her by her aunt.

Censorship prevented Ozu from explicitly presenting this as an arranged marriage but it has the look of one, and Noriko does not want to enter into it.[12] However, there is also a glimpse of the new dispensation: earlier in the film Noriko accompanies her father's assistant on a date of sorts, as they ride their bicycles to the seashore.[13]

Almost ten years later, love marriages were over a third of all marriages and still rising in popularity. In the 1958 film *Equinox Flower*, Fumiko explicitly rebels against an arranged marriage in favor of a love marriage with a musician, while Setsuko tries to persuade her father to permit her own love match with a salaryman. Setsuko's father approves of love marriages in theory (in response to a question posed by her friend Yukiko) but not for Setsuko. However, he finally relents and gives his blessing to the happy couple. Fumiko's father does likewise, and we see a new custom well on its way to becoming pervasive.[14]

Consider a Japanese girl born after World War II, say, in 1949, the year of *Late Spring*. She would likely have spent her entire time in elementary, middle, and high school in the presence of boys. She might have taken part in the newly-invented Japanese custom of girls giving "love chocolates" to boys on Valentine's Day. She might have had a steady boyfriend, gone on dates with him, and even kissed him.

She would have been quite aware of the growing popularity of love marriages. If she entered into a marriage in the early to mid-1970s (perhaps after attending university and then being employed for a few years), it would have been more likely to be a love marriage than an arranged marriage. (The crossover point between the two S-curves was around 1967.)

Given this life experience, would it be any wonder that the idea of an S relationship would have seemed to her like something from the distant prewar past and Class S literature of little or no appeal to her? She would likely have been much more interested in the emerging genre of *shōjo* manga targeted to her and her contemporaries and perhaps even have dreamed of becoming a *shōjo* manga artist herself. But that's a topic for the next chapter.

1. Erica Friedman, "On Defining Yuri." In "Queer Female Fandom," edited by Julie Levin Russo and Eve Ng, special issue, *Transformative Works and Cultures* 24, https://journal.transformativeworks.org/index.php/twc/article/view/831/835.

2. Erica Friedman, *By Your Side: The First 100 Years of Yuri Manga & Anime* (Vista, CA: Journey Press, forthcoming).

3. Verena Maser, "Beautiful and Innocent: Female Same-Sex Intimacy in the Japanese Yuri Genre." PhD diss., Universität Trier, 2015. https://ubt.opus.hbz-nrw.de/frontdoor/index/index/docId/695.

4. Shamoon, *Passionate Friendship*, 84.

5. Again my argument echoes that of Yukari Fujimoto: "One explanation that I might give [for the absence of lesbians in *shōjo* manga] is that the closed, girls-only time and space that comprised Yoshiya Nobuko's world does not exist as a communal object any more." Fujimoto, "Where Is My Place in the World?," 26.

6. Joseph C. Trainor, *Educational Reform in Occupied Japan: Trainor's Memoir* (Tokyo: Meisei University Press, 1983), 148.

7. Mark McLelland, *Love, Sex, and Democracy in Japan during the American Occupation* (New York: Palgrave Macmillan, 2012), chap. 1, Kindle.

8. McLelland, *Love, Sex, and Democracy in Japan*, chap. 4.

9. National Institute of Population and Social Security Research, "Marriage Process and Fertility of Japanese Married Couples / Attitudes toward Marriage and Family among Japanese Singles: Highlights of the Survey Results on Married Couples/ Singles" (Tokyo: National Institute of Population and Social Security Research, 2017), 12, http://www.ipss.go.jp/ps-doukou/e/doukou15/Nfs15R_points_eng.pdf.

10. The earliest figures leave many marriages unaccounted for (15 percent or so). That may be due to people not recalling exactly how they met their spouse or not being sure how to categorize the meeting. Also, the survey results likely understate the extent to which marriages were informally arranged by others acting as matchmakers, for example, by corporate managers acting on behalf of their employees.

11. *Late Spring*, directed by Yasujirō Ozu (1949; New York: Criterion Collection, 2012), 1 hr., 48 min., Blu-ray Disc, 1080p HD.

12. Like other films at the time, *Late Spring* was censored by the American occupation authorities. They rejected explicit mentions of arranged marriage as a feudal relic. Mars-Jones, *Noriko Smiling*, 190–91.

13. Ozu included in this scene images referencing American military and cultural power: a sign in English on a bridge marking its "30 Ton Capacity" for drivers of tanks and other military vehicles, and a second sign in English encouraging consumers to "Drink Coca-Cola." *Late Spring*, 22:56.

14. *Equinox Flower*, directed by Yasujirō Ozu, in *Eclipse Series 3: Late Ozu (Early Spring / Tokyo Twilight / Equinox Flower / Late Autumn / The End of Summer)* (1958; New York: Criterion Collection, 2007), 1 hr., 58 min., DVD.

The Yuri Tribe

The last chapter discussed how Class S literature declined to near extinction in the postwar period. That decline may have occurred because the social context that had given rise to S relationships had, for the most part, disappeared with the advent of coeducation, Western-influenced dating behaviors, and "love marriages" as an increasingly popular alternative to arranged marriages.

How then did things change so as to create an identifiable genre of works featuring relationships between women, what we now know as "yuri," and a subgenre within the yuri genre of works like *Sweet Blue Flowers* that feature relationships between schoolgirls?

As before, I point readers to the histories of yuri in Friedman[1] and Maser[2] for a full treatment and discuss only the trends of most interest to me, starting with the rise of magazines featuring manga targeting the *shōjo* demographic of girls and young women.

The production of *shōjo* manga recapitulated the development of prewar magazines featuring Class S literature: Initially, men were featured prominently not only as *shōjo* magazine editors but also as creators of a substantial fraction of *shōjo* magazine content. However, over the 1960s, as a new generation of girls grew up reading *shōjo* manga, and some tried their hand at writing it, almost all *shōjo* manga came to be written by women.[3]

Eventually, the production of *shōjo* manga assumed its present form: edited primarily by older men—supplemented by a younger cadre of women editors not on the career track—and created almost exclusively by younger women.[4] Magazines sought out these female artists for their supposed superior knowledge of what girls would be interested in and actively recruited them via "manga schools" sponsored by the magazines themselves.[5]

During the 1960s, the content of *shōjo* manga also changed, with the family dramas of the 1950s replaced with a broader range of stories, including romances: stories based on Hollywood romances, romances featuring boys and girls in America and other countries, and romances involving Japanese schoolgirls and boys—in other words, stories featuring relationships that might have arisen in the coeducational school environments that most Japanese girls of that time experienced.[6]

In the early 1970s a new group of manga artists, the so-called Year 24 group, took the styles and conventions established in 1960s *shōjo* manga and used them to produce innovative works that stretched genre boundaries and introduced new themes. Many of these themes directly or indirectly influenced the yuri genre.

The first was the revival of Class S themes of doomed love among adolescent students, as seen in Moto Hagio's *The Heart of Thomas*.[7] The twist was that instead of featuring girls, it featured boys, and instead of being set in Japan, the action took place in an imagined European setting.

In writing her earlier story "November Gymnasium," a predecessor to *The Heart of Thomas*, Hagio did a draft of it as a story of love between girls. However, she found substituting boys for girls more in accord with the story she wanted to tell: "When I wrote it as a boys' school story, everything fell into place smoothly. But when I wrote the girls' school version it came out sort of giggly. ... [That] sort of nastiness distinctive to girls worked its way into the story."[8]

The Heart of Thomas was followed by other works in a similar vein, including Keiko Takemiya's *Kaze to ki no uta* (which has never received an official English release). These eventually came to constitute a new genre, "boy's love" or "BL," which became popular among the adolescent girls who made up the core audience for *shōjo* manga.

Even before *The Heart of Thomas* Ryoko Yamagishi had published her manga *Shiroi heya no futari* (unreleased in English), also featuring doomed love in a European setting but between two girls. This is considered among the first, if not the first, yuri manga.[9] However *Shiroi heya no futari* did not immediately lead to a flood of similar works, possibly due to what I've hypothesized: that the social context of traditional Class S works was no longer present in postwar Japan. From this point of view, most adolescent girls would likely have been more interested in reading stories featuring romances involving boys, including BL works, than stories featuring romances between girls.

This included reading stories about girls who appeared to be boys, or vice versa, which brings me to other major themes influencing the yuri genre: gender crossing, gender nonconformance, and transformations more generally. These themes have relatively deep roots in Japanese artistic culture—including the cross-dressing *onnagata* performers in all-male kabuki performances and (more recently) the *otokoyaku* of the all-female Takarazuka Revue—as well as in Japanese life—witness the chronicling by the popular postwar "perverse press" of the cross-dressing *dansho* sex workers or the effeminate *gei boi*.[10]

Themes of gender crossing and gender nonconformance featured in such manga as *Rose of Versailles* (recently released in English)[11] and *Dear Brother* (adapted as an anime subsequently released in English),[12] both by Riyoko Ikeda, both featuring women presenting as male, and both containing at least hints of romances between women.

However, the more impactful embodiment of these themes, at least in the West, was Naoko Takeuchi's popular 1990s manga *Pretty Guardian Sailor Moon*[13] and its anime adaptations. *Sailor Moon* featured the "magical girl" transformations of Usagi Tsukino and her friends (the "guardians" of the title), multiple instances of gender-nonconforming or gender-ambiguous characters (for example, the Sailor Starlights), and—most relevant in this context—the relationship between Haruka Tenoh (Sailor Uranus) and her partner Michiru Kaioh (Sailor Neptune).

Sailor Moon was followed by other works combining magical girl plots with yuri elements, most notably *Revolutionary Girl Utena*, which featured the pairing of prince-like Utena Tenjou and her "Rose Bride" Anthy Himemiya.[14] *Revolutionary Girl Utena*, directed by *Sailor Moon* veteran Kunihiko Ikuhara, was more explicitly feminist than its predecessor, featuring key themes I see echoed in *Sweet Blue Flowers*: a critique of dominance hierarchies arising from patriarchy and how they can warp relationships between women, and a search for alternative relationships grounded in equality.[15]

Moving beyond the realm of fiction and fantasy, the 1990s also saw a marked increase in the public visibility of lesbians in Japan, part of a "gay boom" of increased mainstream media coverage of gay culture.[16] This increased visibility coincided with the publication of the first commercial magazines targeted at lesbians themselves and (in those magazines) the publication of manga by lesbians for lesbians, including Rica Takashima's exploration of lesbian life in Tokyo.[17]

At the turn of the twenty-first century, these works and themes combined to form a recognized genre, a genre acquiring the name "yuri" ("lily") by which we know it today.[18] But for my purposes, the most significant work was one that revived Class S tropes of schoolgirl relationships at all-girls schools and without which *Sweet Blue Flowers* likely would not exist. That work, *Maria Watches Over Us*, deserves its own chapter.

1. Friedman, "On Defining Yuri."
2. Maser, "Beautiful and Innocent."
3. Dalma Kálovics, "The Missing Link of Shōjo Manga History: The Changes in 60s Shōjo Manga as Seen Through the Magazine *Shūkan Margaret*," *Journal of Kyoto Seika University* 49 (2016), 11–13, https://www.academia.edu/36310321/The_missing_link_of_sh%C5 %8Djo_manga_history_the_changes_in_60s_sh%C5%8Djo_manga_as_seen_through _the_magazine_Sh%C5%ABkan_Margaret.
4. Jennifer S. Prough, *Straight from the Heart: Gender, Intimacy, and the Cultural Production of Shōjo Manga* (Honolulu: University of Hawai'i Press, 2011), 90–93.
5. Prough, *Straight from the Heart*, 81–87.
6. Kálovics, "The Missing Link of Shōjo Manga History," 13–15.
7. Moto Hagio, *The Heart of Thomas*, trans. Rachel Thorn (Seattle: Fantagraphics Books, 2012).
8. Moto Hagio, interview by Rachel Thorn, in Moto Hagio, *A Drunken Dream and Other Stories*, trans. Rachel Thorn (Seattle: Fantagraphics Books, 2010), xxi.
9. Erica Friedman, review of *Shiroi heya no futari*, by Ryoko Yamagishi, *Okazu* (blog), June 3, 2004, https://okazu.yuricon.com/2004/06/03/yuri-manga-shiroi-heya-no-futari.
10. Mark McLelland, *Queer Japan from the Pacific War to the Internet Age* (Lanham, MD: Rowman & Littlefield, 2005), chap. 2, Kindle.
11. Riyoko Ikeda, *Rose of Versailles*, trans. Mori Morimoto, 5 vols. (Richmond Hill, ON: Udon Entertainment, 2019–21).
12. *Dear Brother*, directed by Osamu Dezaki (1991–92; Altamonte Springs, FL: Discotek Media, 2021), Blu-ray Disc, 1080p HD.
13. Naoko Takeuchi, *Pretty Guardian: Sailor Moon*, trans. William Flanagan, 12 vols. (New York: Kodansha, 2011–13).
14. *Revolutionary Girl Utena*, directed by Kunihiko Ikuhara (1997; Grimes, IA: Nozomi Entertainment, 2017), Blu-ray Disc, 1080p HD.
15. There are other parallels between *Revolutionary Girl Utena* and *Sweet Blue Flowers*, including incorporating elements taken from the theater (including the Takarazuka Revue) and investigating the limitations of the "girl prince" archetype. Perhaps not

coincidentally, Kunihiko Ikuhara also directed the opening sequence of the anime adaptation of *Sweet Blue Flowers*.

16. McLelland, *Queer Japan*, chap. 5.

17. Rica Takashima, *Tokyo Love ~ Rica 'tte Kanji!?*, trans. Erin Subramanian and Erica Friedman (ALC Publishing, 2013), Kindle.

18. Erica Friedman, "Why We Call It 'Yuri,'" Anime Feminist, August 9, 2017, https://www.animefeminist.com/history-why-call-yuri.

Loving Hierarchy

Maria Watches Over Us (*Maria-sama ga miteru*, or *Marimite* to its fans) looms like a colossus over the twenty-first-century yuri genre, including *Sweet Blue Flowers* in particular. Understanding what *Sweet Blue Flowers* might be saying thus requires our first understanding what kind of work *Maria Watches Over Us* is.

Beginning with a short story by Oyuki Konno in 1997, *Maria Watches Over Us* eventually grew into a multimedia franchise. It includes a series of over three dozen light novels by Konno (published from 1998 to 2012, overlapping serialization of *Sweet Blue Flowers*), a nine-volume manga adaptation, a four-season anime adaptation (the only version released in English translation),[1] a live-action film, audio CDs, and other products.[2]

At first glance, the existence of *Maria Watches Over Us* poses a problem for the thesis I advanced in an earlier chapter: that postwar changes in Japan, including in particular the introduction of coeducation and the decline in arranged marriages, removed the social context within which the Class S literature of the early twentieth century had flourished. *Maria Watches Over Us* also features "passionate friendships" between students at an all-girls Catholic school and thus seems to conform to the traditional Class S template pioneered by Nobuko Yoshiya and others. Why then is it so popular in twenty-first-century Japan?

To resolve this seeming paradox, we need to look more closely at *Maria Watches Over Us* and the differences between it and traditional Class S works. First, even though not all girls in early twentieth-century Japan attended high school, much less Catholic high schools, those who did attended all-girls schools. Thus the settings of typical Class S works were not too far removed from their own experiences.

However, in the early twenty-first-century timeframe of *Maria Watches Over Us* the upper-class all-girls Catholic school environment portrayed in the series would likely be foreign to almost all of its readers and viewers. Though depicting events in contemporary Japan, the exotic setting of *Maria Watches Over Us* makes it more akin to a work of fantasy.

Second, the life prospects of the characters in *Maria Watches Over Us* are not nearly as constrained as those of the girls in traditional Class S stories. In particular, with one exception (Sachiko Ogasawara), no girls are depicted as being compelled into an arranged marriage—and it appears that even Sachiko may escape that fate. Almost all of the characters are implied to have a fair amount of freedom in making their life choices after high school, even to take somewhat unusual paths (like pursuing a widowed man with a young child, as Eriko Torii does).

As I interpret it, the core theme of traditional Class S works is that a girl's time at an all-girls school is a brief period during which she can exercise a measure of free choice in entering into a deep and fulfilling relationship with another girl, before she is called to fulfill her assigned duty as a "good wife and wise mother," serving a husband chosen for her by others and a Japanese state that envisions no other role for her. At best, that fleeting period of happiness must end in permanent separation from the one she loves. At worst, it will end in death for her or her partner.

That theme is echoed in the "Forest of Briars" episode of *Maria Watches Over Us*, which features a novel initially thought to be written by Sei Satō about her relationship with her younger classmate Shiori Kubo.[3] But, in fact, that novel was written by a woman who attended Lillian Girls' Academy many years ago—a plot twist that serves to distance that Class S story from the very different tale told by *Maria Watches Over Us*.

So, if *Maria Watches Over Us* is not simply a traditional Class S story updated to modern Tokyo, what is it? I contend that *Maria Watches Over Us* is best thought of as a utopian fantasy featuring a benevolent hierarchically-ordered society sustained by kindness, empathy, and love—a fantasy rendered at least superficially plausible by the fact that the society's members are all women. The central concerns of *Maria Watches Over Us* are how to find a suitable place for oneself in such a hierarchically-ordered society and, having done so, how best to perpetuate that society by bringing others into its embrace.

That hierarchical order is sustained through the *sœur* ("sister") system, in which older girls enter into relationships of close friendship and affection with younger girls. Those younger girls then take on *sœurs* of their own, advancing up the ranks of the age-based hierarchy as their seniors graduate.

There are many attractive features of this hierarchically-ordered society. First, it is relatively inclusive, with girls able to find a place in it irrespective of their family wealth or social status. Thus, for example, the main protagonist, everygirl Yumi Fukuzawa, finds herself chosen as the *"petite sœur"* of Sachiko, the aristocratic scion of one of the wealthiest families of Japan.[4]

The *sœur* system also accommodates relationships between girls with very different personalities (for example, Yumi and Sachiko) and relationships of varying characters and degrees of intensity, like the superficially distant but actually deep relationship between Sei Satō and her *petite sœur* Shimako Tōdō.

The system is also flexible enough to survive occasional "problems of succession," like Sei delaying her selection of a *sœur* and picking someone two grades below herself (instead of one grade, as is the usual practice) or Yoshino Shimazu picking as a *petite sœur* Nana Arima, a girl who hasn't yet graduated from middle school into high school. Even choices of a successor made almost at random, like Sachiko's selection of Yumi as her *sœur* or Yoshino's selection of Nana, work out fine in the end, as if guided by the hand of the Virgin Mary herself.

Finally, and perhaps most important, the *sœur* system also offers the opportunity for positive personal growth. As a new *petite sœur* Yumi must learn what Sachiko needs from her, and what she must learn to properly be a *grande sœur* herself to Tōko Matsudaira, to grow "from an 'average' young woman to a commander among her peers, guiding with gentle pressure."[5] And through Yumi's relationships with Sachiko and Tōko, they become better people as well.

Maria Watches Over Us thus embodies in contemporary fiction Nobuko Yoshiya's contention that relationships between younger girls and older ones (or, for that matter, between girls and their teachers) are critical to their developing "a beautiful, moral, social, and non-self-centered character."[6]

But no matter how benign it may be, the social order of *Maria Watches Over Us* is still one organized as a relatively rigid hierarchy based on age and seniority, one that in some respects is reminiscent of traditional

Confucian teachings or the ideologies of imperial Japan. Like the hierarchies promoted by those, the society of Lillian Girls' Academy is a hierarchy of hierarchies.

First, there are the groups of girls linked together by *sœur* relationships (a girl, her *petite sœur*, that girl's *petite sœur*, and so on). These are analogous to the extended family unit of the traditional Japanese household (*ie*), with each generation deferring to those above it.

Then there are three groups of *sœurs* that are set apart from other girls as a sort of hereditary aristocracy, the so-called "Rose families." The heads of these families, that is, the oldest girls within each of these three sets of *sœurs*, even have the equivalent of titles of nobility: Rosa Chinensis, Rosa Foetida, and Rosa Gigantea.

The student council of the school is supposedly chosen in democratic elections. In practice, the Roses control the council, just as the governments of Meiji-era Japan were dominated by the former samurai who became part of the newly-(re)constituted Japanese nobility. In *Maria Watches Over Us* there are two challengers who seek election to the council, but both are easily defeated and the system of hereditary succession preserved. (See also below.)

As student council members, the Roses are shown to be enlightened rulers. Unlike the student councils in many manga and anime, they do not lord it over the students, seek to shut down clubs, or attempt to restrict students' behavior through petty regulations.

Instead, they seek to narrow the perceived distance between themselves and other students. For example, Sachiko's *grande sœur* Yōko Mizuno shows concern that ordinary students are afraid to approach the Roses and expresses her desire to open up the Rose Mansion (the building that serves as their gathering place) to anyone who wishes to visit.

However, the scope of this benevolent order is limited in both space and time. First, these hierarchies are themselves embedded in the larger hierarchies of Japanese society. Erica Friedman claims that "fans [of *Maria Watches Over Us*] are treated to a world in which women are assumed to be able to lead and to command without question."[7] But that world ends at the gates of Lillian Girls' Academy, the boundary beyond which the patriarchy reigns. The nuns who run the school are subject to the authority of the local (male) bishop, who is himself a mid-rank figure in the (male) church hierarchy presided over by the Pope.

Likewise, Sachiko, the epitome of aristocratic grace and ability, rules supreme within the school in concert with her fellow Roses. However, though she is the sole child of the family, she is apparently deemed unfit to lead the Ogawasara corporate empire as an adult. Her proposed marriage with Suguru Kashiwagi would lead to his taking over the companies. If that engagement ends, some other man would presumably be found to take his place, whether through marriage to Sachiko or adoption into the Ogasawara family.

For the most part, the hierarchical order of *Maria Watches Over Us* goes unquestioned by those who participate in it—and almost all of the girls do participate in it. There are at least four exceptions to this, two political and two personal, each illustrating various aspects of the social order and how it is preserved against potential threats.

The first political challenge is brought by Shizuka Kanina, also known as Rosa Canina—analogous to a usurper granting themselves a royal title.[8] She runs for the student council essentially to get the attention of Sei. Having achieved that goal, she leaves school to study voice in Italy, exiling herself from Japan and (by implication) its social hierarchies.

The second challenger is Sachiko's cousin Tōko. Insecure in her position in her family due to her having been adopted into it, Tōko's story resembles the stories of bastard sons of the aristocracy, born of nobility but estranged from it by the circumstances of their birth, of the elite but at the same time not of it.

In some stories, this results in the bastard son leading a revolution against the class of which they are ostensibly a member. This finds echoes in Tōko's student council run, in which she apparently seeks to overthrow the tradition of the Rose families running the council.[9] However, Yumi's kindness wins Tōko over, Yumi makes Tōko her *petite sœur*, and she becomes part of the Rosa Chinensis family, one day to assume the position of Rose that she had dreamed of as a child. Thus, like many past rebellious sons of nobility, she ends her story co-opted into the hierarchical order against which she had once inveighed.

As for personal challenges to the social order, the more significant is the relationship of Sei and Shiori, the intensity and passion of which reads as being lesbian in nature.[10] However, they are not criticized for engaging in lesbian activity specifically.

Rather Sei and Shiori are criticized, explicitly by their elders and implicitly by the story framing, for letting their absorption in each other lead to their neglecting their roles in the two hierarchical orders to which they have respectively committed themselves: Sei to her *sœurs* and the *sœur* system, and Shiori to the Church that she intends to join as a nun. (Note that despite her affection for Shiori, Sei explicitly rejects making Shiori her *sœur*.) To put it another way, Sei and Shiori's true sin is the sin of individualism, and their subplot is resolved by their repenting of it.

The other case of rejecting the hierarchical order is not a rejection at all. The "ace of the photography club," Tsutako Takeshima, who loves to photograph others but hates to be photographed herself, exists outside of the *sœur* system, observing it closely but not participating in it herself. She is a fairly transparent stand-in for the author, and as such does not constitute a threat to the social order.

Given the above, why might *Maria Watches Over Us* be so popular, both with the teenaged girls for whom it was originally written and the older all-genders audience that makes up a significant part of *Marimite* fandom?

For teenaged girls, besides the emotional drama (tending to melodrama) for which *shōjo* manga, anime, and light novels are known and loved, *Maria Watches Over Us* offers a vision of a charmed school existence, in which bullying is seemingly nonexistent and almost all troubles are ultimately dissolved in a sea of mutual kindness and support.[11] I can see many a girl picturing herself in Yumi's place, plucked from obscurity to become the valued companion and helpmeet to the elegant and cultured Sachiko, who seemingly has everything but desperately needs what only Yumi can provide.

This emotional identification can extend to other characters: *Maria Watches Over Us* features such a wide variety of personalities and relationships that almost any young reader or viewer can find some aspect of the story that speaks to them personally.

As for the older audience, it may be no accident that the popularity of *Maria Watches Over Us* grew as Japan was entering its second "lost decade" of economic stagnation. *Maria Watches Over Us* offers an appealing vision of an alternative Japan, of a Japan as some like to think of it. The world of Lillian Girls' Academy is a hierarchical social order that works for all those who are part of it. Those on the lower rungs of the ladder are valued and cared for, not ignored or exploited—comfort food for "freeters" and others for whom the traditional Japanese promise of lifetime corporate employment (never extended to all of society, especially women) will remain forever unfulfilled.

The popularity of the *Maria Watches Over Us* franchise led to others creating works inspired by it. Independently-published *dōjinshi*, fan fiction, and other types of unofficial derivative works sought to extend the story, explore different pairings of the characters, or show favorite "ships" in more compromising positions. Among others, *Strawberry Panic* reused the Catholic girls' school setting and other *Marimite* tropes to tell a story of schoolgirl affections more directed at the male gaze.[12]

And, of course, there's *Sweet Blue Flowers*, which seems to have been something of a side project for Takako Shimura while she was creating *Wandering Son*. She began serialization of *Sweet Blue Flowers* in 2004, about a year and a half after serialization of *Wandering Son* began. She ended it in 2013, a month before *Wandering Son* ended, having published one chapter every other month instead of the monthly schedule for *Wandering Son*.

Thus Shimura had enough spare time to do a second manga (albeit on a less demanding schedule), an available outlet in *Manga Erotics F* (*Wandering Son* was being serialized in *Comic Beam*), an all-genders adult audience familiar with tales of love between schoolgirls, a story structure to echo and adapt, and presumably something she wanted to say.

What was that something? As noted previously, I think it was about presenting a model of loving relationships between women that does not conform to a hierarchical framework like that in *Maria Watches Over Us*, relationships in which two girls come to each other not as *grande sœur* and *petite sœur*, not as *senpai* and *kōhai*, not as superior and inferior, but rather as equal individuals.

1. *Maria Watches Over Us*, directed by Yukihiro Matsushita and Toshiyuki Kato (2004–2009; Houston: Sentai Filmworks, 2020), Blu-ray Disc, 1080p HD.

2. For an overview of the franchise and an assessment of its significance, see Erica Friedman, "*Maria-sama ga miteru*: 20 Years of Watching Mary Watching Us," *Okazu* (blog), January 28, 2018, https://okazu.yuricon.com/2018/01/28/maria-sama-ga-miteru-20-years-of-watching-mary-watching-us.

3. *Maria Watches Over Us*, season 1, episode 10, "The Forest of Briars."

4. However, this spirit of inclusion extends only so far. None of the girls in *Maria Watches Over Us* appear to be genuinely lower-class—not surprising given the presumed expense of attending an exclusive private school. In particular, Yumi's father owns a small design firm and is thus solidly situated within the *petite bourgeoisie*.

5. Friedman, "*Maria-sama ga miteru*: 20 Years."

6. Suzuki, "The Translation of Edward Carpenter's *Intermediate Sex*," 208.

7. Friedman, "*Maria-sama ga miteru*: 20 Years."

8. *Maria Watches Over Us*, season 1, episode 6, "Rosa Canina."

9. *Maria Watches Over Us*, season 4, episode 9, "The Masked Actress."

10. *Maria Watches Over Us*, season 1, episode 11, "The White Petals."

11. The most serious instance of attempted bullying is perpetrated on Yumi by three wealthy girls whose families are friends with Sachiko's. This, however, occurs outside the walls of Lillian Girls' Academy, and is thoroughly defeated by a wise elder charmed by Yumi's sincerity and artlessness. *Maria Watches Over Us*, season 3, episode 1, "Vacation of the Lambs."

12. Sakurako Kimino, *Strawberry Panic*, trans. Michelle Kobayashi and Anastasia Moreno, 3 vols. (Los Angeles: Seven Seas Entertainment, 2008).

A Manga by Any Other Name

Why is *Sweet Blue Flowers* named "Sweet Blue Flowers"? We can try to answer this by starting at the end of the title and working backward.

As mentioned previously, *Sweet Blue Flowers* was originally published in Japanese as *Aoi hana*. "Hana" means "flower"—or "flowers," Japanese not having plural forms as English and other languages do. Shimura's name-checking of Nobuko Yoshiya and her titling her first chapter "Flower Story" indicates that "hana" in the title references *Hana monogatari* or *Flower Tales*, the short story collection previously discussed.

Next, "aoi." This means "blue," so we have "blue flower" or "blue flowers." Is there a significance to the color blue in this context? Unfortunately, I can't find a list in English of the titles of the stories in *Hana monogatari*, so I don't know if this is a reference to a specific story of Yoshiya's.

Is the reference to something else? The most well-known reference to a blue flower in Western literature is from the unfinished novel *Heinrich von Ofterdingen* by the eighteenth-century German Romantic poet and philosopher Novalis (Georg Philipp Friedrich Freiherr von Hardenberg), translated into English as *Henry of Ofterdingen*. It begins with young Henry lying in bed, beguiled by an image from a tale told by a stranger: "I long to behold the blue flower. It is constantly in my mind, and I can think and compose of nothing else."[1]

The blue flower (*blaue Blume*) of Novalis has connotations both sacred and profane. On the one hand, as Wikipedia puts it, it "stands for desire, love, and the metaphysical striving for the infinite and unreachable. It symbolizes hope and the beauty of things." It later became a symbol for the entire German Romantic movement.

But the blue flower also has a worldly incarnation in the person of the young girl Matilda, the fictional counterpart of Sophie von Kühn. Novalis met Sophie when she was twelve and he twenty-two, and secretly became engaged to her just before her thirteenth birthday. The marriage never took place: Sophie died of illness just over two years later, shortly after her fifteenth birthday.

In the manga, Fumi compares her budding romance with Akira to "a small flower. A very small flower. ... And you might not know what to do with a flower like that" (*SBF*, 1:188). Whether or not Shimura was thinking of the "blaue Blume" of the German Romantics when she titled her manga *Aoi hana* is not clear, but certainly the age and status differences found in the relationship between Henry and Matilda (and between Novalis and Sophie) are rejected in *Sweet Blue Flowers*.

What about the word "Sweet"? When *Aoi hana* was translated into French and Spanish, its title was straightforwardly translated as *Fleurs bleues*[2] and *Flores azules*[3] respectively. So why is the English title "Sweet Blue Flowers," and not just "Blue Flowers"?

I don't know for sure, but I *can* say that "Sweet Blue Flowers" was used as an alternate English title on the Japanese edition of *Aoi hana* when the manga was published as eight collected volumes. (I believe this alternate title was also used when the manga began serialization in *Manga Erotics F*, but I have not found any confirmation of this.) This title was then carried over when *Aoi hana* was first published in a (partial) English translation and used again for the VIZ Media edition.

Finally, what kind of blue flowers might the title refer to? Blue flowers are somewhat uncommon in nature, one of the reasons for their symbolic resonance. (For example, there are no naturally occurring blue roses, and attempts to create them via genetic engineering have been only partially successful.)

Shimura may have intended to leave the identity of the blue flowers to our imaginations: in the color pages of the manga there are only two instances I could find of blue flowers, a seven-petal blue blossom in the character profile at the beginning of volume 1, and a four-petal blossom on the back cover of volume 1 of the Japanese edition.

Therefore we're free to amuse ourselves by identifying a type of flower to go with the title. A lily would be an obvious choice since "yuri" is the Japanese word for "lily," and lilies are associated with the Class S genre. However, there are no true lilies (of genus *Lilium*) that are blue. This is perhaps a tell on Shimura's part: that *Sweet Blue Flowers* pays homage to but ultimately breaks from the traditional narratives of Class S and yuri.

Another possible choice of flower is wisteria, which has purple blossoms that often appear bluish in color. The kanji for "wisteria" appears in both "Fujigaya" and "Fujisaki," the city next to Kamakura where Fujigaya appears to be located. "Wisteria" is also the name of Akira's class in her first year at Fujigaya (*SBF*, 1:26). But *Sweet Blue Flowers* is at heart Fumi's story, and Fumi attends a different school.

In the end, the identity of the blue flower remains mysterious, at least to readers in English. Though I have chosen an illustration of blue flowers to adorn the cover of this book, I'm uncertain which species it's intended to depict. I prefer to think of those flowers, and *Sweet Blue Flowers*, as being uniquely themselves.

1. Novalis, *Henry of Ofterdingen: A Romance*, trans. John Owen (Cambridge, MA: Cambridge Press, 1842; Project Gutenberg, 2010), chap. 1, https://gutenberg.org/ebooks/31873.
2. Takako Shimura, *Fleurs bleues*, trans. Satoko Inaba and Margot Maillac, 8 vols. (Paris: Kazé, 2009–15).
3. Takako Shimura, *Flores azules*, trans. Ayako Koike, 8 vols. (Colombres, Spain: Milky Way Ediciones, 2015–16).

Lizzy-chan and Darcy-san

It seems to be obligatory for reviewers of translated manga to comment on the quality of the translation. Since I don't speak or read Japanese, my opinions on the English translation of *Aoi hana* are next to worthless. However, it *is* worth noting that compared to other manga I've read, the VIZ Media edition of *Sweet Blue Flowers* is very westernized: signage and sound effects are converted to English only (as opposed to leaving them as is and adding a translation), and except for some food names the characters don't use any Japanese vocabulary or expressions.

That aspect of the translation shows up most strongly in the complete absence of honorifics. The English subtitles for the anime adaptation of *Sweet Blue Flowers* use "A-chan" and "Fumi-chan," "Manjome-san" and "Sugimoto-senpai," but here it's just "Akira," "Fumi," "Manjome," and so on.

Manga critic and translator Rachel Thorn has expressed her opposition to indiscriminately retaining honorifics in English translations, for example, in volume 1 of her translation of Takako Shimura's *Wandering Son*: "Retention of Japanese honorifics without good reason seems to me to be an affectation intended to make self-described *otaku* feel part of an exclusive club ...."[1] I've always thought keeping honorifics in translations was pretty harmless, but I'm beginning to see her point.

Suppose as a fan your concern is that the translation show the subtleties of interpersonal relationships. In that case, there's a perfectly good way to do that in English, one that's quite familiar to anyone who's read a lot of eighteenth and nineteenth-century English literature. For example, Jane Austen's *Pride and Prejudice* contains English equivalents for almost all typical usages of Japanese honorifics (*-senpai* being the major exception): Mr. Darcy is almost always "Mr. Darcy," is plain "Darcy" to his friend Mr. Bingley, and is never referred to by his given name "Fitzwilliam." (We do not learn it until almost halfway through the novel, when Elizabeth Bennet's aunt, Mrs. Gardiner, mentions it.)[2]

Similarly, Elizabeth Bennet is at different times and to different people

"Miss Bennet," "Miss Elizabeth Bennet," "Miss Elizabeth" (used by the pompous Mr. Collins, who presumes too much), "Miss Eliza Bennet" (used condescendingly by Miss Bingley, Elizabeth's more well-born rival), and (to her friend Charlotte and her sister Jane) "dear Eliza" or "dearest Lizzy" (similar to "A-chan" for Akira). It is a mark of his affection and the deepening of their relationship that at the conclusion of the novel Darcy addresses her simply as "Elizabeth." However, for her he is "Mr. Darcy" to the end.[3]

Why don't manga translators use this strategy? Probably because fans accustomed to ubiquitous informality in modern English usage would find such language incredibly stilted. They don't want their manga to read like a Regency novel, instead preferring the satisfaction of knowing the difference between -san and -sama. The John Werry translation of *Sweet Blue Flowers* does have characters address each other either by given name or family name to distinguish degrees of formality, and Mr. Kamagi is always "Mr. Kamagi." But otherwise it's directed to the non-*otaku* reader.

This translator's choice also bears on what I believe to be one of the themes of *Sweet Blue Flowers*: Western fans of anime and manga happen to live in societies that are relatively unmarked by hierarchies of age, class, gender, and so on—at least by historical standards. They do not know what it is like to live day-to-day in a society in which the very language makes explicit these hierarchies.

For example, Rachel Thorn notes that Japanese people will query others if needed to ascertain which of them is older, so that they may adopt the correct mode of speech. "There are no 'brothers' or 'sisters' in Japan: only 'older brothers,' 'younger brothers,' 'older sisters,' and 'younger sisters.' Even in the case of twins, one is arbitrarily defined as the 'elder.'"[4]

I wonder how many Western fans of anime and manga would truly want to live in a society organized by age and seniority—just as, for example, I wonder how many present-day readers of Jane Austen would want to live in a society organized by class, with everyone expected to abide by a strict code of expression in speaking to their "inferiors" and deferring to their "betters."

Moreover, the use of honorifics is not always a harmless exoticism (as Western fans might view it) or a mark of respect (as people in Japan or other Asian countries might consider it). Often they serve not just to mark hierarchies but reinforce them. In Yasujirō Ozu's film *Late Autumn*, a young woman confronts three middle-aged men she accuses of meddling in the affairs of her friend's mother. They invite her to sit, but she insists on remaining standing. One of them tries to regain the upper hand by addressing her as "Yuri-chan," but she angrily retorts, "Call me Yuriko."[5]

How does *Sweet Blue Flowers* view such hierarchies? I'll have more to say about this further on, but I think this particular feature of the English translation provides a hint.

1. Rachel Thorn, "Snips and Snails, Sugar and Spice: A Guide to Japanese Honorifics as Used in *Wandering Son*," in Shimura, *Wandering Son*, 1:iii.

2. Jane Austen, *Pride and Prejudice* (London: 1813; Project Gutenberg, 2013), vol. 1, chap. 3, vol. 2, chap. 2, https://gutenberg.org/ebooks/42671.

3. Austen, *Pride and Prejudice*, vol. 1, chap. 10, vol. 1, chap. 6, vol. 1, chap. 18, vol. 1, chap. 8, vol. 1, chap. 22, vol. 1, chap. 6, vol. 3, chap. 16.

4. Thorn, "Snips and Snails, Sugar and Spice," 1:iii.

5. *Late Autumn*, directed by Yasujirō Ozu, in *Eclipse Series 3: Late Ozu (Early Spring / Tokyo Twilight / Equinox Flower / Late Autumn / The End of Summer)* (1958; New York: Criterion Collection, 2007), 1:41:24, DVD.

Notes on Volume 1

A Rude Awakening

Content note: This chapter discusses child sexual abuse.

Often when we encounter the cultural products of other countries we are brought up short by certain features of them. Manga and anime are no exception. Here we are expecting a sweet tale of cute schoolgirls, and no sooner do we begin reading *Sweet Blue Flowers* than we find Akira Okudaira's brother being caught in her bed (*SBF*, 1:8). This is no case of prepubescent siblings cuddling together: since she's starting high school, we know Akira is fifteen years old, and since he has a driver's license, we know her brother is at least eighteen if not older.

What's going on here? One possibility is that Shimura is making fun of a common manga and anime trope: the older brother with a "sister complex." Akira's brother pretty much fits the "siscon" template to a T: no girlfriend to be seen, still living at home, no apparent job or anything else to keep him occupied, and last but not least, no evident realization that he's doing something wrong and unwanted.

Shimura gets a laugh out of Akira's brother hypocritically warning her to "watch out for gropers!" (*SBF*, 1:11) and a subsequent chapter makes fun of his overprotectiveness in following her as she goes on a planned group date (1:102). The joke seems somewhat off, though: if the point of the story is to show the evolving relationship between Akira and Fumi, why undercut that at the very beginning by putting her brother front and center?

Instead of being a joke, one could speculate that Shimura's intent is much darker, in particular, that she is implying that Akira is the victim of ongoing sexual abuse from her brother. Under this interpretation, Akira's disinterest in relationships might not be simply a reflection of the way she is, but rather the result of childhood trauma that leaves her emotions numbed. But this seems somewhat at odds with the relatively light-hearted portrayals of both Akira and her brother elsewhere in the manga—though I'll defer to the judgment of abuse survivors regarding this question.

My interpretation is somewhat in the middle: beyond being a nod to a familiar trope that could be exploited to humorous ends, Shimura may have also intended this as an example of how women have reason to distrust men and turn to other women (in this case, Akira's mother) in response for their protection. The subsequent scene on the train reinforces this, as discussed in the next chapter.

"Commuting is Rough"

Content note: This chapter discusses sexual harassment.

No sooner does Akira take leave of her brother than she has another unpleasant encounter. While she stands on the platform waiting to board a train to Fujigaya, a salaryman stands too close to her, an invasion of her personal space not justified by the area being overly crowded. She then notices another girl (Fumi, though Akira does not know this) and stands next to her for protection: "She's so tall! I'll stick close to *her*" (*SBF*, 1:13–14).

However, Fumi's height does not protect her from harassment. Once on the train, someone (perhaps the same man?) gropes Akira and then Fumi. Fumi is too embarrassed to say or do anything, but Akira comes to the rescue, whacking the perpetrator with her schoolbag. Akira sympathizes with Fumi ("Commuting is rough, *huh?*") and then accepts her thanks, after which Fumi takes her leave and walks away crying (*SBF*, 1:15–17).

Shimura's audience would, of course, be familiar with the problem of men groping women and girls on trains (*chikan*), given its prevalence in Japan. In various surveys, over a quarter to up to seventy percent of Japanese young and adult women have reported experiencing groping. The problem is severe enough that several Japanese railway operators added women-only cars to their trains.[1]

Akira and Fumi's plight would also have been familiar to the schoolgirls of late Meiji-era Japan, whose lives gave rise to *shōjo* culture and Class S literature. As Japan's economic growth led to an increase in Tokyo's population and the creation of new suburbs to house new arrivals, railway operators built a series of rail lines to serve white-collar workers and others commuting to the city center.[2]

Schoolgirls also used these railway lines to travel from their homes to the rapidly expanding system of public and private high schools for girls. "From the last decade of the nineteenth century, the number of female students (*jogakusei*) increased, and the image of the teenage schoolgirl dressed in *hakama*, wearing hair ribbons, and traversing Tokyo or its suburbs on a bicycle or by train frequently appeared in popular literature and the mass media."[3]

Commuter trains and streetcars brought together people of all classes and genders into a shared space: "Passengers holding different tickets rode together, and the train car became a travelling universe, grouping unrelated people for a brief moment. For the first time, men and women of various social classes were forced literally to look upon each other in new ways." Not all of this attention was benign. In particular, "female students became both idealised as model modern women and eroticised as sexual objects. ... their fashions and figures could be observed and even evaluated by other passengers on commuter trains."[4]

The obsession of male commuters with commuting schoolgirls found literary form in Tayama Katai's 1907 short story "The Girl Watcher." The story chronicles the life of a man (an editor at a Tokyo publisher and former writer of girls' literature) who spends his daily train journeys not looking at the scenery but instead finding ways to surreptitiously observe the young women who share his railway carriage. In his late thirties, married with two children, he neglects his wife, whom he thinks has "passed her prime," though she is only in her mid-twenties. Instead he indulges in "this bad habit of getting obsessed with young women."[5]

The story's protagonist confines his activities to looking at the girls. For that, his friends condemn him as a coward: "Now if it was us, well, we wouldn't be satisfied with just *thinking* about them—the force of instinct would soon raise its head, wouldn't you say?" They speculate that "he couldn't fool his instincts, so finally he had to resort to self-abuse for his pleasures," and conclude that "you can't live unless you follow your instincts!"[6]

Other men of the period thought the same, so much so that writers of the period warned parents not to let their daughters ride the trains during workers' commuting hours. To preserve their innocence, a railway operator introduced a "Flower Train" (*hana densha*), designated "For Use by Women Only."[7]

And so it went for the next hundred years, as new generations of schoolgirls had to deal with the unwanted attentions of new generations of salarymen and other male workers. Train groping goes unmentioned in *Sweet Blue Flowers* past the first chapter. However, it is no doubt an ongoing possibility during the daily commutes of Fumi, Akira, and their classmates, a low-level but ever-present hazard in their lives—as Akira is well aware: "I guess they target girls from Fujigaya" (*SBF*, 1:15).

Like rape, child sexual abuse, and related crimes, "*chikan* victimisation is likely to damage victims' sense of self-control over their own environment and make them believe that they live in a dangerous world. This constructs women's fear of crime victimisation greater than men's ... [and] discourages women from using public transport."[8]

This discouragement has real consequences for the women involved. In another country with an even more severe problem with street harassment, women enrolling in university seek safety at the expense of their education. To have a significantly safer commuting route, they choose lower-quality colleges, ranked several places lower than the colleges that their entrance examination scores would otherwise qualify them for. They also pay much more in travel expenses to take safer commuting routes—up to twice what they pay in tuition.[9]

This puts women at an economic disadvantage: "Choosing a worse ranked college is likely to have long-term consequences since college quality affects a student's academic training, network of peers, access to labor opportunities, and lifetime earnings."[10] Although Japan is overall safer for women, Fumi and Akira will likely also find that train groping and related street harassment impose an invisible tax that they must pay as women—a tax made more onerous because Fumi at least will likely never marry, and hence will not have the economic support of a husband.

Whether they intend to or not, train gropers also enforce a central patriarchal norm: every woman must ally with and commit herself to a "good" man to secure the protection of her person from "bad" men. For example, in the romantic comedy manga *My Love Story!!* (*Ore monogatari!!*), the brawny high-school student Takeo Gōda rescues the petite Rinko Yamato from a train groper, after which she falls for him and becomes his girlfriend.[11]

Unlike his *bishōnen* friend Makoto Sunakawa, Takeo is not conventionally attractive. But his physical strength ensures that he can protect both himself and Rinko from people and things that might harm them. In contrast, Rinko cannot even defend herself and must always depend on Takeo.

When contrasting good and bad men above, I wrote "good" and "bad" in quotes because which men are good and which are bad can often be ambiguous. For example, *My Love Story!!* and many other manga and anime depict train gropers as clearly criminal, unattractive, perverse, and by implication set apart from the "good guys."

But in *Sweet Blue Flowers* the man invading Akira's personal space on the platform appears perfectly innocuous at first glance, just another typical salaryman on his way to work. Indeed he may act as a devoted husband and father at home, just as a man who jumps in to protect women on the train may beat his wife and children if they anger him.

By implication, *Sweet Blue Flowers* questions this division of men into "good" and "bad" and rejects the norm that a woman must ally herself with one man for protection from others. It is not a man who comes to the aid of the two girls, but rather Akira who acts to protect herself and Fumi—and recall that at this point in the story, Akira is coming to the aid of a girl otherwise unknown to her. To repeat what I wrote in the previous chapter, whether Shimura consciously intended this or not, the incidents on the station platform and the train, in combination with the actions of Akira's brother (countered by Akira's mother), serve "as an example of how women have reason to distrust men and turn to other women ... in response for their protection."

1. Mitsutoshi Horii and Adam Burgess, "Constructing Sexual Risk: 'Chikan,' Collapsing Male Authority and the Emergence of Women-Only Train Carriages in Japan," *Health, Risk & Society* 14, no. 1 (2012), 42, https://doi.org/10.1080/13698575.2011.641523.

2. Alisa Freedman, "Commuting Gazes: Schoolgirls, Salarymen, and Electric Trains in Tokyo," *Journal of Transport History* 23, no. 1 (March 2002), 23, https://doi.org/10.7227/TJTH.23.1.4.

3. Freedman, "Commuting Gazes," 23.

4. Freedman, "Commuting Gazes," 26, 30.

5. Tayama Katai, "The Girl Watcher," in *The Quilt and Other Stories by Tayama Katai*, trans. Kenneth G. Henshall (Tokyo: University of Tokyo Press, 1981), 171, 173. Freedman translates the story's title as "The Girl Fetish," on the basis that "the original Japanese [*Shôjobyô*] includes the word *byô*, which connotes an illness or psychological disorder."

Freedman, "Commuting Gazes," 34n4.

6. Katai, "The Girl Watcher," 174–75.

7. Freedman, "Commuting Gazes," 30–31.

8. Horii and Burgess, "Constructing Sexual Risk," 44–45.

9. Gorija Borker, "Safety First: Perceived Risk of Street Harassment and Educational Choices of Women," (job market paper, Department of Economics, Brown University, 2018), https://data2x.org/wp-content/uploads/2019/11/PerceivedRiskStreetHarassmentandEd ChoicesofWomen_Borker.pdf.

10. Borker, "Safety First," 3.

11. Kazune Kawahara, *My Love Story!!*, vol. 1, trans. Ysabet Reinhardt MacFarlane and JN Productions (San Francisco: Viz Media, 2014), 1:17–21.

Old School, New School

As I mentioned earlier, *Sweet Blue Flowers* pays homage to and (to some extent) subverts traditional Class S and yuri tropes. One of the first ways that shows up is in the contrast drawn between Fujigaya Women's Academy and Matsuoka Girls' High School, the schools attended by Akira Okudaira and Fumi Manjome, respectively.

Fujigaya is the type of all-girls school made famous in works like *Maria Watches Over Us*: separated from the normal world by a tunnel at the end of a long uphill path (*SBF*, 1:20), a Catholic-flavored hothouse in which (according to the trope) the students engage in never-ending rounds of crushes and potential crushes. As Akira's mother tells her, "Soon you'll bring home a girlfriend!" (1:27).

(The call-out to *Maria Watches Over Us* is even more explicit in the Digital Manga translation, in which Akira's brother asks her, "So does everyone say 'good day to you'?," a common English translation of the formal expression "*gokigenyō*" made famous by *Maria*.)

However, despite the association with Class S relationships, Fujigaya is better thought of as an institution whose primary purpose is promoting and propagating traditional values around marriage and class. Michi Kawai, who ran a Christian school in Tokyo in the 1930s and 1940s, wrote: "There is an increasing tendency for well-to-do Protestant families in Japan to send their children, especially girls, to Catholic institutions. ... Is it the policy of Catholics to gather the children of the wealthy and those of high station in life?"[1]

Kawai's conclusion: "The families who are socially ambitious wish to send their children to exclusive schools so that after graduation their daughters may be married into families of social standing. This is a natural desire for any parent, and Catholic educationists were clever enough to diagnose the need and the church rich enough to start one or two very exclusive schools in large cities with lovely big campuses and many consecrated Sisters of different orders, working together with efficient Japanese staffs."[2]

Kawai also noted the recent founding of the Catholic-sponsored Nogi Girls' High School near Kamakura: "Very soon the school will be overflowing with pupils because it again meets the demand of the people who have the money and the leisure to live all the year round in that exclusive neighborhood."[3]

Nogi Girls' High School was subsequently renamed Shonan Shirayuri Gakuen High School, and under that name exists to this day, its junior and senior high school campus located only a short distance inland from Enoshima.[4] It also has an affiliated kindergarten and elementary school. Although the history of Shonan Shirayuri Gakuen High School dates back only to just before World War II, its setting, mission, and target demographic make it the closest real-life equivalent to Fujigaya Women's Academy.[5]

The most notable difference is that as a more recent institution Shonen Shirayuri Gakuen has more modern architecture. As Shimura mentions in the afterwords to parts 1 and 2 of volume 1, she used the Kamakura Museum of Literature as the model for the physical appearance of Fujigaya (SBF, 1:193, 1:378). The museum grounds even feature a tunnel like the one Akira walks through on her first day of school (1:20).[6]

In contrast to Fujigaya, Matsuoka appears to be a typical nondenominational single-sex high school. Akira's mother sees it as particularly academically rigorous (SBF, 1:36), but it's otherwise indistinguishable from other modern educational institutions. Based on evidence in other volumes (2:309, 3:311–12), Matsuoka appears to be located near the Kamakurakōkō-Mae station on the Enoden railway, near the site of the real-life Kamakura Senior High School, a coeducational public high school.

Unlike Fujigaya, which names its classrooms after flowers (Akira is in the Wisteria class),[7] Matsuoka uses a more prosaic naming scheme (Fumi starting in class 1-A). To further enhance the contrast, Matsuoka students wear dark jumpers with blouse, tie, and (optional) jacket—a handsome but severe uniform that's a far cry from the (often fetishized) sailor-style uniforms worn at Fujigaya and countless other schools in anime and manga.[8]

When schools like Fujigaya were first established during the Meiji era,

I'm sure that the first generation of students saw them as excitingly modern. However, in the twenty-first-century timeframe of *Sweet Blue Flowers* the manga's characters perceive Fujigaya as a bastion of traditional values. When Fumi and her friends from Matsuoka visit Fujugaya, they admire it for its refined atmosphere and elegant trappings: tea parties! a chapel! bay windows in the library! (*SBF*, 1:85–86). If *Sweet Blue Flowers* were a traditional yuri work, I'm sure that the story would never stray beyond its ivied walls.

But although *Sweet Blue Flowers* pays homage to traditional yuri, the trajectory of this first volume points beyond it. I don't think that it's a coincidence that its most modern character, Fumi Manjome, is a student at Matsuoka and not at Fujigaya, or that her first kiss with Yasuko Sugimoto takes place among the austere steel shelves of Matsuoka's library, not the stylish wooden shelves of Fujigaya's (*SBF*, 1:114–16).

1. Michi Kawai, *My Lantern*, 3rd ed. (Tokyo: privately-pub., 1949), 224.
2. Kawai, *My Lantern*, 225.
3. Kawai, *My Lantern*, 225. Nogi Girls' High School was named after Count (or General) Maresuke Nogi, a Japanese war hero of the Meiji era, subsequent head of the Peers' School that educated the sons of Japan's noble families, and a mentor to the future Emperor Hirohito.
4. Shonan Shirayuri Gakuen, "History of the School," accessed December 5, 2021, using Google Translate, https://www.shonan-shirayuri.ac.jp. "Shonan" refers to the coastal area centered on Enoshima, while "Shirayuri Gakuen" translates literally as "White Lily Academy."
5. It's also worth noting that "Fujigaya" shares its initial kanji with Fujisawa, the city west of Kamakura where Shonan Shirayuri Gakuen's various schools are located.
6. "Category:Literature Museum of Kamakura," Wikimedia Commons, Wikimedia Foundation, last modified June 23, 2018, https://commons.wikimedia.org/wiki /Category:Literature_Museum,_Kamakura.
7. As previously noted, the kanji for "wisteria" is the same as that in "Fujigaya" and "Fujisawa."
8. And in real life, too: the uniforms worn by the girls at Shonan Shirayuri Gakuen High School resemble the Fujigaya uniforms. They feature a fleur-de-lis, the lily-derived design that is the school's emblem.

Ten(?) Years After

What is the chronology of *Sweet Blue Flowers*? How old are Fumi and Akira? When did they first know each other? And why were they separated for such a long time? Attempting to answer these questions can help us explore how *Sweet Blue Flowers* works as a narrative and why Takako Shimura made the choices she did.

In chapter 1, Fumi Manjome and Akira Okudaira meet again for the first time in several years (*SBF*, 1:34). To be precise, they meet knowing who the other person is—when they met at the train station on their first day in high school, they were effectively strangers to one another (1:12). How long had it been since they had last been together?

After their reunion, Fumi thinks to herself about "the ten years we'd spent apart" (*SBF*, 1:44). Is this consistent with the rest of the manga? In volume 1, Fumi and Akira are beginning their first year of (senior) high school. In the Japanese educational system, students spend six years in elementary school, three years in junior high school (lower secondary school), and three years in senior high school (upper secondary school).[1]

In the flashbacks to Fumi and Akira's childhood together, their class year is given as "year 1," with Fumi and Akira in the "Cherry Blossom" and "Plum Blossom" classes, respectively (*SBF*, 1:29–30). If these are elementary school classes, then nine years (not ten) would have elapsed between their entering year 1 of elementary school and year 1 of senior high school.

If this were the case, the time since Fumi and Akira last saw each other would be even less: they also appeared in a Christmas performance together (*SBF*, 3:68), so they would have been in school together almost an entire year. (The school year presumably started on the standard date of April 1.) Assuming that Fumi's parents moved away sometime after that, their time apart would be closer to eight years than nine.

The alternative explanation is that the manga depicts young Akira and Fumi in kindergarten rather than elementary school. I don't know enough to judge whether this is a reasonable explanation. But I will note that since Akira and Fumi must be fifteen years old to be entering high school, a ten-year separation would put them at five years old when they separated and four years old when they first met. These ages seem a bit young given the characters' appearances in the manga and make it a bit implausible that they would even have memories of that time.

Also, in a flashback in volume 3, Fumi is depicted as having started at a new school in what appears to be a typical elementary school classroom, numbered "2-2" (*SBF*, 3:116, 3:123). Therefore the most reasonable conclusion is that this scene depicts Fumi entering the second grade of elementary school relatively soon after her separation from Akira at or near the end of first grade.

On balance, I believe that Fumi and Akira met in elementary school and that the "ten years apart" was poetic license on the part of Fumi—or perhaps just her not doing the math correctly.

The more interesting question is, why did Shimura choose the plot device of girls separated in childhood and reunited in high school? I think the most straightforward explanation flows from two key elements of the manga: the contrast between Fujigaya and Matsuoka and the relationship between Funi and Chizu.

As discussed in the last chapter, I think Shimura thought it essential to the manga's themes that Fumi and Akira go to different schools. Having Fumi and Akira both go to Fujigaya would have made *Sweet Blue Flowers* just another conventional "schoolgirl yuri" story, while having them both go to Matsuoka would have denied Shimura an opportunity to comment on Class S tropes and attitudes.

But if Fumi and Akira were to attend different high schools, that raises the question of how they would have met in the first place. One obvious solution is for their respective families to have known each other in the past, either because they were related in some way or because they lived near each other and had daughters going to the same school.

There are already two incestual or potentially incestual relationships in *Sweet Blue Flowers* (Fumi and her cousin and Akira and her brother), neither of which the story portrays in a positive light. Thus having Fumi and Akira be related would be a non-starter. Shimura chose a better solution: the two families previously lived together, Fumi and Akira went to school together, and then Fumi's family moved away, presumably due to the demands of her father's work.

But then the story also has to account for the relationship between Fumi and Chizu. This relationship occurred before Fumi entered high school, presumably while attending junior high school. In this case, it does make sense for Chizu to be related to Fumi, providing an excuse for them to know each other well enough to have sleepovers. And since they were related, they likely spent time together well before then.

It wouldn't make sense for Fumi to be going to school with Akira during the period in which Fumi was having sex with Chizu. Among other things, this would eliminate the conceit that Akira was Fumi's "first love." So, that pushes the timeframe for Fumi's and Akira's time together past junior high into elementary school and likely into early elementary school.

Having Fumi and Akira meet in the first grade supports the plot device of Fumi coming to recall her "first love." It provides enough time for Fumi and Akira to have forgotten what each other looked like—and even each other's names—while still making them old enough to have retained some detailed memories of the time they spent together.

1. Ministry of Education, Culture, Sports, Science, and Technology, "Overview," MEXT website, accessed January 2, 2022, https://www.mext.go.jp/en/policy/education /overview/index.htm.

Abusive Relations

Content note: This chapter discusses child sexual abuse.

Having learned about Akira's brother's bad behavior, now it's time for Fumi's cousin Chizu to give readers a double dose. First, the facts as presented thus far in the series: Fumi is now fifteen years old. (See my previous discussion on this point.) Chizu is getting married, so presumably she's finished high school and is at least eighteen, perhaps even older if she went to university. Chizu wanted to (and apparently did) have sex with Fumi at a time when (judging from appearances) Fumi was younger than fifteen (*SBF*, 1:65).

Fumi seems to have had genuine feelings for Chizu and consented to her advances. But regardless of Fumi's feelings, to my mind, this is clearly a case of abuse: Chizu used Fumi for her own purposes and then abandoned her when she got married. As with Akira's brother, we can ask, what is this episode doing in this "schoolgirl yuri" story?

Unfortunately, the subplot with Chizu might imply to some that Fumi is a lesbian only because she was "recruited" as a child. This notion defames lesbians as predators on children and lessens the emotional impact of Fumi's journey to coming out. It casts her as a victim "groomed" to a role and unable to move beyond a past trauma, not as a person with agency expressing her inherent identity.

As an outsider to the culture, I can only guess at Takako Shimura's thinking here, but I doubt that was her intent. Here are my guesses as to what's going on, for what it's worth:

Recall again that *Sweet Blue Flowers* was originally serialized in *Mango Erotics F*. Shimura (or her editor) may have felt that including this sort of subplot made the series more appealing to the magazine's target audience of adults.

Also, other Shimura works published in *Manga Erotics F* and elsewhere include questionable content of this general type. For example, readers of *Wandering Son* will recall the scene when an adult character grabs a trans youth's crotch to investigate their genitals.[1]

Are there any ways in which Chizu's subplot contributes to the story? I presume that one purpose was to use the relationship and its end as a trigger for Fumi's rebound relationship with Yasuko Sugimoto. Having Fumi's prior relationship be with a schoolmate closer to her age would complicate the narrative of Akira's being Fumi's first love and (perhaps) her true love. Her time with Chizu also means Fumi is more sexually experienced than Akira—a factor in future volumes as their relationship evolves.

Finally, whether Shimura intended this or not (and I suspect she may have), Chizu's relationship with Fumi serves as a dark mirror of Class S and yuri narratives that feature older girls or women entering into relationships with younger girls. (For example, Nobuko Yoshiya's story "Yellow Rose" features a twenty-two-year-old teacher and a seventeen-year-old student.)[2]

These traditional tropes reflect an age-based social hierarchy in which one partner is senior to and (in social terms, at least) dominates the other. As the senior members of the pairings graduate or marry, they leave the world of intimate female-female relationships to live in a male-dominated and -centric world. The junior members, in turn, become the seniors to a new crop of girls in a never-ending cycle. (See, for example, my previous discussion of the workings of the *sœur* system in *Maria Watches Over Us*.)

In contrast, based on the evidence thus far *Sweet Blue Flowers* seems to valorize relationships between equals and implicitly criticize unequal relationships based on age or other hierarchies. Clearly, the relationship between Fumi and Akira is becoming more important to the story than Fumi's relationship with her senior Yasuko, with Kyoko's unrequited crush on Yasuko and Yasuko's on Mr. Kagami providing additional negative takes on unequal relationships. From this point of view, Chizu's relationship with Fumi offers the reader another example of the potential harms inherent in and inseparable from some classic yuri tropes.

1. Shimura, *Wandering Son*, 2:100–101.
2. Yoshiya, *Yellow Rose*, chap. 2.

Cry Baby

Fumi Manjome is a crybaby. That's pretty much the extent of the characterization she gets in the early chapters of *Sweet Blue Flowers*: she cries on the train when a man sexually harasses her (*SBF*, 1:16–17). In a flashback, she cries when she wets her pants in elementary school (1:30) and when she moves away from Akira (1:32). She cries (on multiple occasions) after she learns that her cousin Chizu is getting married and has abandoned her (1:43, 1:50, 1:62–63, 1:66). She cries before Yasuko kisses her for the first time (1:115), when she tells Akira about dating Yasuko (1:139–40), when Yasuko breaks up with her at the Sugimoto house (1:314), and while commiserating with Kyoko Ikumi afterward (1:376).

If this were all there were to Fumi's character, *Sweet Blue Flowers* would be a pretty depressing and uninteresting manga. But although Fumi is very prone to crying, she's more than the sum of those instances. It's not that she suffers from a debilitating emotional condition: it's more that she feels things very deeply and doesn't hold back expressing her emotions.

And as we're beginning to see, there's a steel core to Fumi's personality: she doesn't wallow in her tears but (typically with help from Akira) goes on to deal with whatever's upsetting her. She doesn't cling to Chizu after her abandonment, and she moves to get out of the Sugimoto house as soon as possible once she sees how things are with Yasuko.

This is why Fumi is my favorite character in *Sweet Blue Flowers*: she doesn't hold things in and present a false front to the world. She doesn't get passive-aggressive and lash out at people. Instead, she cries, spends a bit of time deciding what to do, and then gets on with her life.

Akira Questions

The acronym LGBTQIA and its more pronounceable near-anagram QUILTBAG were invented to be more inclusive than the phrase "gay and lesbian" or the more commonly used acronym LGBT. It's easy to make fun of piling letter upon letter in this way, but there's a serious point behind these neologisms: the rich variety of people's identities, orientations, and emotions can't be adequately described by a restricted set of labels. Akira Okudaira is a prime example of that.

Like Fumi Manjome, Akira's outer impression doesn't always match her inner expression. At first glance, she seems to fit the typical "*genki girl*" stereotype: lively and energetic, self-confident and enthusiastic. Her level-headedness and can-do confidence are indispensable to Fumi, helping her dry her tears and get on with life.

But at the same time, Akira isn't nearly as confident and assured when it comes to herself and her feelings, including her feelings concerning Fumi. When Fumi tells Akira that she's dating Yasuko Sugimoto, it throws Akira for a loop: "It's okay to like a girl, right? Or am I too dumb to know better?" (*SBF*, 1:144).

At this point in the story, it's not so much that Akira is questioning her orientation (one possible meaning of the "Q" in LGBTQIA)—although she does experience first-hand the "lady-killer" aura of Yasuko (*SBF*, 1:233–34)—it's more that she's questioning the conventional narrative of heterosexuality. Akira was familiar with the stories told about girl-girl friendships at a place like Fujigaya —"that really happens?!" she marvels when Kyoko Ikumi gets a letter from a junior high girl (1:78)—but now she's encountering the emotional reality of it in the person of someone she cares about.

Things are not made easier due to Akira herself being inexperienced in terms of relationships. She doesn't seem to have had crushes on anyone or been on a date of any sort. She welcomes the opportunity to go to the "singles party" arranged by Kyoko and Ko Sawanoi, but whether due to her brother's tagging along or for other reasons, nothing comes of it

(*SBF*, 1:97–98, 1:102–3). The comments from Akira's brother and Kyoko about Ko's interest in her elicit a response of "I'm not ready for that yet" (1:129–30).

Will Akira ever be ready? It's too early in the story to say definitively one way or another. Thus far the evidence hints that Akira may be asexual or aromantic (two possible meanings of the "A" in LGBTQIA). Unfortunately, the siscon subplot with her brother clouds the picture here with its implication of something darker causing this, instead of this just being the way Akira is. And what about Fumi, who seems to be beginning to see Akira (or re-see, given the "first love" memory) as more than just a friend? We'll have to look to future volumes for possible answers to these questions.

The Melancholy of Kyoko Ikumi

In another story, Kyoko Ikumi would be the main character. Her life thus far has followed a trajectory associated with many Class S and early yuri stories: apparently destined for an arranged marriage with an older man for whom she seems to have little if any real feeling, seeking refuge in an unrequited crush on an older girl, then meeting clear and unequivocal rejection from the object of her affections. If this were a traditional story, the only suspense would be whether her remaining life would be short and unhappy or long and unhappy.

But Kyoko is not the main character of *Sweet Blue Flowers*, which tells us something about what kind of story this is: "S for a new generation," as Erica Friedman put it in her review.[1] That new generation will presumably identify more closely with Akira and (especially) Fumi, whom Friedman called in another context a "Heisei girl," born after the Shōwa period ended in 1989 with Emperor Hirohito's death.[2]

So, why is Kyoko featured so prominently in *Sweet Blue Flowers* (almost as prominently as Yasuko Sugimoto in this first volume)? For one, she serves as a friend and classmate to Akira, a guide to her as she navigates the new world of Fujigaya Women's Academy. As Kyoko tells Akira, the women in her family have always attended Fujigaya, from elementary school on (*SBF*, 1:287).

Kyoko is also both a (would-be) rival to Fumi for Yasuko's affections and eventually a fellow sufferer (*SBF*, 1:375–76). I'll have more to say about Yasuko later, but clearly Kyoko's transparent neediness and Yasuko's own problems poisoned the possibility of any real relationship between them.

Where will Kyoto go from here? Thematically she seems destined to represent the past, as Fumi represents the future. Personally she still has Ko Sawanoi waiting in the wings, and perhaps their relationship (strained as it is) is her own best hope for escaping the unhappy fate of many a Class S protagonist.

1. Erica Friedman, review of *Sweet Blue Flowers*, vol. 1, by Takako Shimura, *Okazu* (blog), October 4, 2017, http://okazu.yuricon.com/2017/10/04/yuri-manga-sweet-blue-flowers-volume-1-english.

2. Erica Friedman, review of *Sweet Blue Flowers*, disc 1, *Okazu* (blog), May 6, 2013, https://okazu.yuricon.com/2013/05/06/yuri-anime-sweet-blue-flowers-aoi-hana-disk-1-english.

Takarazuka Time

It's time for the cultural festival, that staple of manga and anime set in high schools. However, the point of this festival isn't the festival per se, but the plays within it, put on by the Fujigaya drama club.

The school play is a frequently appearing element in Takako Shimura's work. It serves as a source of, well, drama, but more specifically, is used to put the characters into situations that allow them to imagine themselves as they wish to be, or show how others perceive them. Recall, for example, the performance of *Romeo and Juliet* in *Wandering Son*, in which Shiuchi envisions herself in (but does not get) the part of Juliet.[1]

Unlike Matsuoka (where the drama club consists only of Fumi's three friends), at Fujigaya the drama club is a long-standing institution ("they take it very seriously," Akira tells Fumi) that includes at least a couple of dozen students. The three divisions of Fujigaya each put on a production: *The Little Prince*, *Little Women*, and (for the high school) *Wuthering Heights*. The first two are interesting if only for their titles ("princes" and "little women" being a theme here, as we'll see), but the main focus is on *Wuthering Heights* (*SBF*. 1:74).

The play, and the casting of Yasuko Sugimoto in the male role of Heathcliff, evoke the Takarazuka Revue, an all-woman musical theater group formed in the early twentieth century (the same period that saw the creation and popularization of the Class S genre). To ensure readers get the connection, Shimura has the characters twice explicitly reference the Revue (*SBF*, 1:55, 1:241).[2]

The image of the Takarazuka Revue in Japanese popular culture is multi-faceted and shot through with ambiguity, with the Revue "the focus of heated debates about the construction and performance of gender."[3] It embodies a tension between the idea of women performing a male role for entertainment and instruction and the idea of women behaving in stereotypically masculine ways (including having women as romantic and sexual partners) as part of their core identity.

The Takarazuka Revue was founded as a corporate venture (to promote tourism and sell railroad tickets) and remains such today. It was and is motivated to conform to both popular ideals and government policy dictating the proper roles of men and women in society. The theory was that "by performing as men, females learned to understand and appreciate males and the masculine psyche [so that] when they eventually retired from the stage and married ... they would be better able to perform as 'good wives, wise mothers,' knowing exactly what their husbands expected of them."[4]

However, at the same time, a large part of the attraction of Takarazuka productions to their mainly female audience is the frisson of seeing women act in non-feminine ways both socially and sexually: "female fans of all ages, classes, and educational levels do not see a man on stage, but rather *acknowledge* a female body performing in a capacity that transgresses the boundaries of received femininity."[5]

This history of tension and conflicting visions of women's place replays itself in *Sweet Blue Flowers*. As a traditional educational institution, Fujigaya's mission is to prepare women for their "proper" place in Japanese society. The *Wuthering Heights* production and other plays are intended as socially-approved entertainment and instruction suitable for students and their parents. As such, they are designed to minimize anything that hints of transgression.

That strategy is implemented in large part through productions that are isolated in time and place from modern Japan, and thus avoid direct commentary on contemporary Japanese society: *Wuthering Heights* in late eighteenth and early nineteenth-century England, *Little Women* in mid-nineteenth-century America, and *The Little Prince* in a French-influenced science-fictional setting. (See also the ubiquity of Takarazuka productions in foreign historical settings, most notably *The Rose of Versailles*, set in late-eighteenth-century France.)

But despite Fujigaya's "official" intent regarding these all-girls plays, unofficially they evoke similar responses to Takarazuka productions: the students ooh and aah over the poster showing Yasuko in a glamorous pose as Heathcliff, take and exchange photographs of "Heathcliff" and "Catherine" in romantic poses, and speculate whether they'll kiss (*SBF*, 1:210–11).

Like the Class S relationships discussed in previous chapters, this aspect of Fujigaya productions remains universally known and discussed but never officially acknowledged, let alone accepted or endorsed. Given Shimura's love of plays as devices to drive the plot and highlight themes, we'll undoubtedly see more of them in future volumes of *Sweet Blue Flowers*. It will be interesting to see whether and how these productions depart from the standard Takarazuka template.

1. Shimura, *Wandering Son*, 6:20–24, 6:99–100.
2. Shimura also has an ongoing manga *Awashima hyakkei* (sometimes romanized as *Awajima hyakkei*) set in a girls' school resembling the school that trains Takarazuka performers. (The title is a play on *Fugaku hyakkei*—better known in the West as *One Hundred Views of Mount Fuji*—Hokusai's famous series of woodblock prints.) Unfortunately, *Awashima hyakkei* has not had an official release in English. Takako Shimura, *Awashima hyakkei*, 3 vols. (Tokyo: Ōta Shuppan, 2015–).
3. Jennifer Robertson, "The Politics of Androgyny in Japan: Sexuality and Subversion in the Theater and Beyond," *American Ethnologist* 19, no. 3 (August 1992), 422, https://doi.org/10.1525/ae.1992.19.3.02a00010.
4. Robertson, "The Politics of Androgyny in Japan," 427.
5. Robertson, "The Politics of Androgyny in Japan," 433. Italics in the original.

Yasuko Acts Out

If you read (only) the first volume of *Sweet Blue Flowers*, or if you've only watched the anime adaptation, you'd be forgiven for thinking that Yasuko Sugimoto was the most important character other than Fumi Manjome. Although Akira Okudaira is on the cover, through most of the first volume Akira primarily serves as a companion for Fumi, lending her a sympathetic ear and a shoulder to cry on. Fumi's coming out drives the plot in this volume, and Yasuko is the key driver of that development.

With that in mind, it's worth thinking about who Yasuko actually is and what she represents. What Yasuko represents is relatively easy to discern: she's (at least superficially) the *Sweet Blue Flowers* version of the "girl prince" archetype, whose evolution over the years has been explored by Erica Friedman.[1]

The girl prince's attributes include a somewhat masculine presentation and appearance (Yasuko's short hair and above-average height), excellence at sports or other pursuits not thought of as traditionally feminine (Yasuko is a star on Matsuoka's basketball team), a somewhat cool and distant attitude (most pronounced in Yasuko's relationship with Kyoko Ikumi), and attractiveness to other girls and women (as noted in my previous discussion of the *Wuthering Heights* production).

As Friedman notes, a classic example of the girl prince is Haruka Tenoh, Sailor Uranus in *Sailor Moon*, dashing race-car driver and lover of Michiru Kaioh (Sailor Neptune). The archetype is common enough to be parodied, for example, in the character of Yū Kashima in *Monthly Girls' Nozaki-kun*,[2] or to be critically interrogated, for example, with Utena Tenjoh in *Revolutionary Girl Utena*.

I believe that the character of Yasuko is an example of the latter. More specifically, *Sweet Blue Flowers* presents several examples of common yuri tropes and then inverts or critiques them (see, for example, my previous comments on Fumi and Chizu). As far as the students at Matsuoka and Fujigaya are concerned, Yasuko totally has her act together, just like any other proper girl prince.

But it becomes clear from the events of the first volume that Yasuko is as messed-up as any teenaged girl, veering between an emotional breakdown when Mr. Kagami appears at the *Wuthering Heights* cast party and rebelliousness and feigned bravado during Fumi's visit to the Sugimoto home (*SBF*, 1:249–51, 1:306–8). Even her sexual orientation gets questioned (somewhat cruelly) by her sisters: "So you're a lesbian? ... So *at the moment*, this is who you like? ... Then I guess you're bisexual, huh?" (1:307–8).

At the same time, Yasuko can step back and diagnose her situation and accept some responsibility for herself and her actions toward others. See, for example, her comments toward the elementary school student starring in *The Little Prince*, in which Yasuko may be comparing herself to Heathcliff: "a troubled man," prone to "cause other people trouble," but not exactly a "bad guy" (*SBF*, 1:225–27).

She also acknowledges to Fumi that "My feelings are a mess ... and I took it out on you," and tells her they should stop seeing each other—although even here it's not clear at all that Yasuko is entirely forthcoming about the background to all this (*SBF*, 1:320). It's Akira, not Fumi, that figures out the connection with Mr. Kagami (1:347).

But, in the end, Yasuko is a failure as a girl prince. Where in another yuri work she might end up as the senior partner in a foregrounded relationship with a junior girl, here she seems to represent a dead end for Fumi. And not just for Fumi either: the end of the volume sees Fumi and Kyoko commiserating with each other over their being "dumped" by Yasuko (*SBF*, 1:375–76). Whatever part Yasuko is destined to play in the remainder of *Sweet Blue Flowers*, it will not be that of the prince.

1. Erica Friedman, "Overthinking Things 05/03/2011: 40 Years of the Same Damn Story, Part 2," *The Hooded Utilitarian* (blog), May 2, 2011, http://www.hoodedutilitarian.com/2011 /05/21840

2. Izumi Tsubaki, *Monthly Girls' Nozaki-kun*, trans. Leighann Harvey, 12 vols. (New York: Yen Press, 2015–).

S Is for Sugimoto

From Yasuko Sugimoto, I now turn to her family: her sisters Kuri, Kazusa, and Shinako, and her mother Chie (who is not named in volume 1). The Sugimoto family occupies a particular place in the story of *Sweet Blue Flowers*, related to the overall theme of the work as I see it.

First, as Fumi marvels when she first visits Yasuko's home, "Her family's rich!" (*SBF*, 1:303). To be clear, Fumi's and Akira's families are far from poor. They live in detached houses (instead of apartments), own cars, and can afford to send their daughters to exclusive (and presumably expensive) private schools. However, the Sugimotos are in another class entirely. It's no accident that Takako Shimura modeled the Sugimoto family home on a guest house on the Tokyo estate of Marquis Toshinara Maeda, head of a leading samurai clan and (later) general in the Japanese army (1:378).

That wealth presumably comes from the position of Yasuko's father. We've already encountered the fathers of both Fumi and Akira. But the Sugimoto family patriarch is unseen, unnamed, and unmentioned, at least in the story thus far. The only male presence in the Sugimoto household is Mr. Ogino, the family servant Fumi initially mistakes for Yasuko's father (*SBF*, 1:299).

In the father's absence, the Sugimoto women occupy their time with gossip and Mahjong. Except for Kazusa, an artist who formerly taught at Fujigaya for a brief time, they appear to have done little else since graduating from school. Of course, they all went to Fujigaya, and appear to have been part of that school's Class S milieu. Shinako appears in the side story "Little Women" as the unrequited love interest of other girls ("everyone admires her," Orie sighs) (*SBF*, 1:379), and (as Kuri remarks) "Mother wants to brag about how popular she was as a girl," rather like a former high school sports star who continually retells stories of his exploits (1:305).

To my mind, the Sugimoto sisters and their mother represent another of Shimura's critiques of Class S and yuri tropes. The Sugimoto women have achieved a sort of freedom from the patriarchal culture of Japan, to speak frankly about intimate relationships between women (much to Fumi's embarrassment and consternation, after she's outed by Yasuko), and to indulge in such relationships themselves.

However, it is a freedom that is open to only to a wealthy few (who do not have to worry about discrimination against LGBTQ people at work or elsewhere), is limited in time and place, and is ultimately at the sufferance of the men who wield financial and other control over these women's lives. When those men return from their company headquarters, or golf courses, or mistresses, like Sir Thomas Bertram returning from Antigua in *Mansfield Park*,[1] they will reassert their authority and that of the male-dominated culture of Japan.

In other words, this is not the sort of freedom that Fumi needs or wants, even if she could achieve it in the first place. The Sugimoto women may be catalysts whose actions inadvertently help Fumi realize her identity and desires, but they can never be her models.

---

1. Jane Austen, *Mansfield Park* (London: 1814; Project Gutenberg, 1994), chap. 19, https://gutenberg.org/ebooks/141.

Girl Friends and Girlfriends

Now that I've come to the end of my commentary on volume 1 of *Sweet Blue Flowers*, it's a good time to consider some of the side characters in this volume. First up are Fumi's three classmates and friends at Matsuoka: Yoko Honatsugi ("Pon"), Miwa Motegi ("Mogi"), and Misako Yasuda ("Yassan"). They aren't very fleshed out as characters, so much so that it can be difficult keeping their nicknames straight, much less their full names. Their introduction at the beginning of volume 1 identifies them merely as "lively girls." They aren't featured at all in the character list at the beginning of part 2 of volume 1 (volume 2 of the Japanese edition) (*SBF*, 1:3, 1:198–99).

The main functions of Pon, Mogi, and Yassan seem to be giving Fumi someone else other than Yasuko to interact with at Matsuoka, drawing Fumi out of her introversion, and getting her involved with the *Wuthering Heights* production and other activities at Fujigaya. Time will tell whether they emerge as developed characters in their own right or simply exist to drive the plot in various directions.

Last but not least are Orie and Hinako (no family names given), who appear in the side story "Little Women" at the end of volume 1, along with Yasuko's sister Shinako, here portrayed in high school. Orie has a crush on Shinako, apparently her senior, and confides in Hinako, only to find that Hinako has a crush on her. "Soon after, I fell in love with Hinako," Orie recalls (*SBF*, 1:379–81), as she and Hinako enact Erica Friedman's "Story A" on a single page: "There is a girl, she likes another girl. The other girl likes her. They like each other. The end."[1]

Is there more to Orie's and Hinako's story than this? A story beyond "Story A"? That will have to wait until future volumes. In the meantime, it's worth noting two things: First, other than Fumi and Yasuko, Orie and Hinako are the only two girls referenced as being in a relationship. Second, and perhaps even more important, unlike Fumi and Yasuko, Orie and Hinako's appears to be a relationship of equals, between girls in the same class and of the same age. This means that they may break out of the straitjacket of age-based hierarchy in which Class S and yuri works often bind women who love women.

1. Erica Friedman, "Overthinking Things 04/03/2011: 40 Years of the Same Damn Story, Pt. 1," *The Hooded Utilitarian* (blog), April 3, 2011, https://www.hoodedutilitarian.com/2011/04/overthinking-things-04032011.

Notes on Volume 2

Shinobu and Ko

Despite being nominally an example of "schoolgirl yuri," *Sweet Blue Flowers* deviates from many works in that genre in featuring several male characters. The first to be encountered—and in less than pleasant circumstances—was Akira Okudaira's brother, who got kicked out of his sister's bed on the second page of volume 1 (*SBF*, 1:8). He spent the remainder of that volume being absurdly overprotective of his sister, to Akira's great annoyance, and creepy in general (1:102–3, 1:109).

In volume 2, Takako Shimura finally gives Akira's brother a name: "Shinobu" (*SBF*, 2:182). It's a name that (if Wikipedia is any guide) tends to be roughly equally used for both men and women. (For example, see Shinobu Oshino of Nisio Isin's *Monogatari* series, an ancient vampire in the form of an eight-year-old girl.)

Shimura may have meant this as a subtle comment that Shinobu does not measure up to traditional male standards: at this point in the story, he's still living at home, doesn't appear to have a job or to attend school (although a subsequent volume does refer to him being a university student), has no girlfriend (or any hint of having had one in the past), and seems to have nothing to do in life other than pestering his sister.

Be that as it may, he now starts shedding his siscon ways and, at least to some degree, repenting of them. Much of this is not through his own initiative, but instead comes about as a result of the actions of others.

This applies, in particular, to Shinobu's burgeoning relationship with Fumi's classmate Miwa Motegi ("Mogi"). As he drives the girls to a sleepover at Ko Sawanoi's aunt's estate (which, of course, he has free time to do), Mogi finds herself attracted to him, not by anything Shinobu actively does or says, but just because she thinks "he's cool" (*SBF*, 2:8–9, 2:62–63).

Mogi eventually takes the initiative of confessing to Shinobu (*SBF*, 2:133–35). We don't ever see his reaction or much of any other signs of his attraction to her; it's as if he simply passively entered into the relationship. Whether that's true or not, it's all very convenient from

Akira's point of view because it gets her brother out of her hair—though she continues to think of him as "super creepy" (2:44).

Shinobu does show at least some self-awareness and potential for emotional growth. As Ko attempts to initiate him into the mysteries of golf (that classic sport of upper-middle-class men), he admits to Ko that he's overprotective and that Akira will inevitably begin dating at some point (*SBF*, 2:22–24). (In other words, any siscon dreams he had are doomed to remain just that.)

However, I won't go out of my way to praise Shinobu's emotional growth or, for that matter, Ko's suitability as an instructor and role model for him. I'll comment on this more in a subsequent chapter, but it's not as if Ko, an adult (or nearly so) man fixated on entering into a relationship with a (now) second-year high school student, is an examplar of mature masculinity himself. To be uncharitable for a moment, from the evidence at hand, it seems that mostly what Shinobu learned from Ko is that it's OK for an older man to pursue a girl much younger than himself, as long as she's not his biological relative.

Ko and Kyoko

Though they didn't name her, one reviewer of volume 1 questioned Kyoko Ikumi's place in the overall plot: "There is also a character whose importance to the story fluctuates in such a way that it's unclear whether they are a side character or if they are a fourth, but underdeveloped, lead."[1]

My take is that Kyoko is indeed intended as a lead character and arguably is more important to the overall story and its themes than Yasuko Sugimoto. First, it's clear that Kyoko is Akira's closest friend other than Fumi, and given her status as Akira's same-year classmate at Fujigaya, that's likely to remain the case. Kyoko has also grown closer to Fumi after volume 1 ended with them dissolving into tears together over their respective infatuations with Yasuko (*SBF*, 1:374–76).

Thematically Kyoko and Ko's relationship somewhat mirrors that of Akira and Fumi, beginning in childhood and marked by one depending on the other. However, the situations are subtly different, in a way that echoes traditional gender roles: Fumi's love for Akira was first sparked by Akira's helping her, but Ko's love seems to date to his helping Kyoko.

But there are more differences beyond that. The age difference between Ko and Kyoko introduces a note of inequality into their relationship, unlike the inherent equality between Akira and Fumi. (Kyoko is nominally the person who has the power to say yes or no to the relationship, with Ko wanting it more than she does. However, this is just an example of the traditional "man the seeker, woman the sought" dynamic, and it remains unclear exactly how much freedom of action Kyoko has.)

Even more significant is that Ko and Kyoko's relationship is ultimately rooted in familial and societal expectations: that they will be married and that their marriage will cement an alliance between families. Ko's mother's concerns about his relationship with Kyoko emphasize this: "It looks bad for someone like that to join the family." She may feel sorry for Kyoko herself, but from her point of view, Kyoko's mother's (ambiguously described) condition and its possible reoccurrence in Kyoko and her children threaten the future of the Sawanoi family (*SBF*, 2:49–51).

In contrast, if Akira and Fumi eventually enter into a relationship, they will be doing so as equal individuals, acting on their own in defiance of social norms and the possible disapproval of their families or even their friends.

It's clear where Takako Shimura's sympathies lie: Despite the increased focus on Kyoko, Akira and Fumi are the "stars" of *Sweet Blue Flowers*, and everything we've seen to date, including Fumi's rejection of Yasuko, indicates that the manga valorizes equality and individuality in relationships. From this point of view, Kyoko and Ko, like Fujigaya, represent the past, with Fumi and Akira representing, if not the future, at least the promise of it.

1. Alex Cline, review of *Sweet Blue Flowers*, vol. 1, by Takako Shimura, Adventures in Poor Taste, October 19, 2017, http://www.adventuresinpoortaste.com/2017/10/19/sweet-blue-flowers-vol-1-review.

Speaking Up

As I wrote in a previous chapter, despite her tendency to break out in tears, "there's a steel core to Fumi's personality." That steel core is shown most clearly in the aftermath of Kazusa's wedding when Yasuko tries to escape her feelings about Mr. Kagami by tagging along with Akira and her brother to meet Fumi in Enoshima (*SBF*, 2:100–101).

Despite her past involvement with Yasuko and her meeting Kazusa at the Sugimoto home, Fumi did not attend Kazusa's wedding for various reasons, including not being a Fujigaya student and breaking up with Yasuko. Akira seems not to have even told Fumi about the wedding ("Oh, but I guess you couldn't," observes Kyoko), and Fumi appears to have forgotten all about it until reminded of it by Akira's mother when trying to call Akira at home (*SBF*, 2:92, 2:76–77).

Fumi decides to go to Enoshima on the spur of the moment. Her initial motivation seems to be to have some time to herself (*SBF*, 2:90–91). Although she initially protests, Fumi appears happy to have Akira come to meet her. However, when Yasuko invites herself as well, things come to a head, especially after Yasuko inserts herself into a dispute between Akira and her brother over his wanting to stay with the group (2:100, 2:106).

The overall sequence of events seems to be driven by the *senpai-kōhai* dynamic characteristic of Japanese school life (and indeed Japanese life in general). Students in lower grades defer to those in upper grades, and as students advance in grade they will be in turn deferred to by those coming up behind them.

Many manga and anime set in high schools (including *Sweet Blue Flowers*) are structured around this progression. New first-year students arrive, former first-years advance to their second year and have the new first-years to be *senpai* to, former second-years enter their third and final year and reach the top of the school hierarchy, and third-year students leave to face a world in which they will have new *senpai* to defer to. It's common for establishing shots of school classrooms to show the external signs marking the class year of the students within so that the viewer can keep track of the students' place in the hierarchy.

At this point in the story, Yasuko is a third-year student, and Akira and Fumi are only first-years, so the status gap between them is as large as it is possible to be within a high school. Yasuko exploits her *senpai* status, first in inviting herself to go with Akira and her brother to Enoshima, then in taking Akira's brother's side in his argument with Akira over his staying ("Why is she taking the lead?!" Akira fumes), and finally in proposing they "all hang out together" as a group (*SBF*, 1:100, 106–7).

Akira is clearly unhappy with the turn of events but remains silent. Instead, it is Fumi who actually verbalizes her opposition, with a single word: "No." She goes on to tell Yasuko, "I don't want to walk with you," and commands her to "stop bothering Akira" (*SBF*, 2:108).

Akira is shocked, and I think rightly so. Fumi's words seem to be a significant breach of the standard *senpai-kōhai* protocol. Fumi goes on to compound it later in the trip by rejecting Yasuko's attempt to make up ("I wanted to see you, Fumi." "Well, *I* didn't want to see *you*.") and then uttering a final and crowning insult: "Grow up" (*SBF*, 2:121–23).

Fumi later has second thoughts about the exchange ("I'm pretty selfish … aren't I?" she asks Akira) (*SBF*, 2:128). But her prior words to Yasuko can't be unsaid, and I believe that in Shimura's framing Fumi was absolutely right to say them. First, Yasuko was, in fact, abusing her position as *senpai* in her attempt to get back together with Fumi, inserting herself into a private outing she had no inherent right to participate in.

Second, and I think more important, these scenes are consistent with Shimura's framing of other relationships in the manga thus far, including Fumi's with Chizu and Kyoko's with Yasuko. To quote myself again: "*Sweet Blue Flowers* seems to valorize relationships between equals and implicitly criticize unequal relationships based on age or other hierarchies."

The difference here is between criticizing bad actions within a hierarchical system seen as otherwise promoting harmony within society versus criticizing the very idea of hierarchy itself. I believe that Shimura is doing the latter: she is implicitly criticizing the dominance hierarchies characteristic of traditional Class S and yuri works (hierarchies which are themselves embedded in larger hierarchies), and proposing a new model of yuri based on individualism and equality.

Fumi is the primary embodiment of this model within the world of *Sweet Blue Flowers*. But, as we shall see, she is not the only one, or even the first one.

Exit the Prince

Having discussed Fumi Manjome's side of the question, let's turn back to Yasuko Sugimoto. I earlier noted Yasuko as an example of the "girl prince" archetype who was nonetheless "as messed-up as any teenaged girl." Volume 2 of *Sweet Blue Flowers* continues that picture and (presumably) concludes Yasuko's time as a significant character in the story.

We already know the basic outlines of Yasuko's story from volume 1. While a student at Fujigaya, she had a crush on Mr. Kagami, a teacher who was her older sister's boyfriend and eventual husband (*SBF*, 1:162–63). After being rebuffed by him, she subsequently left Fujigaya to attend Matsuoka, where she met Fumi (1:164, 1:57–58). After a brief relationship, they broke up, apparently because of Yasuko's lack of honesty with Fumi about her continued feelings towards Mr. Kagami and Fumi's consequent jealousy and anger (1:320).

Volume 2 adds two new elements to the fallout from Mr. Kagami's wedding to Kazusa: a (presumably) definitive rejection by Fumi of Yasuko's attempt to get back together (discussed in the last chapter), and a view into Yasuko's past and inner feelings, apparently occasioned by Yasuko's self-reflection after being stung by Fumi's words.

The flashback starts with Yasuko's remembrance of being "treated ... like a prince" and growing used to that role, meeting her sister's boyfriend Mr. Kagami, and cutting her hair short to imitate her sister's "tough personality," finding herself becoming popular with other girls, and becoming "pretty stuck-up" (*SBF*, 2:110–13). The whole sequence is consistent with what we know from volume 1, so what if anything new do we learn in volume 2?

I don't think it's so much new information as a deeper look into things only hinted at before. Most notably, the backstory explains very well the fraught relationship between Yasuko and Kyoko Ikumi: Kyoko reminds Yasuko of what she herself is, a needy person obsessed with another person who will not return her affections. Yasuko's brusque and at times cruel behavior toward Kyoko resembles Kagami's treatment of Yasuko:

"He laughed when I confessed my feelings" (*SBF*, 2:115–16).

Seeing Kyoko cutting her hair and otherwise mimicking her, Yasuko considers it "cute but annoying" and concludes, "She never thinks about what's right for her" (*SBF*, 2:116). But this is often just as true of Yasuko herself, who veers between recognizing that her own behavior is destructive and then going ahead and behaving that way anyway, only to suffer yet another reverse.

There are a couple of other aspects worth noting about Yasuko's story. First, it's not clear exactly why she finds Mr. Kagami attractive. He praises her talent (at painting presumably) and encourages her to join the drama club, but that seems a thin motivation for what appears to be a years-long crush (*SBF*, 2:114). And when she's faced with the actual reality of Mr. Kagami, she seems put off: "You think like an old guy," she tells him, "You just aren't cool," and then berates him in her thoughts: "Even now, he says flirty things!" (2:87–89).

Maybe it's just as Yasuko tells him, referring to herself and her sisters, "We must have a genetic weakness for guys like you" (*SBF*, 2:88). Whether this is true or not, it does bring up a second key point about Yasuko.

For Yasuko, and apparently for her sister Kuri (another frustrated Mr. Kagami admirer), relationships with other women function as substitutes for the relationships with men they cannot have and are ultimately secondary to their relationships (or potential relationships) with men. See, for example, the "Little Women" story of Kuri and her classmate Komako, who laments, "I don't think we like each other the same way" (*SBF*, 2:176–77).

At an all-girls school, girls are more available for relationships than boys, and for Yasuko (and perhaps Kuri as well) they offer a less-stressful alternative—as Yasuko says to herself, "Girls are easy to handle" (*SBF*, 2:113). This again echoes the traditional Class S idea that relationships with women are "just a phase," appropriate for the hothouse atmosphere of an all-girls environment, but not something that can or should continue beyond graduation.

So what of Yasuko now? With Fumi's rejection of her, Yasuko's primary role in Fumi's story appears to be over (although Fumi still wonders for a bit whether she's genuinely over Yasuko). Yasuko has another scene with Kyoko (who also appears to be getting over Yasuko, though more quietly) and ultimately flies off to England, "as beautiful and brilliant as ever" (*SBF*, 2:146–48, 2:187–88).

Her final achievement at Matsuoka is to take the school's basketball team to the national championship game. However, she was not able to lead them to a final victory—somewhat of a metaphor perhaps for Yasuko's life thus far (*SBF*, 2:187).

Where will she go from here? Her worst fate, perhaps, would be to end up like her sisters Shinako and Kuri: wealthy and carefree, but having no visible purpose in life beyond gossip and flirtation with their old schoolmates, apparently unable or unwilling to commit to a deep relationship. Whatever one might think of her choice, Kazusa at least has made one and is committed to it. We'll have to see whether the same is true of Yasuko.

Patriarchy by the Book

In commenting on Fumi's visit to Yasuko's family, I noted the absence of Yasuko's father, the head of the Sugimoto household: "unseen, unnamed, and unmentioned." Now, at last, we catch a glimpse of him, albeit an exceedingly brief one, in a single panel in the chapter set at Kazusa's wedding (*SBF*, 2:94). However, though seen, he remains unnamed and unmentioned.

Determining the intent of an author is always tricky. Still, this omission may be deliberate on Takako Shimura's part, her version of the "curious incident of the dog in the night-time"—significant not for what is said or shown but rather for what is not. The creators of the *Sweet Blue Flowers* anime adaptation added an extra scene to humanize Yasuko's father: before the wedding, he sits on his back porch, sighs, and looks to the heavens as if he were a father in an Ozu film, mourning the loss of his daughter.[1]

I believe this violates the intent of the manga. In the context of everything else we know about the Sugimoto family and the evolving themes of the manga, this particular father is not supposed to be a character with emotions and an inner life. The Sugimoto sisters have a father, here he is, but he is not integral in any way to the plot, and hence we need know nothing more about him.

He is simply embodying a role, that of the family patriarch. More specifically, he is an entry in a book, the person listed as the "first registrant," the de facto head of the Sugimoto family, in the household register (*koseki*) maintained by the Japanese state. The *koseki* lists the other family members after him, in a representation of the family's age-based hierarchy: his wife Chie, "eldest daughter" Shinako, "second daughter" Kazusa, "third daughter" Kuri, and "fourth daughter" Yasuko.

Although precursors to the *koseki* system existed for many centuries, the *koseki* in its present form originated in the desire of Meiji-era governments to bring the entire Japanese population under their purview. The *koseki* system, as established in 1871 and revised and elaborated in 1898, enforced as normative an ideal patrilineal family. In this ideal family, a male head of household presided over a multi-generational family consisting of his wife, his unmarried daughters, his sons and their wives, their children in turn, and so on—replicating in miniature the Japanese "family nation" ruled over by the emperor.[2]

The postwar reforms imposed by the occupation authorities included a constitution that ostensibly treats the Japanese people as individuals. To accompany that change, the *koseki* system was reformed to eliminate its patrilineal character, at least in theory. The postwar period also saw several administrative and legal changes made to accommodate evolving family structures and practices, including divorces, intermarriage between Japanese nationals and foreign nationals, and the use of assisted reproductive technologies.[3]

However, in practice, the "reformed" *koseki* still reflects the patriarchal and heteronormative ideal of a nuclear family headed by a husband with a wife and one or more legitimate biological children.

For example, consider the (only) context in which we see Sugimoto *père*: he leads Kazusa down the aisle before her being wed to Mr. Kagami. In Anglo-American parlance, he is "giving the bride away," a phrase that implies that men own women and that in marriage that ownership is transferred to other men. Under the Meiji-era *koseki* system, this transfer would have been made literal by Kazusa's name being removed from the Sugimoto register and added to that of the Kagami household, headed by Mr. Kagami or his father or grandfather (if one of them were still alive).

The postwar *koseki* system is ostensibly more egalitarian and less patriarchal. Instead of Kazusa being transferred from the Sugimoto register to the Kagami register, she and Mr. Kagami would together leave their previous household registers and enter themselves into a new register corresponding to their newly-formed nuclear family. However, one of them would still be required to be the "first registrant," whose family name would become the name on the *koseki*. If they followed typical practice, this would be Mr. Kagami.[4]

If Kazusa wished to continue to use the Sugimoto family name, she would encounter a significant obstacle: which name she uses is not simply a matter between her as an individual and the Japanese state. The logic of the *koseki* dictates that she must enter herself into some register, she and her husband must register together as a household unit, and the household registration must be made under only one family name. She could retain her original family name by not registering her marriage with Mr. Kagami (in effect, entering into a common-law marriage). However, their children might then not be considered legitimate. One couple endured a lengthy legal battle over precisely this issue.[5]

The Japanese state forces everyone into the Procrustean bed of the *koseki* and has been willing to adjust its dimensions only slightly, slowly, and grudgingly. Likewise, Japanese society has come to identify the household as defined in the *koseki* with the concept of family itself: to be in a family means being registered together in the *koseki* and not being registered together means not being a family. We can see this especially in the case of LGBTQ individuals.

Consider, for example, Shuichi Nitori, the transgender protagonist of Shimura's *Wandering Son*. If she were to transition in accordance with Japanese law, she would be forced off the Nitori *koseki* and required to register herself separately—in effect, severing her from her family of birth.[6]

Some have justified this according to the logic of the *koseki*. If Shuichi's sister Maho were younger than Shuichi (instead of one year older), after Shuichi's transition there would be two "eldest daughters" on the Nitori *koseki*. The claim is that the state needs "to prevent such confusing *koseki* entries." However, this logic is not applied in other cases more aligned with patriarchal norms—for example, the case of a man who marries and has a daughter with one woman, divorces her and remarries, and then has another daughter with his second wife, all the while acting as the "head" of his register. Here the *koseki* also contains two "eldest daughter" entries, but the state does not care.[7]

Consider also Fumi and Akira, should their relationship ever progress to becoming life partners. Japanese law does not explicitly prohibit two women from marrying each other, but the logic of the *koseki* is again deployed against them: when two people marry and start their own register, one must designate as the husband and one as the wife. In combination with ambiguous wording in the Japanese Constitution and other aspects of Japanese law relating to gender, this fact has heretofore provided the justification for Japanese judges to reject marriage equality.[8]

One way to work around this restriction is for the older person to adopt the younger, as Nobuko Yoshiya did her partner Chiyo Monma. This allows them to access some of the benefits usually denied to unmarried couples, such as access to insurance and the ability to make medical decisions for each other. However, such arrangements can be contested by the partners' families.[9] They also promote the idea of an age-based hierarchy in relationships, an idea that *Sweet Blue Flowers* implicitly (and, at times, explicitly) opposes.

It's true that men also can be harmed by the *koseki* system. Witness the case of the man rejected by his biological father, who refused to acknowledge the existence of his son in the *koseki*. Living outside the system and unable even to attend public school, the man was released from legal limbo only at age 36 upon his father's death and the successful conclusion of a subsequent legal proceeding.[10]

But it's clear that the system in which Kazusa is embedded (along with all the other women of *Sweet Blue Flowers*) is ultimately of men, by men, and for men. (In the story mentioned above, the man's mother and her household register were irrelevant in establishing his legal existence.) In entering into a relationship, Fumi and Akira would be living outside the law, or more precisely trapped by rules and regulations that, for the most part, refuse to recognize their lives except in the context of their relationships to men.

The typical "schoolgirl yuri" work slides over this reality in its quest to portray a fantasy world of female relationships in which men are invisible. Though *Sweet Blue Flowers* has the outward form of schoolgirl yuri, like a Jane Austen novel it hints at a deeper and darker reality beneath its allegedly frivolous surface.

I previously likened Yasuko's father to another absent father, Sir Thomas Bertram of *Mansfield Park*, who spends much of the story away at his plantation on the Caribbean island of Antigua. In that novel, after the demure heroine Fanny Price is reproved by others for being "too silent in the evening circle," she says of Sir Thomas, "Did not you hear me ask him about the slave-trade last night?"[11]

It is but one sentence in a very long novel. Still, in combination with a reader's knowledge of early nineteenth-century British society, it speaks volumes about the socioeconomic system that supports the aristocracy into which Fanny will ultimately marry. Whether Shimura intended this or not, to someone like myself with at least a superficial knowledge of contemporary Japanese society, *Sweet Blue Flowers* similarly says a great deal with a single image.

1. *Sweet Blue Flowers*, episode 10, "The Happy Prince," 00:17.

2. David Chapman, "Geographies of Self and Other: Mapping Japan through the *Koseki*," *Asia-Pacific Journal: Japan Focus* 9, no. 29 (July 19, 2011), 6–7, https://apjjf.org/-David-Chapman/3565/article.pdf.

3. For an overview of how the *koseki* system has operated from the immediate postwar period to the present, see Vera Mackie, "Birth Registration and the Right to Have Rights: The Changing Family and the Unchanging *Koseki*," in *Japan's Household Registration System and Citizenship: Koseki, Identification, and Documentation*, ed. David Chapman and Karl Jakob Krogness (London: Routledge, 2014), 203–17.

4. At the time that *Aoi hana* was being serialized, wives adopted their husbands' names in over 96 percent of Japanese marriages. Linda E. White, "Challenging the Heteronormative Family in the *Koseki*: Surname, Legitimacy, and Unmarried Mothers," in Chapman and Krogness, *Japan's Household Registration System and Citizenship*, 253n16.

5. White, "Challenging the Heteronormative Family in the *Koseki*," 239–40, 249–51.

6. Shūhei Ninomiya, "The *Koseki* and Legal Gender Change," trans. Karl Jakob Krogness, in Chapman and Krogness, *Japan's Household Registration System and Citizenship*, 169–71.

7. Ninomiya, "The *Koseki* and Legal Gender Change," 177–78.

8. Claire Maree, "Sexual Citizenship at the Intersections of Patriarchy and Heteronormativity: Same-Sex Partnerships and the *Koseki*," in Chapman and Krogness, *Japan's Household Registration System and Citizenship*, 190–91.

9. Maree, "Sexual Citizenship at the Intersections of Patriarchy and Heteronormativity," 194–96.

10. Kana Yamada, "Now with a Legal Father, Saitama Man, 36, Ready to Start Own Life," *Asahi Shimbun*, February 21, 2018, https://web.archive.org/web/20180222034739/http://www.asahi.com/ajw/articles/AJ201802210043.html. The man's father was an aide to a member of the Japanese Diet, the legislative body responsible for the continued existence of the *koseki* in its present form.

11. Austen, *Mansfield Park*, chap. 21.

New Year, New Girl

We're now into the second half of volume 2 of *Sweet Blue Flowers* (volume 4 in the original Japanese edition). Fumi's and Akira's first years at their respective high schools have ended, and they are now second-year students. Yasuko Sugimoto has left the scene (as discussed in a previous chapter), making room for a new secondary character, Haruka Ono (*SBF*, 2:182).

Haruka continues the *Sweet Blue Flowers* tradition of having interesting secondary characters beyond the central duo of Fumi and Akira. (This isn't universal, though: Fumi's Matsuoka friends Mogi, Yassan, and Pon continue to have relatively little to do, and their characterization remains thin.)

Haruka performs several critical functions within the story. First, she's entertaining in her own right, with her outsized personality and vocal brashness. She also provides a pair of fresh eyes to view the goings-on at Fujigaya, especially because she transferred in and did not attend Fujigaya's elementary or middle schools.

In this respect and others (including her height), she resembles Akira. It's almost as if she's a younger version of Akira, with her wide-eyed admiration of all things Fujigaya. She's even visually framed the same way as she enters the tunnel leading to the school and repeats Akira's comments to herself about being a "Fujigaya lady" almost word for word (*SBF*, 2:194–95). "She's just like you were!" Kyoko marvels (2:195).

One might ask, why do we need an Akira clone when we already have Akira? The most straightforward answer is that second-year Akira is much changed from first-year Akira. She's been thrown for a loop by Fumi's interest in her and seems somewhat uncertain and almost lost, not knowing what to do about the situation and not knowing whom to turn to for advice and a sympathetic ear. "You seem so distant," Fumi tells her (*SBF*, 2:249).

Haruka reminds us of the most appealing traits of Akira: her energetic and impulsive nature, her sense of justice, and her willingness to speak and act in support of what she thinks is right. Even their motivations in attending Fujigaya are similarly ditzy: Akira seems to have done it almost on a whim, while Haruka was moved by her admiration of Yasuko—not realizing that Yasuko didn't attend Fujigaya (*SBF*, 2:288–90). It's no surprise that Fumi becomes friends with Haruka, despite their age difference and their attending different schools. Many of the things that attract her to Akira attract her to Haruka as well.

Haruka is also in a way going through a similar self-assessment as Akira. Just as Fumi's confession to her prompts Akira to question both her feelings toward Fumi and her feelings about lesbian relationships generally, Haruka's discovery of her sister's love letter causes her to think about the issue as well, involving as it does someone close to her (*SBF*, 2:322).

Haruka also helps drive the plot in various ways, both large and small. She discovers Ryoko Ueda reading in the library and urges she be cast in the school play, encourages and counsels Fumi in her (ultimately unsuccessful) attempt to play a role as well, and then apologizes to Fumi for her pushiness after Fumi calls it quits (*SBF*, 2:259–60, 2:262, 2:291, 2:294, 2:314–16).

Finally, Haruka's conversation with Fumi about her sister ("I think my sister is in love with a girl!"), Fumi's response to Haruka about that revelation, and Fumi's regret over what she feels is the inadequacy of that response, set up the climactic scene of volume 2, Fumi's confession to Akira of her true feelings (*SBF*, 2:328–31, 2:33–38).

Altogether Haruka is a most amusing and appealing character. By the end of volume 2, she's become a force to be reckoned with at Fujigaya ("You sure have a lot of older friends," remarks Akira) and reinforces the theme of the subversion of hierarchy that I discussed in previous chapters (*SBF*, 2:318). Where her character will go in volume 3 remains to be seen, but her presence is certainly one of the highlights of volume 2.

Rokumeikan

Now that a new school year has begun at Fujugaya, it's time for the school's drama club to choose a new play to put on. This year they decide to put on *Rokumeikan*, a 1956 play by the Japanese author Yukio Mishima.[1] I'll defer talking about the play's plot and characters and how they integrate with the themes of *Sweet Blue Flowers*; that will have to wait until the next volume when the drama club will perform the play. For now, I'll concentrate on its author and setting.

Any discussion of *Rokumeikan* inevitably starts with its author. Non-Japanese readers are far more likely to know the name "Yukio Mishima" than they are to know the play itself. Mishima is most famous for the way he died, committing *seppuku* in 1970 at the age of 45 after an unsuccessful attempt to rally the soldiers at a Japan Self-Defense Forces base to revolt in the name of the emperor.

Non-Japanese readers are also likely to know that Mishima was almost certainly a closeted gay man (though his widow strenuously denied this). This constitutes subtext for *Sweet Blue Flowers*, but I don't think it's the most relevant aspect of the choice of *Rokumeikan*. (Among other things, I think one of the themes of *Sweet Blue Flowers* is the rejection of subtext.)

Instead, I think we can best understand the significance of *Rokumeikan* to *Sweet Blue Flowers* by looking not at its author but at the play itself.

Although Mishima is best known outside Japan as a novelist, he was also a major playwright with several dozen plays to his credit. He occupied a position in 1950s and 60s Japan comparable to that of his contemporaries Tennessee Williams and Arthur Miller in America. Far from being a Takurazuka-style fantasy, *Rokumeikan* is a serious literary work. Fujigaya putting on a production would be like an American high school putting on a production of *A Streetcar Named Desire* or *Death of a Salesman*.

Like those plays, *Rokumeikan* caught the imagination of audiences. After its initial production in 1956, the play went on tour to thirty-five cities. It was produced again in 1962 and 1963, and then in 2006 was revived to celebrate the 50th anniversary of the premiere.[2] A television adaptation aired in January 2008 while Takako Shimura was writing *Sweet Blue Flowers*. This TV movie would likely have been the form in which Akira encountered it, hence her comment to Ryoko Ueda: "Oh, right! It was originally a play" (*SBF*, 2:230).

Unlike a typical Takurazuka production, *Rokumeikan* is not set in a foreign land but in Japan itself, during one of the most critical eras of its history, and touches on key issues still relevant in Japan today. Before Rokumeikan was a play, it was a building ("Deer-cry Hall") constructed in the 1880s as a guest house cum meeting center for foreign diplomats visiting Japan. The Rokumeikan was designed by a British architect working in the French style and featured balls and banquets attended by Japanese nobles and bureaucrats dressed in Western suits and gowns.

The Rokumeikan could thus be seen as either a sign of Japan's emergence as a recognized equal to Britain, France, and other Western powers or an attempt by Japan to mimic Western ways to the detriment of native Japanese traditions.

This harks back to the chapter contrasting Fujigaya and Matsuoka. How should modernity and tradition be balanced? Should one be bound to tradition? Celebrate it but move on? Actively repudiate it? What is lost, and what is gained, with each approach? Over the years, Fujigaya itself has gone from an emblem of modernity in the Meiji era—established by representatives of a foreign religion and based on a Western model—to a bastion of tradition in twenty-first-century Japan.

These tensions display themselves in the setting of *Rokumeikan*, the characters' actions within the play, and the lives of the girls who portray those characters. I'll discuss this topic in more depth when we get to volume 3.

---

1. Yukio Mishima, "The Rokumeikan: A Tragedy in Four Acts," in *My Friend Hitler, and Other Plays of Yukio Mishima*, trans. Hiroaki Sato (New York: Columbia University Press, 2002). The lines from the play quoted in *Sweet Blue Flowers* are not from Sato's translation. They were presumably translated by John Werry, translator of the manga.

2. Mami Harano, "Anatomy of Mishima's Most Successful Play *Rokumeikan*" (master's thesis, Portland State University, 2010), https://pdxscholar.library.pdx.edu/cgi /viewcontent.cgi?article=1386&context=open_access_etds, 55.

Adult Concerns

I earlier speculated that Shimura was promoting a "new model of yuri based on individualism and equality," and noted that Fumi was neither the only nor the first example of this in the world of *Sweet Blue Flowers*. I was thinking specifically of Hinako Yamashina and Orie Ono.

Orie and Hinako (as they were introduced initially) first showed up at the very end of volume 1, as junior students to Shinako Sugimoto who eventually fell in love with each other (*SBF*, 1:379–81). I wrote in a previous chapter that "Orie's and Hinako's appears to be a relationship of equals" and speculated that they might "break out of the straitjacket" imposed by traditional Class S and yuri tropes.

That speculation is confirmed in the second half of volume 2, as Orie and Hinako re-enter the story as full-fledged adults (with family names to boot). Hinako Yamashina is the homeroom teacher for Akira's second-year class, and Orie Ono is the elder sister of first-year student (and friend to Akira and Fumi) Haruka Ono. Their (re)appearance is significant for multiple reasons:

First, Orie and Hinako represent a group that in classic schoolgirl yuri tales is not supposed to exist, namely adult women who have relationships with other adult women after graduation. Their very existence puts the lie to the idea that "it's just a phase" and that in the end, every girl-turned-woman must conform to the prevailing heterosexual ideal.

Second, Hinako is a potential role model for students attracted to other girls, reassuring them that they are not alone or abnormal. This is highlighted in the "Orie and Hinako" segment in the middle of volume 2, in which the student Kawakubo (only her family name is given) talks with Hinako and complains about her parents thinking her "sick" for liking girls. After hearing her out, Hinako affirms that she too "liked a girl" (leaving unsaid the fact that she still does) (*SBF*, 2:165–67).

It's worth stopping for a moment here to re-emphasize a point I've made previously about *Sweet Blue Flowers*. Although Kawakubo tries her best to get Hinako to reciprocate her feelings, Hinako shuts her down cold: "I don't want a student as my girlfriend." Her response echoes Mr. Kagami's previous rejection of Yasuko's advances. Their actions seem to me to reflect more than just caution on the part of Hinako and Mr. Kagami, or a feeling on their part that student-teacher relationships are unhealthy.

To my mind, it's consistent with the repeated framing in *Sweet Blue Flowers* of equal relationships as superior to relationships marked by age, status, and power differentials—a clear rejection of the idea promoted by both Nobuko Yoshiya and *Maria Watches Over Us*, that a relationship with an older girl (or a teacher, as Yoshiya adds) is essential to a girl's proper socialization and emotional development.

Finally, the fact that Hinako and Orie are adults with adult concerns introduces a note of realism into a genre often marked by fluffy fantasies. As Akira listens to her fellow students talk, it's clear that she's worried about the consequences of reciprocating Fumi's feelings (2:206–9). But the stakes are much higher for Orie and Hinako.

Orie's refusal to marry has caused conflicts with her parents and heartbreak for her mother (*SBF*, 2:329). Hinako is presumably at risk of losing her job if the rumors circulating among the students were to come to the attention of the school administration and were then to be confirmed. In this context, Hinako's admission to Kawakubo, even if couched in the past tense, is especially risky. What if, after being rejected, Kuwakubo were to turn against Hinako and seek revenge?

The presence of Hinako and Orie does not make *Sweet Blues Flowers* an adult yuri work. The primary focus is still on the budding relationship between Fumi and Akira. However, I think it's fair to say that although *Sweet Blue Flowers* is still an example of "schoolgirl yuri," it's schoolgirl yuri that is increasingly concerned with issues that can only be called adult.

Stuff like That

I've come to the end of volume 2, and I still haven't said much about what's going on with Fumi and Akira. Allow me to remedy that, in my last comments before I wrap up this volume.

Like many schoolgirl yuri relationships, Fumi and Akira's progresses relatively slowly, with only three significant developments across the entire volume.

The first is Fumi's rejection of Yasuko. Her relationship with Yasuko firmly cemented Fumi's identity as a lesbian (to the reader, but I also think to Fumi herself). At the same time, its ending and her subsequent recovery left her open to the (re)kindling of her feelings toward Akira (*SBF*, 1:88–92, 1:135–40, 1:333–35).

That led directly to the next significant development, Fumi's telling Akira that she was her "first love" (*SBF*, 2:138–41). Since this was not an unambiguous confession, it leaves both Akira and Fumi at loose ends: Akira cannot discern precisely what Fumi's present-day feelings are toward herself. She also wonders about both her feelings (or perceived lack of them) toward Fumi and her more general feelings about girl-girl relationships.

Meanwhile, Fumi is tortured about what Akira's feelings are, even to the point of being led astray, imagining that something is going on between Akira and Ko Sawanoi. She struggles to regain the self-confidence she evinced when rejecting Yasuko.

We see this in Fumi's ultimately unsuccessful attempt to participate in the Fujugaya drama club's production of *Rokumeikan* (*SBF*, 2:279–86, 2:308–10). It's unclear why Fumi actively persists with this, given her evident discomfort and feelings of inadequacy. She tells Haruka Ono that she "wanted to show her up" ("her" meaning Yasuko), but what exactly did Fumi mean by this (2:316)?

Perhaps Fumi wanted to mimic Yasuko's smooth self-confidence, the attitude that initially swept Fumi off her feet. Being in the play as Kiyohara (a supporting role but a major one) would put her in a similar position to Yasuko in *Wuthering Heights*. With Akira also in the play, she'd have plenty of opportunities to impress her, just as Yasuko impressed the girls of Fujigaya the year before.

But, as Fumi ultimately concludes, she's in no way equipped to step into Yasuko's role, much less to "show her up." "I'm simply not like Sugimoto. This is just ... the way I am" (*SBF*, 2:308). Fumi walking away from the play relieves her of that burden. In combination with her dissatisfaction with her answer to Haruka, it also leads to the third and final significant development: Fumi's confession to Akira, which in essence concludes the volume (2:335). (The final scene at the Kamakura rail station is inconclusive.)

So where do things stand now, at the end of volume 2? We've already had a kiss (between Yasuko and Fumi) and a confession. In a typical schoolgirl yuri work, a confession and a kiss would be the climax, and we'd be ready to call it a success and go on to the next thing. Yet here we are with another two volumes still to come.

From Fumi's point of view, things are relatively straightforward: she knows who she is (a woman who loves women), knows what she wants (both an emotional and physical relationship with Akira), and has come right out and asked Akira for just that. The major suspense in subsequent volumes will be whether Fumi gets what she wants.

As for Akira, she still reads as asexual and (mostly) aromantic, so whether she's even able to have that sort of relationship with Fumi is still in doubt, let alone whether she's interested in doing so. However, there are some points we can contemplate.

First, Akira isn't repulsed by the idea of two girls having a relationship. Her fear seems to be more that she'll be embarrassed if she quizzes Fumi and finds out Fumi's not interested in her (*SBF*, 2:221). She mainly appears to be somewhat confused and unsure what to think (2:219–20).

Second, it's also clear that Akira has no interest in boys or men. Whatever interest Ko Sawanoi might have had in her, it's apparent that she feels nothing towards him—which makes Fumi's insecurities about Akira and Ko a bit unrealistic, even if jealousy does make her temples hurt (*SBF*, 2:156).

Finally, it's been intimated that girls can arouse some sort of response in Akira. The first instance was in volume 1 with Yasuko ("I can see how she's such a lady-killer.") (*SBF*, 1:234). The second was arguably in volume 2 in her reaction to seeing Fumi and Ryoko standing next to each other ("... seeing Fumi and Ueda together felt strange.") and to Ryoko's "key-chain" comment (2:276, 2:212–13). Given that all three girls are tall, and both Fumi and Ryoko have long hair, I don't think it's too much to conclude that Akira may have a "type." If so, Fumi fits it to a T.

Where will Akira and Fumi go from here? That is the primary question to be addressed in the final two volumes.

Notes on Volume 3

All Japanese

Before I get to the main attraction (i.e., *Rokumeikan*), let me take a moment to consider the other plays presented at the Fujigaya drama festival. The first point worth noting (as Kazusa does while reading the flyer) is that all the plays are Japanese in origin and on Japanese themes (*SBF*, 3:10).

This contrasts with the previous year, when (as I previously wrote) the plays seemed "designed to avoid as much as possible anything that hints of transgression ... through productions that are isolated in time and place from modern Japan, and thus avoid direct commentary on contemporary Japanese society." None of this year's plays take place in modern Japan, but a play like *Rokumeikan* is certainly more relevant to contemporary Japanese society than *Wuthering Heights*.

What about the other two? *The Bamboo Cutter* is based on a thousand-year-old Japanese folktale (*Taketori monogatari*), also known as *The Tale of Princess Kaguya* (*Kaguya-hime no monogatari*), about an old childless couple who discover a baby in a stalk of bamboo and raise her as their own. As she grows to become a young woman, she is beset by suitors, including the emperor, but refuses them all and is eventually carried away to the moon to rejoin her people.

The Bamboo Cutter seems simply a charming tale fit for elementary school students. But as Caroline Cao points out, it can be interpreted as implicitly criticizing a father driven by "patriarchal obsessions" to seek social status for himself through his daughter's marriage. "Had Kaguya's father not been oblivious to her evident pain and so presumptuous of her welfare, perhaps Kaguya would have lived happily in an earthly life ... away from the greed of men seeking to make a wife out of her."[1]

The Izu Dancer (*Izu no odoriko*) is a more modern tale, based on a 1926 short story by the famous Japanese author Yasunari Kawabata. Better known in the West as "The Dancing Girl of Izu," the story was an early highlight in a career that eventually saw Kawabata win the Nobel Prize for Literature in 1968.

"The Dancing Girl of Izu" has been translated into English by Edward Seidensticker[2] and later by J. Martin Holman.[3] (The Holman translation is supposedly more faithful to the Japanese, but I think the Seidensticker translation reads better as English.) The Wikipedia article for the story calls it "a lyrical and elegiac memory of early love," but to my Western eye it's also more than a bit creepy.

Why might I think that? Let's look at a summary of the plot (from an anonymous contributor to Answers.com): "The nineteen year old narrator, an introspective student on a holiday from an upper class school in Tokyo, ... meets and becomes infatuated with a young dancer in a traveling family of entertainers. At first he feels a vague erotic attraction to her. But when he sees her in the nude in a public bath, he realizes that she is still a [thirteen-year-old] child, still pure and innocent. This changes his feelings for her to a loving brother-like protector. He is accepted by and becomes close to the family. ... At the end the narrator and the little dancer part with the promise that they will meet again. Yet we understand, as the narrator seems to realize, that this will never happen; this sweet tender moment in life has passed, and the love they feel is impossible."[4]

(The Seidensticker version gives the student's and the girl's ages as nineteen and thirteen respectively, the Holman version as twenty and fourteen. I presume this is because Holman is literally translating ages written according to the older Japanese system, in which a child is considered to be one year old at birth and their age increases by one year at every New Year.)

On the one hand, one could agree with critic Mark Morris that this is a story "about cleansing, purification ... [a] narrative vision that ... generates impulses of release, near jouissance, by means of an effacement of adult female sexuality and its replacement by an impossible white void of virginity ....," and see it as a worthy literary accomplishment.[5] On the other hand, if one is familiar with the many anime and manga featuring prepubescent "waifus" worshiped for their purity and innocence then the story can be a bit harder to take.

So, how has *The Dancing Girl of Izu* been able to inspire at least six films, three television dramas, and (in *Sweet Blue Flowers*) an adaptation for the stage deemed suitable for a production by middle schoolers in a stodgy girl's academy? Some adaptations side-step the implications of the plot by aging the dancing girl up. For example, in the 1933 silent film version, the girl's age goes unmentioned, and the twenty-four-year-old star Kinuyo Tanaka is hard to mistake for a minor.[6]

Other adaptations age the student down, as the Fujigaya production presumably does. And some may not care, just as many people watching the anime adaptation of *Sailor Moon* don't seem to care that thirteen-year-old Usagi Tsukino has a boyfriend who's a university student.

The more interesting question is, does Takako Shimura care? I have no way of knowing. But I will repeat what I have written multiple times now, that *Sweet Blue Flowers* seems to implicitly endorse relationships between equals (Akira and Fumi, Orie and Hinako) relative to relationships between those unequal in age or other aspects (Chizu and Fumi, Yasuko and Fumi, and Ko and Kyoko). So from that point of view, I hope you'll forgive me if I interpret Shimura's reference to *The Izu Dancer* as a subtle hint that contemporary Japanese society still has some issues when it comes to young girls and older guys.

1. Caroline Cao, "The Patriarchal Pains of Womanhood in the Films of Studio Ghibli's Isao Takahata," Anime Feminist, January 25, 2019, https://www.animefeminist.com/feature -the-patriarchal-pains-of-womanhood-in-the-films-of-studio-ghiblis-isao-takahata.

2. Yasunari Kawabata, "The Izu Dancer," trans. Edward Seidensticker, in *The Izu Dancer, and Other Stories*, Yasunari Kawabata and Yasushi Inoue, trans. Edward Seidensticker and Leon Picon (Tokyo: Tuttle, 2011). Kindle.

3. Yasunari Kawabata, "The Dancing Girl of Izu," in *The Dancing Girl of Izu, and Other Stories*, 3–33, trans. J. Martin Holman (Washington, DC: Counterpoint, 1998).

4. "What Is a Plot Summary of The Izu dancer'?," Answers.com, accessed November 28, 2019, https://www.answers.com/Q/What_is_a_plot_summary_of_The_Izu_dancer.

5. Mark Morris, "Orphans," review of *The Dancing Girl of Izu, and Other Stories*, by Yasunari Kawabata, trans. J. Martin Holman, *New York Times*, October 12, 1997, https://archive .nytimes.com/www.nytimes.com/books/97/10/12/reviews/971012.12morrist.html.

6. *The Dancing Girl of Izu*, directed by Heinosuke Gosho (Shochiku, 1933), 1 hr., 32 min., https://www.youtube.com/watch?v=yd36RJ0nzdM.

Setting the Stage

Before I comment on the play itself, I think it's helpful to discuss the historical context around *Rokumeikan*. The play is set in 1886, in the middle of the Meiji era (1868–1912), one of the most tumultuous and consequential eras in the history of Japan. The historical setting of *Rokumeikan* would be as familiar to modern Japanese schoolgirls like those at Fujigaya and Matsuoka as the Civil War period is to us in the US.

This chapter is in the service of my commentary on *Sweet Blue Flowers* and the girls who populate its pages. I therefore thought it appropriate to discuss the history of Meiji-era Japan and the Rokumeikan from the point of view of Sutematsu Yamakawa, Shige Nagai, and Ume Tsuda,[1] three ordinary girls whose extraordinary lives were documented by Janice Nimura[2] and by Akiko Kuno, one of their great-grandchildren.[3] Yamakawa, the oldest of them, was born in 1860, only a few years after Commodore Matthew Perry and his "black ships" showed up in Tokyo harbor in 1853, demanding that Japan open its ports to the US.

With no navy and no national military, the Tokugawa shogunate struggled to resist pressures from the US and other countries. In 1858 it signed a series of "unequal treaties" that favored Western powers and impinged upon Japanese sovereignty. Resentment of Western influence and long-standing grievances with the Tokugawas then led to a prolonged period of civil strife, ending in 1867–68 with a civil war in which forces fighting in the name of the emperor decisively defeated pro-government forces. Sutematsu Yamakawa, daughter of a mid-rank samurai on the losing side, was slightly wounded by shrapnel in one of the final battles, and her sister-in-law was killed.[4]

Fourteen-year-old Prince Mutsuhito became emperor in 1867, with the new "Meiji" ("enlightened rule") era proclaimed in 1868 with the fall of Edo (now Tokyo) and the formation of a new government populated by many energetic and relatively young mid-rank samurai. They embarked upon a crash course of importing Western knowledge, technology, and experts to make Japan a modern power as fast as possible.

One of those men, Kiyotaka Kuroda, had been impressed with American women while visiting the US. He conceived the fantastical scheme of sending a group of Japanese girls to the US for a ten-year stay to learn American ways and come back to educate a new generation of Japanese girls. After an initial recruitment effort failed, the government succeeded in finding five low- to mid-rank samurai families who had been on the losing side, were living in relative poverty, and were therefore willing to let their girls leave home so as not to have to support them.[5]

The five girls left Japan in 1871 as part of the famous Iwakura mission along with a group of high-ranking government officials, scholars, and male students charged to visit foreign nations and bring back information of use to Japan. The oldest two girls soon returned to Japan due to ill health and homesickness. However, Sutematsu Yamakawa (eleven years old), Shige Nogai (ten), and Ume Tsuda (six) found places with American families. They soon learned English, made close American friends, and became socialized in a manner typical of upper-middle-class American girls of the period.[6]

While the girls were away, Japan saw a blooming of intellectual discourse, the formation of grass-roots political movements, and the creation of nascent political parties, as elements within society and government contended over what political and cultural ideas and institutions were most appropriate for Japan.

The three girls returned in the early 1880s, Sutematsu Yamakawa having graduated from Vassar College (the first Japanese woman to receive an American college degree) and Shige Nogai having earned a certificate in music from Vassar. All three girls experienced severe culture shock, with Ume Tsuda having completely forgotten how to speak Japanese. They also found that foreign ideas were not as popular as when they left for America, as a conservative backlash was building.[7]

Shige Nogai soon entered into a love match with a fellow Japanese student who had attended the US Naval Academy. She went to work as a music teacher, continuing her career while bearing and raising six children. At one point, she was the highest-paid female employee in Japan. Some scholars contend that she's depicted in a woodblock print showing a dance at the Rokumeikan—the pianist on the right to whom the other pianist seems to be looking for cues.[8] Her husband eventually became a baron and an admiral in the Imperial Japanese Navy, and she a baroness.[9]

Sutematsu Yamakawa struggled to find work suitable to her upbringing and education and ended up accepting an offer of marriage from Iwao Ōyama, minister of war and a former general in the Imperial Japanese Army. Ōyama, twenty years her senior, was looking for a wife familiar with Western ways to assist him in his political and diplomatic activities. In time, Sutematsu became a pillar of the Japanese aristocracy, advising the empress herself on Western culture and fashion.[10]

As Countess (later Princess) Ōyama, she became known as the "Lady of the Rokumeikan" for her role in hosting events there after its construction in 1883. (In fact, she appears as a minor character in the play *Rokumeikan*.) Ōyama also introduced American-style philanthropy to Japan, including a charity bazaar held at the Rokumeikan.[11] This event was also memorialized in a woodblock print, depicting Countess Ōyama and her daughter Hisako in the center of the image.[12]

One of the primary beneficiaries of Sutematsu's philanthropy was Ume Tsuda, who had the worst time adjusting to life in Japan. She first obtained employment as a private tutor to the children of Hirobumi Itō, soon to become Japan's first prime minister. She then taught at the Peeresses' School, which Itō set up (with assistance from Countess Ōyama) to educate the daughters of the Imperial family and Japanese nobility.[13] (Prestigious girls' schools like Fujigaya Women's Academy would later offer an equivalent experience for the daughters of Japan's upper and upper-middle classes.)

Ume Tsuda became frustrated by the conservatism of the Peeresses' School and the expectations of her family and others that she marry. Due to her youth, she had not been able to attend college while in America, and hence she applied for and was granted permission and funding to go back to the US to complete her education. Tsuda enrolled at the recently-opened Bryn Mawr College for women and graduated with a bachelor's degree. She then returned to Japan, having also found time to (anonymously) assist an American friend, Alice Mabel Bacon, in writing a book critical of Japanese laws and educational policies relating to girls and women.[14]

After some time and assistance from Countess Ōyama, Ume Tsuda realized her dream of opening her own school, the Women's Institute for English Studies (*Joshi Eigaku Juku*). Its mission was to train teachers for Japan's newly-mandated middle schools for girls. Tsuda was soon joined by Anna Cope Hartshorne, her close friend from Bryn Mawr, who became her partner in both work and life. (Like Nobuko Yoshiya and her partner Chiyo Monma, Tsuda and Hartshorne bought a cottage together in Kamakura.)[15]

In 1905 the Women's Institute for English Studies enrolled nearly a hundred and fifty students. It was so highly regarded that its graduates received a government exemption from taking the teaching certification exam.[16] Those women, in turn, taught the schoolgirls of the late Meiji and Taishō eras who created *shōjo* culture, and introduced them to Western literature and ideas. In Nobuko Yoshiya's 1923 Class S story "Yellow Rose," Misao Katsuragi, the protagonist, is an English teacher newly-graduated from Tsuda's institute.[17]

Ume Tsuda spent her last years in ill health, living in Kamakura with Anna Hartshorne. After she died in 1929, the Women's Institute for English Studies was renamed in her honor, eventually becoming Tsuda College and then (more recently) Tsuda University. Hartshorne herself left Japan in 1940, on the brink of war, never to return. She died in 1957, a year after the first production of *Rokumeikan* and almost a century after the beginning of the Meiji era.[18]

The Rokumeikan itself was long gone by then. Its use had declined with the rise of conservative sentiment and anti-Western feeling, and it was sold in 1890 to become a private club for the aristocracy. The building fell into disuse and was eventually demolished in 1941, as Japan went to war with the Western powers whose diplomats it had once invited to dance at the Rokumeikan.

There's an intriguing parallel between the three twenty-first-century girls who are the main characters in *Sweet Blue Flowers* and the three nineteenth-century girls of *Daughters of the Samurai*. Kyoko resembles Sutematsu Yamakawa, thwarted in her original desire and falling back on marriage with an older man of higher social status. We can only hope that

Kyoko will find happiness in such a marriage, as Yamakawa did in hers.

Fumi resembles Ume Tsuda. She will remain unmarried, as Tsuda did (unless marriage equality comes to Japan). Our hope for Fumi is that, like Tsuda, she will also find a woman, whether Akira or another, who will be her lifelong companion.

As for Akira, her fate is not yet clear—though I doubt she'll have six children, like Shige Nogai. We can only hope that Akira also finds someone to love, just as Shige did.

1. As adults, Ume Tsuda and Shige Nagai changed their given names to Umeko and Shigeko, respectively, reflecting the increasing use of the suffix -ko for women's names in the late Meiji era, a trend that saw almost universal use of -ko by the end of the Taishō era. See, for example, Yuri Komori, "Trends in Japanese First Names in the Twentieth Century: A Comparative Study," *International Christian University Publications 3-A, Asian Cultural Studies* 28 (2002), 75–76, https://icu.repo.nii.ac.jp/?action=repository_action_common _download&item_id=1637&item_no=1&attribute_id=18&file_no=1.

2. Janice P. Nimura, *Daughters of the Samurai: A Journey from East to West and Back* (New York: W. W. Norton, 2015), Kindle.

3. Akiko Kuni, *Unexpected Destinations: The Poignant Story of Japan's First Vassar Graduate*, trans. Kirsten McIvor (Tokyo: Kodansha International, 1993).

4. Nimura, *Daughters of the Samurai*, chap. 2.

5. Nimura, *Daughters of the Samurai*, chap. 3.

6. Nimura, *Daughters of the Samurai*, chap. 4, 6–7.

7. Nimura, *Daughters of the Samurai*, chap. 9–10.

8. Toyohara Chikanobu, *Kiken butō no ryakuzu*, 1888, https://en.wikipedia.org/wiki /Rokumeikan#/media/File:Chikamatsu_Kiken_buto_no_ryakuke.jpg.

9. Nimura, *Daughters of the Samurai*, chap. 10.

10. Kuni, *Unexpected Destinations*, 118–22, 133–50. Nimura, *Daughters of the Samurai*, chap. 10.

11. Kuni, *Unexpected Destinations*, 162–64.

12. Toyohara Chikanobu, *Rokumei-kan ni okeru kifujin jizenkai no zu*, 1884, https://en .wikipedia.org/wiki/File:Rokumei-kan_ni_okeru_kifujin_jizenkai_no_zu.jpg.

13. Nimura, *Daughters of the Samurai*, chap. 11.

14. Nimura, *Daughters of the Samurai*, chap. 13.

15. Nimura, *Daughters of the Samurai*, chap. 14–15.

16. Nimura, *Daughters of the Samurai*, chap. 14.

17. Sarah Frederick, translator's introduction to *Yellow Rose*, by Nobuko Yoshiya. The story identifies Katsuragi's alma mater as "a certain English Academy … in Gobanchō, near the British Embassy in Tokyo." The Women's Institute for English Studies moved to that location in 1903. Nimura, *Daughters of the Samurai*, chap. 15.

18. Nimura, *Daughters of the Samurai*, chap. 15.

The Play's the Thing

Takako Shimura's use of Yukio Mishima's 1956 play *Rokumeikan* in volume 3 of *Sweet Blue Flowers* is probably the best example of her fondness for using theatrical plays as elements in her manga. The interplay between the events and characters of the play and the events and characters of the manga contributes to that volume being, to my mind, the best of the series.

The bits of the play presented in *Sweet Blue Flowers* are somewhat fragmentary. Shimura assumes a readership familiar with at least the basic outline of the play and its main characters. For those who have not read the play, here's a summary of the plot:

Act 1. On the emperor's birthday, November 3, 1886, a group of aristocratic women gather at a teahouse on the estate of Count Hisatoshi Kageyama, a high-ranking government minister, and watch the military review being held in the emperor's honor. (This first scene is also the first depicted in the manga (*SBF*, 2:233–35).) Kageyama's wife Asako (played by Kyoko Ikumi in the performance shown in *Sweet Blue Flowers*) joins them. Asako, an ex-geisha elevated to the aristocracy by her marriage, is uncomfortable with her new status and never appears in public.[1]

One of the women appeals to Asako on behalf of her daughter Akiko (played by Akira Okudaira in *Sweet Blue Flowers*) and Akiko's lover Hisao. Hisao supports the opposition party, and Akiko fears that he will disrupt that night's ball at the Rokumeikan and attempt to assassinate Count Kageyama. Perturbed at hearing Hisao's name, Asako agrees to help, and after the ladies depart, she meets with him.[2]

Asako reveals to Hisao that she is his mother by her former lover Einosuke Kiyohara, leader of the opposition party, who took Hisao in after his birth. Hisao expresses his resentment of his father's neglect of him and his treatment compared to Kiyohara's legitimate children and reveals that he plans to kill not Kageyama but Kiyohara.[3]

Act 2. After Hisao leaves, Asako reaches out to Kiyohara (played by Ryoko Ueda in *Sweet Blue Flowers*) and meets him at the teahouse. She tells him she knows about the plan to disrupt the ball and urges him to abandon it. Kiyohara resists until she tells him that she plans to leave her private sphere and attend the ball herself.[4]

Kiyohara leaves as Count Kageyama and his retainer Tobita enter the scene. Overheard by Asako, their conversation reveals that Kageyama knows about the plot to disrupt the ball and, with Tobita as his intermediary, is the mastermind behind Hisao's plan to kill Kiyohara. The bloodthirsty Tobita protests that Kageyama did not give him the task of assassination.[5]

Asako reveals herself and tells Kageyama that there will be no disturbance at the ball, and after Tobita leaves, tells Kageyama of her plan to attend. She then urges Kageyama to persuade Hisao to abandon his plan to kill his father, explaining her interest as simply that of helping a friend's daughter. Kageyama agrees on the condition that the ball not be disrupted. After Asako leaves, he grabs her maid Kusano and forces himself upon her.[6]

Act 3. Upstairs at the Rokumeikan before the ball, Akiko and Hisao talk of Asako's role in bringing Hisao to the ball. They kiss, after which Asako enters and busies herself with directing the workers decorating the rooms. Meanwhile, having seduced Kusano with the promise of his favor, Kageyama extracts from her the information that Asako is Hisao's mother and Kiyohara's former lover.[7]

After conversing briefly with Asako, Kageyama seeks out Tobita and tells him that plans have changed: since Kiyohara called off the original plot to disrupt the ball, Tobita should now arrange a disruption himself. Kageyama then tells Kusano to summon Kiyohara to the Rokumeikan that evening in Asako's name.[8]

Akiko and Hisao talk of their plans to elope together and leave for a foreign tour. Kageyama interrupts them and upbraids Hisao for his giving in to romance and abandoning his plans. He tells Hisao that (contrary to what Asako told Hisao) a break-in will occur, and the (unnamed) target of Hisao's assassination plot will be present on the grounds outside the Rokumeikan. Kageyama hands Hisao a pistol, and he accepts it.[9]

Kageyama rejoins Asako and her friends, and they drink a toast to the emperor's health—marred by the ill omen of Asako accidentally dropping her glass.[10]

Act 4. As Asako, Kageyama, and their fellow aristocrats talk among themselves, the invited dignitaries begin to arrive at the ball. These include Prime Minister Hirobumi Itō, Minister of the Army Iwao Ōyama and his wife, the former Sutematsu Yamakawa (see the previous chapter), and various foreign guests.[11]

After the guests enter the ballroom, a report comes up from downstairs of men brandishing swords and destroying decorations. Asako goes to the head of the stairs and faces them down, after which Kageyama quietly directs Tobita to have the men withdraw. Meanwhile, thinking that his father has betrayed both him and Asako in ordering the plot to proceed, Hisao flies into a rage and leaves the building.[12]

Soon after, shots are heard, and a distraught Kiyohara enters, explaining that Hisao is dead: Kiyohara was fired upon by an assailant hiding in the dark and fired back in self-defense, subsequently discovering that he had killed his son. Perceiving that Hisao had deliberately misdirected his shot, Kiyohara concludes that Hisao wanted to be killed by his father as an act of revenge upon him.[13]

Kiyohara declares himself done with politics and sardonically congratulates Kageyama on achieving his goal of eliminating a political enemy. He also tells Asako that the men who broke into the Rokumeikan were not his own, declares that he kept his promise (implying that in calling him to the scene, Asako had not kept hers), swears that he will never see her again, and exits.[14]

Tobita exits as well ("with a conspiratorial air," per the stage directions), as do Akiko and her mother after Asako attempts to comfort them, leaving Asako and Kageyama to face each other. Kageyama taunts Asako for believing in "fairy tales" of trust and cooperation between people, in ignorance of the real world of politics, while Asako accuses him of knowing and wanting nothing but power.[15]

Asako declares her intention to leave Kageyama for Kiyohara, the arrival of the Imperial Princess is announced, the orchestra plays while Asako and Kageyama dance, and Asako thinks she hears a pistol shot in the distance. The music stops, Kageyama tells Asako the sound was only fireworks, and then the music and dance continue as the curtain falls.[16]

1. Mishima, *Rokumeikan*, 5–8.
2. Mishima, *Rokumeikan*, 9–12.
3. Mishima, *Rokumeikan*, 14–16.
4. Mishima, *Rokumeikan*, 16–23.
5. Mishima, *Rokumeikan*, 23–27.
6. Mishima, *Rokumeikan*, 27–31.
7. Mishima, *Rokumeikan*, 32–37.
8. Mishima, *Rokumeikan*, 37–41.
9. Mishima, *Rokumeikan*, 41–45.
10. Mishima, *Rokumeikan*, 45–46.
11. Mishima, *Rokumeikan*, 46–47. Mami Harano incorrectly refers to Count Kageyama as the prime minister. Harano, "Anatomy of Mishima's Most Successful Play," 1, 11, 17, 36–37, 39, 42, 46–47.
12. Mishima, *Rokumeikan*, 48–49.
13. Mishima, *Rokumeikan*, 49–50.
14. Mishima, *Rokumeikan*, 50–51.
15. Mishima, *Rokumeikan*, 51–53.
16. Mishima, *Rokumeikan*, 53–54.

Akiko and Akira

I now come to the actual performance of *Rokumeikan*, in which Akira Okudaira plays Akiko Daitokuji, the lover of Hisao Kiyohara.

Like almost all the characters in *Rokumeikan*, Akiko is a member of the Japanese aristocracy. As a marchioness, her mother is the wife of a marquess, the second-highest rank in the hierarchy of Japanese noble families (*kazoku*) established in the early Meiji era.

Akiko's social status may thus seem far above that of Akira, but it's worth noting that at least some of Akira's ancestors may have been equally high-born. The family name Okudaira is shared by Nobumasa Okudaira, a feudal lord who fought with Ieyasu Tokugawa and Nobunaga Oda in the wars that established the Tokugawa shogunate. Tokugawa gave his eldest daughter in marriage to Okudaira, so Akira herself may be descended from one of the most influential figures in Japanese history.

Akiko is also the youngest character in *Rokumeikan*. Her age is not given in the play, but I guess that she is around sixteen or seventeen years old, or in other words, about the same age as Akira. Since the play takes place in 1886, Akiko would thus be a "Meiji girl" in the same sense that Akira is a "Heisei girl," born in the new era and knowing nothing of life before it—in contrast to all the other characters in the play.

It's therefore no coincidence that Akiko is the character most in tune with the new spirit of Meiji Japan, and the one who looks most to the West rather than to traditional Japan. As her mother says, "she loves radical things." Hisao is one of those "radical things," not "a man of the lower class, but ... on the side of that class." Akiko first meets him not at an arranged meeting but rather by chance at a performance of "Charine's circus horses," where Hisao picks up the imported European handbag her mother had accidentally dropped.[1]

That evening at the Rokumeikan, Akiko plans to leave Japan in the morning with Hisao on a trip to Europe arranged by her mother, to return only when (or if?) her father gives her permission to marry. It's not clear if Akiko's mother intends to accompany the couple. If not, this would presumably be a decided breach of social norms on Akiko's part: not only to refuse an arranged marriage and marry for love, but to travel alone with a man not her husband or father. Similarly, Akira is considering her own breach of contemporary Japanese social norms in contemplating entering into a lesbian relationship with Fumi.

In her disregard for social norms, Akiko is not condemned by her mother and her friends, but instead receives their support. They too seem to welcome "this new wonderful age," as Akiko's mother's friends call it, "this age where women are able to bask in the sun for the first time in hundreds of years." It is to help Akiko that her mother requests Asako meet with Hisao, the event that kicks off the play's action. As her mother says, in a line quoted in *Sweet Blue Flowers* (*SBF*, 3:92), "I want my daughter to experience a full life in the new era, and have the life that I never had."[2] So too will Akira's friends support her in her own "new era," though she initially fears they will not.

Continuing the parallels between Akira and the character she plays, even their names are similar, though with a twist: Akiko's name has the *-ko* ending often used for girls' given names in Japan, while Akira's name is (if Wikipedia is any guide) more traditionally used for boys and men (e.g., the film director Akira Kurosawa). It's possible that Shimura chose this name specifically to echo that of Akiko and to emphasize how Akira might go beyond Akiko in violating the strictures Japanese society has historically placed on women.[3]

In the end, Akiko's hopes come to naught. Hisao is dead, and the best Asako can do is to advise Akiko to live on: "Hisao did not die for you. So it would be useless for you to follow him in death."[4] Consistent with the themes of *Sweet Blue Flowers*, there is also an implied message here for Akira and her fellow students: though there may be men in your life, don't make your existence dependent on theirs.

---

1. Mishima, *Rokumeikan*, 9–10.
2. Mishima, *Rokumeikan*, 8–9.
3. With respect to Akira's name, it's worth noting that "Akiko" is also the name of the younger and more immature woman in Nobuko Yoshiya's *Yaneura no nishojo*, a character thought to be based on Yoshiya herself.
4. Mishima, *Rokumeikan*, 51.

This Year's Star

Although Akira is one of the most important characters in *Sweet Blue Flowers*, the character Akiko that she plays in *Rokumeikan* is of lesser importance—not exactly a bit part, but not a major role by any means. With Ryoko Ueda we have the reverse: the character she plays, Einosuke Kiyohara, is arguably the second or third most important in *Rokumeikan* (after Asako and comparable to Count Kageyama), but Ueda herself is one of the lesser characters in *Sweet Blue Flowers*.

First, a bit about Kiyohara. In the play, he is described as "the leader of the opposition group," a group described as "the remnants of the Liberal Party."[1] One of the first political parties in Japan, the Liberal Party (*Jiyūtō*) was formed in 1881 as an outgrowth of the Freedom and People's Rights Movement (*Jiyū Minken Undō*), one of Japan's first mass political and social movements. Both the movement and the party advocated for democratically-elected legislatures, though with the electorate restricted to the former samurai and nobility. The Liberal Party was disbanded in 1884 (hence "the remnants of ....").

Kiyohara's son Hisao describes him as "An impeccable idealist. A figure like a leader of the French Revolution. A genuine liberal. ... A believer in Rousseau, a Japanese Jacobin, a man who doesn't give a damn about his life for liberty and equality ...."[2] Mishima may have modeled the character of Kiyohara on Taisuke Itagaki, one of the founders of the real-life Liberal Party. With his colleagues, Itagaki wrote a manifesto modeled on the U.S. Declaration of Independence ("We, the thirty millions of people in Japan are all equally endowed with certain definite rights ...."). Like Kiyohara, Itagaki was the victim of an assassination attempt, in his case unsuccessful, after which he allegedly cried, "Itagaki may die, but liberty never!"

In the play, Kiyohara is less successful in his personal life: he neglects Hisao in favor of his legitimate children and does not speak to Asako in the twenty years after their affair. Though the meeting with Asako rekindles her love for him, Hisao's resentment continues and drives him first to plan to kill his father and then die by his father's hand in a perverse act of revenge upon him.

Unlike the case of Akiko and Akira, there are no real parallels between Ueda and Kiyohara. To the extent Ueda is characterized at all (which is not much compared to even secondary characters like Kyoko or Haruka), it is by explicit and implicit comparisons to Yasuko Sugimoto.

Like Yasuko, Ueda is tall and handsome, and like Yasuko eminently suitable for playing the part of a leading man. Also, like Yasuko (whom Mr. Kagami nicknamed the "library maiden"), Ueda spends her time reading in Fujigaya's library and was discovered there by Haruka acting out the parts of Kiyohara and Asako from *Rokumeikan* (*SBF*, 2:260). Unlike Yasuko, Ueda has long hair, but then Yasuko had longer hair too (though not as long as Ueda's) before she cut it off in an attempt to emulate her sister Kazusa's "tough personality" (2:112).

As Kiyohara, Ueda also speaks a line, "a helpless child resides within me" (*SBF*, 3:102), that Yasuko had previously used in her letter to Mr. Kagami (1:164). Presumably, the drama club was considering *Rokumeikan* for the following year's theater festival, and Yasuko had read the play in preparation for playing Kiyohara. In any case, Mr. Kagami caught the reference, as shown in his thoughts after the play (3:107).

I suspect Takako Shimura introduced the character of Ueda primarily to fill the slot left open by the departure of Yasuko as the "prince" of Fujigaya. She acts opposite Kyoko as Yasuko did opposite Kawasaki in volume 1 and, like Yasuko, inspires admiration and crushes in the younger girls. She is this year's star, as Yasuko was "last year's star" (*SBF*, 3:18). However, unlike Yasuko, Ueda doesn't appear to have any significant hang-ups, other than a bit of shyness. That makes her a better friend for Akira, Kyoko, and Fumi, but it does tend to make her somewhat bland and underdeveloped as a character.

1. Mishima, *Rokumeikan*, 11.
2. Mishima, *Rokumeikan*, 14.

"Such an Old-Fashioned Woman"

Asako Kageyama is the tragic heroine of *Rokumeikan*. Asako was a geisha when she met her former lover Einosuke Kiyohara and later was elevated to the aristocracy by her marriage to Count Kageyama. Such marriages were not uncommon in the Meiji era, as leading politicians looking to host social gatherings sought out geisha used to dealing with men in a social context, making them their mistresses or (as in the case of Prime Minister Hirobumi Itō) their wives.

If this was Count Kageyama's intention in marrying Asako, it was thwarted. Asako proved to be a retiring sort, apparently never venturing outside the Kageyama estate, and certainly not to the Rokumeikan. As she says, "I'm such an old-fashioned woman, I can't possibly go to such a fashionable place."[1]

But she does go to the Rokumeikan to try to save the life of her son Hisao, previously bent on the assassination of Einosuke Kiyohara, his father and Asako's former lover. Her action comes to naught: Hisao dies, shot by his father. It is strongly implied that Kiyohara dies as well, killed by Count Kageyama's henchman Tobita. Asako herself is left to live out her life with Count Kageyama, in a marriage from which all illusions of love and tenderness have been stripped, with only raw power and resentment remaining.

Asako, more than Kiyohara, Hisao, or Akiko, is thus the great tragic figure of Rokumeikan. Akiko is young and still has the possibility of finding happiness. Hisao and Kiyohara are beyond all feelings. But Asako has only a life without hope stretching ahead of her.

Sweet Blue Flowers is not a tragedy, but if anyone in the manga can be said to be a tragic figure, it is Kyoko Ikumi. It's therefore fitting that Shimura selected her to play Asako. She does not look the part—her short brown hair totally unlike Asako's long black hair—but otherwise she fits the role to a T, with her reticence, old-fashioned air, unhappy past, troubled present, and uncertain future. As I wrote of Kyoko in a previous chapter, "If this were a traditional [Class S] story, the only suspense would be whether her remaining life would be short and unhappy or long and unhappy."

In her dissertation on *Rokumeikan*, Mami Harano rhetorically asks why Japanese audiences would continue to flock to a play in which power wins and the heroine loses. Harano answers that audiences see in Asako someone who breaks the bonds of convention and dares to love: to engage in romantic love with her illicit lover Kiyohara, to show maternal love toward her illegitimate son Hisao, to choose affection (*ninjō*) over duty (*giri*).[2]

People often speak of "the power of love." In *Rokumeikan* love has no power, at least in terms of the outworking of the plot. But it still has the power to move us. As Harano writes, "Observing all of the contradictions in her life and seeing all the unfairness and inequality in the world, audiences feel empathy with Asako ...."[3] I think the same can be said of Kyoko in *Sweet Blue Flowers*. Her life is messed up, her mother ill and dependent, her hoped-for relationship with Yasuko thwarted, and her ongoing relationship with Ko in trouble, but she at least has her friendship with Akira and our sympathy as readers.

Sometimes a secondary character will break out from the pack and achieve a special place in the audience's heart (for example, Nanami in *Revolutionary Girl Utena*). Kyoko is such a character for me. Though she is not the star of *Sweet Blue Flowers* as a whole, she is undoubtedly the star of this section of it.

1. Mishima, *Rokumeikan*, 8.
2. Harano, "Anatomy of Mishima's Most Successful Play," 2–3.
3. Harano, "Anatomy of Mishima's Most Successful Play," 45.

Two Characters in Search of an Actor

I previously wrote about the patriarch of the Sugimoto clan, a man notable for the lack of attention paid to him in *Sweet Blue Flowers*. In my final commentary on the Fujigaya production of *Rokumeikan*, I consider two other men notable for their absence in the manga, Hisao and Count Kageyama.

Hisao at least rates a mention in *Sweet Blue Flowers*. In the performance of *Rokumeikan*, Akiko (played by Akira) mentions that he is in danger (though the manga omits the reason why). The girl playing Hisao is subsequently called to the stage, after which the narration explains that he is Asako's estranged son (*SBF*, 3:94–95). But we are left ignorant of who played Hisao and are not made privy to anything he says.

With Count Kageyama, the erasure is (almost) complete. Like Hisao, his actor is never identified, and we never hear his words. Unlike Hisao, he is not referenced at all in the manga, either by his name or by his role in the story.

As with Yasuko's father, we may ask, why might this be? As in that case, the most straightforward answer is that they are peripheral to the story Shimura is telling. They are men, and *Sweet Blue Flowers* is about girls becoming women, specifically women who love women. With Hisao, we have the additional factor that he is explicitly identified as Akiko's lover. It would detract from the story of Akira and Fumi's tentatively blossoming love to have another girl play a love interest opposite Akira.[1]

But, as with Yasuko's father, we can explore this absence further, starting with Hisao. Hisao is a type familiar from Mishima's other works, his life, and Japanese history: the hotheaded young man, whose discontents and violent tendencies alternately affront and are exploited by the Japanese (male) establishment.

Hisao's resentment at his father's treatment of him first leads him to contemplate assassinating Kiyohara. Persuaded to desist only by the intervention of his newly-revealed mother, Asako, he lets himself be goaded again into resentment and action by Kageyama's words and scheming—only to rebel against Kageyama as well by deliberately mis-aiming his shot at Kiyohara, subsequently getting himself killed by Kiyohara's return fire.

I think the term "toxic masculinity" is overused, but if it applies to anything, it applies to Hisao's actions in this play. Hisao has a chance to turn from the path he is taking, to leave Japan with Akiko and make a new life with her. Instead he throws it all away to engage in a self-destructive act—an act that in his mind means a great deal, but in the grand scheme of things makes no difference whatsoever, other than to bring pain to his mother, father, and lover.

This offers another reason why Hisao is downplayed in the manga: to audiences familiar with the play, he is by his omission highlighted as a negative role model, especially for young girls like Akira and Fumi, and especially for a story like *Sweet Blue Flowers*. In older Class S works, suicide (for that is what Hisao's actions amount to) might be the end game for some, frustrated in their inability to escape the strictures of society. However, it has no place in the world of *Sweet Blue Flowers*.

Its message would rather be that of Asako to Akiko after she learns of Hisao's death and despairs of life: "You can't say any such weak-hearted thing. You must by all means try to live."[2] Or in other words: "Don't be Hisao."

What then of Count Kageyama? As I implied above, he is the Voldemort of the *Rokumeikan* production portrayed in *Sweet Blue Flowers*, "he-who-must-not-be-named." But, unlike Voldemort, Kageyama is seemingly successful in his role as the "Big Bad."

When Kageyama's original plan to employ Hisao goes awry, he discovers what Asako has done and arranges a new scheme to achieve his aim. He successfully plays on Hisao's sense of masculinity to persuade him to resume his plan of assassinating Kiyohara—a plan that, even if seemingly unsuccessful, eliminates Kiyohara as a political force (as Kiyohara himself notes). He then (it is strongly implied) has Kiyohara killed to finish the job that Hisao could not. In plain terms, he wins, and everyone else—Asako, Akiko, Hisao, and Kiyohara—loses.

Kageyama is not portrayed in the play as an unrelievedly evil villain. He is jealous of Asako's relationship with Kiyohara, and apparently yearns to have what they have with each other—"I was jealous of that indescribable trust that exists between you and Kiyohara"—even as he scoffs at the possibilities of love and trust between two people: "It is an absurd thing. Human beings can't make pledges or trust each other unconditionally as you and Kiyohara have done. ... That sort of thing should never exist in our human world."[3]

But whatever his feelings, his actions are contemptible, and Asako calls him out for it at the climax of act 4: "Please do not talk about love and human beings any more. Those words are unclean. When they come out of your mouth, they become repellent. You are clean as ice only when you totally isolate yourself from human emotions. Please do not bring in love and humane feelings with your *sticky* hands. This is unlike you."[4]

As it happens, this is the only time Kageyama appears in *Sweet Blue Flowers* even indirectly, as Kyoko rehearses this speech. (I have used Hiroaki Sato's translation here instead of the one in the manga because I think it better conveys the sense of what Asako is saying.) Midway through, Kyoko stops, lost in thought, until prompted by another person—perhaps the anonymous girl playing Kageyama, whom we glimpse only from behind (*SBF*, 3:104-5).

What was Kyoko thinking? Earlier in the manga, she thought to herself, "Did dad fall for a woman like Asako?" (*SBF*, 3:99). Is she comparing her father to Kageyama?

And what of herself? Whatever ardor Ko felt before seems to have cooled, replaced with frustration at Kyoko's behavior towards him—and perhaps also a jealousy born of whatever he might know or guess of Kyoko's feelings toward Yasuko. In turn, Kyoko's renewed desire to get married reeks of desperation and a desire to escape her family situation—as Ko points out to her (*SBF*, 3:90–91).

Perhaps Kyoko stopped to think that what happened to her mother and Asako might one day happen to herself: that she and Ko might enter into a marriage with at least some lingering feelings of love and affection, only to have it all end in cruelty and coldness. Kyoko could not save her mother—"I couldn't stop her from breaking" (*SBF*, 3:101). If it ever came to that, could she save herself?

1. This would be especially true if the Fujigaya performance followed Mishima's stage directions: after meeting Akiko at the Rokumeikan, "Hisao holds her in his arms and kisses her for a long time." Mishima, *Rokumeikan*, 33.
2. Mishima, *Rokumeikan*, 51.
3. Mishima, *Rokumeikan*, 52.
4. Mishima, *Rokumeikan*, 53. Italics in the original.

Abusive Relations Revisited

Content note: This chapter discusses child sexual abuse.

Now that the Fujigaya production of *Rokumeikan* has ended, the story of *Sweet Blue Flowers* moves on to other matters. After the congratulations to the actors and reviews of the performances, the chapter ends with Fumi Manjome being surprised by the news that her cousin Chizu has a new baby and is coming to visit (*SBF*, 3:112–13). The next chapter ("After the Banquet") opens with an image of a young and vulnerable Fumi and is devoted to (re)telling the story of Fumi's childhood relationship with Chizu.

I've already had my say about the abusive nature of this relationship. Does this chapter add anything to our understanding of Fumi and Chizu? Here are my thoughts on this question—which, like all my thoughts on *Sweet Blue Flowers*, are open to correction.

First, Chizu now has a family name, "Hanashiro," as given in the character introductions for volume 3 (*SBF*, 3:5). In Japanese, the first part of her family name is the character for "flower," the same character used in the Japanese title of the manga and the title of Nobuko Yoshiya's *Hana monogatari* Class S series. The second part of the name is the character for "castle," but it shares the same pronunciation as the character for the color "white."

"White" in combination with "flower" evokes the white lily that symbolized passionate but pure romance in Class S culture. Its Japanese name subsequently became the name of the yuri genre. Considering Chizu's history with Fumi, this seems a somewhat ironic pun on Shimura's part.

Second, a brief comment about the title of the chapter. The translator's notes for the VIZ Media edition are silent as to its origin and meaning, but other sources speculate that it references Yukio Mishima's 1960 novel *After the Banquet* (*Utage no ato*). This is appropriate if true since the last few chapters focused on another Mishima work. The novel portrays an ill-fated marriage between an elderly politician and a middle-aged restaurant owner, who first meet at a banquet held at her restaurant. The *New York Times* review summarizes the novel's conclusion as "Love is strong, but too weak to hold disparate natures together."[1]

The theme of "disparate natures" in an equally ill-fated relationship marked by an age gap is certainly apropos here. The purpose of the chapter seems to be to explore the nuances of Chizu's and Fumi's relationship. It also (perhaps deliberately?) contains clues to just how wide the gap in their ages was.

The story starts with Fumi beginning second grade, having moved away from Akira, whom she met in first grade. (See the chapter "Ten(?) years after" for more on the chronology.) Fumi would thus now be seven years old. We see Fumi's introduction to her new class, her feelings of loneliness and thoughts of Akira, her unwillingness to go back to school after the first day, and (after her return) the beginning of what appears to be a budding friendship with two girls in her class (*SBF*, 3:116–23). And then Chizu comes to play.

At this point in the story, Chizu appears to be on the cusp of being a teenager (perhaps twelve or thirteen years old?), "very rebellious," according to her mother, and not "obedient" like Fumi. Fumi clearly looks up to Chizu, looks forward to her visits, and is disappointed that she can't sleep over (*SBF*, 3:124–26).

Then the story skips between pages to a time when Fumi is in fifth grade (*SBF*, 3:126–27), and is thus at least ten years old. Chizu's age is not referenced, but if we take her uniform as that of a high schooler, she is now at least fifteen years old and perhaps as old as seventeen. However, her remark to Fumi that "You're taller than me!" and her comment about "Girls these days!" seem to imply that Chizu herself sees the age gap between herself and Fumi as smaller than the five or more years it actually is (3:127–28).

Soon after, Chizu's family moves closer to Fumi's, implying that the two girls will see each other much more frequently (*SBF*, 3:128). We then time skip again between pages, with Chizu now headed off to university, and thus at least seventeen or eighteen years old, with Fumi therefore around twelve or thirteen years old, or perhaps slightly younger

(3:128–29). The subsequent conversation over dinner and in bed highlights the pressure Chizu feels to marry and Fumi's lack of interest in boys (3:130–32).

Though it's not spelled out in so many words, I sense that the sexual activity between the two begins shortly after this. How frequent it was and long it continued are not clear. However, it ended before the time that Fumi's family moved back to Kamakura, Fumi began attending Matsuoka (at the age of fifteen), had her reunion with Akira, and was then surprised and shocked by Chizu's marriage (*SBF*, 1:20–25, 1:33-40). If we assume that the age gap between Fumi and Chizu is five years, then at the time of her marriage Chizu would have been twenty years old, now officially an adult, and would have completed at least two years of university.

The chapter features one last time skip, as we come back to the present day with an image of Chizu lost in rueful thought (*SBF*, 3:132–33). She's interrupted by Fumi bringing two cups of tea and a piece of cake—a hark back to earlier meetings between the two (3:124, 3:130). Chizu enthuses about the possibility of moving to Kamakura near Fumi, stops and thinks better of it, and then apologizes to Fumi: "Just kidding." Fumi stares at her, drawn in a full-body profile view that echoes but reverses the image of a young and vulnerable Fumi with which the chapter begins (3:133–34, 3:115).

The parallels to earlier scenes continue as Chizu again asks Fumi if she likes anyone. This time Fumi answers, "Yes." When Chizu questions her further regarding the object of her affections, Fumi replies, "A girl." Chizu apologizes again ("I'm the one who made you that way."), but Fumi resists this interpretation ("Don't say it like that.") (*SBF*, 3:134–35).

As the conversation continues, Chizu is overcome with regret and more than a hint of jealousy ("Do you like her more than me?"). She muses on her daughter's resemblance to Fumi and finally breaks down in tears in contemplation of the path her own life has taken compared to Fumi's ("I can't be *that* kind of girl.") (*SBF*, 3:136–37).

The last (unspoken) words are Fumi's. She thinks to herself, "My love for Chizu was real," before drawing a line under the whole affair: "And that's the truth" (*SBF*, 3:138).

But we as readers can't help wondering, what really is the truth here?

Clearly, Chizu thinks of herself, and by implication exonerates herself, as a victim of circumstances beyond her control: that she was pressured into marrying, and that social prejudices and ties of blood ("We're girls ... and cousins.") kept her from having the relationship she wanted to have with Fumi (*SBF*, 3:137).

What is less clear to me is whether Takako Shimura wants us to think of Chizu as a victim. Chizu was certainly hemmed in by the expectations of her family and society, expectations that limited whom she could love and have as a life partner. On the other hand, Fumi was just past childhood, and Chizu was nearly an adult. If Chizu was drawn to women, she could have—and should have—sought out someone closer to her own age, whether at high school or university. Instead, in Fumi she found and exploited a young girl for her own purposes, a girl who was predisposed to look up to her and follow her lead.

As for Fumi, objectively speaking, she was a victim of abuse, but I don't think she regards herself as such. I do not believe this is because she was manipulated into this view, but rather because this is consistent with her overall personality as portrayed in the manga.

To paraphrase what I previously wrote, Fumi is a person with a "steel core," a deeply emotional person who ultimately does not let her emotions distract her from who she is and what she wants. Whether Chizu "made [her] that way" is irrelevant to Fumi. As she tells her friends later in volume 3, she *is* "that type of girl," and that's all there is to it.

The final image of the chapter again echoes and reverses the chapter's initial image of a young and vulnerable Fumi: eyes no longer cast down, she looks straight ahead, her glasses and her ponytail (a change from her typical more childish pigtails) marking the maturity that she is well on the way to achieving (*SBF*, 3:138).

In the end, I'll repeat what I previously wrote about Chizu: "*Sweet Blue Flowers* seems to valorize relationships between equals and implicitly criticize unequal relationships based on age or other hierarchies. ... From this point of view, Chizu's relationship with Fumi offers the reader another example of the potential harms inherent in and inseparable from some classic yuri tropes."

Although Chizu is featured in character introductions later in volume

3 and in volume 4, this is the last time she plays a part in the events of the manga. What happened between Fumi and Chizu is now in the past. What will happen between Fumi and Akira is now the most important question.

1. Faubion Bowers, "Politics and Love in Japan," *New York Times*, April 14, 1963, https:// archive.nytimes.com/www.nytimes.com/books/98/10/25/specials/mishima-banquet .html.

Hot Springs Episode

As they did after the performance of *Wuthering Heights* in volume 1, the students of Fujigaya take advantage of the school break after the performance of *Rokumeikan* to get away for a brief vacation. This time the accommodations are courtesy of Haruka Ono, whose grandparents happen to own a hot springs inn (*onsen*) and are happy to welcome her and her friends, not just from Fujigaya but from Matsuoka as well (*SBF*, 3:141–43, 3:196–98).

The *onsen* visit is a staple of anime and manga set in high schools. It's usually an excuse for comedic hijinks as teenaged boys employ various stratagems to try to catch a glimpse of teenaged girls in the bath. The girls' naked bodies are typically wreathed in strategically-placed plumes of steam—steam that sometimes magically disappears when it comes time for anime DVD or Blu-ray Disk releases.

In *Sweet Blue Flowers*, Shimura too provides the readers of *Manga Erotics F* (and us) with some "fan service," but I think the significance of this section lies in more than mere titillation. Shimura draws Fumi's naked body, but she depicts it from Akira's point of view (*SBF*, 3:204–6).

Akira has listened to Fumi talk about her having sex with Chizu and her desire to have a physical relationship with Akira. However, Akira has not been confronted with the reality of what that implies until now. Underneath Akira's embarrassment and confusion, we sense that she is finding herself physically attracted to a woman's body. ("S... S-Sorry! But you're so pretty—I *had* to stare.") But she doesn't know yet what to do with that feeling.

Although Fumi also gets a chance to see Akira naked, the more significant event for her is after the bath, when her staying too long in the hot springs causes her to almost faint. Her collapsing on the bench attracts the attention of Hinako Yamashina and Orie Ono, who are chaperoning the girls on their visit (*SBF*, 3:214–17).

Since Fumi doesn't go to Fujigaya, she doesn't know Hinako (or she Fumi). However, due to Fumi's friendship with Haruka, she knows that

Haruka's sister Orie has a girlfriend, and Fumi figures out that that girlfriend is Hinako (*SBF*, 2:330). So Fumi takes the opportunity to confide in someone who's a relative stranger but who might understand what Fumi's going through and be a sympathetic listener (3:218, 3:225–27).

Erica Friedman has pointed out the importance of yuri protagonists "[having] an example of an adult woman in a stable [lesbian] relationship ... a person to get advice from and ... a role model."[1] The key phrase here is "in a stable relationship." In other words, Hinako already has a partner and has no romantic or sexual interest whatsoever in Fumi. This marks a clear contrast to other yuri and Class S works in which older women seek out younger women and seduce them.

For example, compare Hinako's behavior toward Fumi with Misao Katsuragi's toward Reiko in Nobuko Yoshiya's "Yellow Rose." The ornate language and concluding heartbreak obscure the fact that, in essence, "Yellow Rose" is a tale of a teacher exploiting her age and superior position to initiate a romantic relationship with a younger student placed in her charge.[2]

Not so with Hinako, who behaves toward Fumi as one would expect a teacher to act toward a student, repeating the scrupulousness she previously showed in her dealings with another student (*SBF*, 2:167). (This is true of other characters in *Sweet Blue Flowers*; see, for example, Mr. Kagami and Yasuko.) Although the manga is silent regarding exactly what advice Hinako provides to Fumi, she does ask Fumi two key questions: "What kind of relationship do you want with [Akira]?" and "Do you want to be a couple?" The unstated implication is, "Do you want you and Akira to be a couple like Orie and me?" (3:243).

We've previously seen that Hinako and Orie were in the same year in high school and began their relationship after Orie's crush on the older Shinako ended (*SBF*, 2:160, 2:163–64, 2:168). Though Fumi has no way of knowing this, their situation thus resembled Akira and Fumi's after Fumi broke up with Yasuko.

However, Fumi does see that Hinako and Orie are two women whose relationship endured beyond graduation, and this has an impact on her. As the chapter concludes, Fumi recalls Hinako and Orie and thinks to herself that she would like a similar relationship with Akira. Not realizing that Akira is not asleep, she speaks aloud of her feelings and is surprised by Akira telling her in turn of hers. Although Akira's feelings toward Fumi are not the same as Fumi's toward her, there's something there. That something is significant enough that Akira wants them to date and explore where their relationship might go next (*SBF*, 3:246–56).

1. Erica Friedman, Review of *Yagate Kimi ni Naru*, vol. 3, by Nio Nakatani, *Okazu* (blog), January 26, 2017, https://okazu.yuricon.com/2017/01/26/yuri-manga-yagate-kimi-ni -naru-volume-3-%e3%82%84%e3%81%8c%e3%81%a6%e5%90%9b%e3%81%ab%e3 %81%aa%e3%82%8b.

2. Yoshiya, *Yellow Rose*, chap. 2. Katsuragi is twenty-two years old and in her first teaching assignment when she meets seventeen-year-old Reiko. Although Katsuragi appears to be an adult already when the story begins, Yoshiya downplays this by repeatedly referring to her as a girl (e.g., "this girl Misao").

Rezubian

It's a truism that the protagonists in typical yuri works are romantically and (in more mature works) sexually attracted to other women but don't necessarily think of themselves as lesbians: "lesbian content without lesbian identity," to quote Erica Friedman's famous definition of yuri.[1] Fumi in *Sweet Blue Flowers* is no exception to this rule; the closest she comes to breaking it is telling her Matsuoka friends that she is indeed "that type of girl." And yet, in volume 3, we find a girl who proudly and defiantly declares herself to be a lesbian (*SBF*, 3:257). What's going on here, and how does it fit into the larger framework of *Sweet Blue Flowers*?

It's noteworthy that this incident occurs in one of the "Little Women" side stories that Takako Shimura sprinkles throughout the various volumes of *Sweet Blue Flowers*. Shimura uses these to provide additional perspectives on the events of the main narrative. In some cases, they relate past events and provide background information on supporting characters, as in the stories featuring Hinako, Orie, and the Sugimoto sisters and their mother (*SBF*, 1:379–81, 2:2–3, 2:159–74, 2:176–77, 2:347–54, 3:165–72).

In other cases, the "Little Women" stories depict events that appear to be roughly contemporaneous with the main storyline but are not directly connected to its events or characters. Instead, these function as commentary on the manga's themes (*SBF*, 3:353–56, 4:173–76).

The scene between self-proclaimed lesbian Maeda and her friend Nakajima is an example of the latter. Judging from their school uniforms, they appear to be students at Fujigaya Women's Academy. So the first and simplest function of the story is to let us know that there are more students at Fujigaya who are attracted to other girls.

Indeed this is almost a mathematical certainty. Fujigaya probably has several hundred students in total, and the three high school grades likely have at least a couple of hundred, assuming two or three classes of students for each year and about twenty to thirty students per class.

In a 2019 Japanese government survey, 0.7 percent of those surveyed identified themselves as "lesbian, gay, or homosexual" (as compared to 3.3 percent of respondents identifying as one or more of lesbian, gay, bisexual, transgender, or asexual).[2] In another more recent survey (conducted by the Dentsu advertising agency), 1.33 percent of those surveyed identified themselves as lesbians (compared to 8.9 percent considering themselves members of a "sexual minority").[3]

Given these figures, we can conclude that in all probability, at least a few Fujigaya high school students would be considered lesbians by any reasonable definition—perhaps more than one could count on the fingers of one hand. Thus Hinako and Orie were likely not alone in their class, nor Maeda in hers.

What other functions does Maeda's story serve? Perhaps the most obvious is to contrast the fictional world of Class S relationships found in many modern yuri works to the real world as young Japanese lesbians might experience it. In the world of yuri fiction (in which *Sweet Blue Flowers* exists as both homage and critique), students in girls' schools swoon over imagined pairings (as with Yasuko and Kawasaki in *Wuthering Heights*). Meanwhile, their parents react with indifference or even enthusiasm—recall Akira's mother's reaction after Akira's first day at Fujigaya: "Soon you'll bring home a girlfriend!" (*SBF*, 1:27).

But in Maeda's world, she gets called a "lesbo" (the English version's translation of *rezu*, a pejorative shortening of *rezubian*) and "ugly" (translating *busu*, which refers to an ugly woman specifically). Fortunately, she manages not to let it bother her, but this is a classic example of homophobic bullying.

One could quibble at Shimura juxtaposing Maeda's treatment with the yuri-inflected goings-on elsewhere at Fujigaya. It seems tonally jarring and inconsistent that both could exist in the same school at the same time. But as I understand it, this is not so different from the situation in Japan before and during the time that Shimura was writing *Sweet Blue Flowers*, and to a large extent, this is still true today.

The distinction here is between lesbians in manga, anime, and other forms of entertainment and lesbians in real life. Lesbians are perfectly acceptable in the context of entertainment, a world in which the unusual and nonconforming are a source of titillation and intrigue. Such entertainment can encompass anything from pornography featuring lesbians to "pure yuri" tales of shy and innocent schoolgirls. (Indeed, *Sweet Blue Flowers* itself is an example of this—recall its publication in a magazine titled *Manga Erotics F.*)

But in Japan, the presence and acceptance of lesbians (or LGBTQ people in general) in entertainment did not carry over to acknowledging and accepting their presence in society. Western ideas of homosexuality as abnormal and depraved influenced Japan in the early twentieth century, but the root problem seems to be different. Lesbians (and LGBTQ individuals more generally) who choose to live as such do not conform to the template of the Japanese family that was institutionalized and propagandized beginning in the Meiji era, and still exerts great influence today.

In that template, the life history of a woman is to attend high school and perhaps university and possibly work full-time at a non-career track job for a few years. She will then leave employment to get married, have children, and devote her life to them. Once her children are grown, she will split her time between part-time work and caring for parents. It is a template for life entirely separate from that seen as the ideal for a man: He will attend school through university, get a corporate job after graduation, and at some point acquire a wife who will keep house and mind children. Meanwhile, he will devote his life to working and socializing within a predominantly male environment.

This rigid conception of women's lives impacts lesbians in at least two ways. First, it limits their long-term employment prospects and therefore their ability to support themselves, much less a partner as well. "In small, medium or large companies there is the assumption that everyone participates in the same kind of kinship relations." Thus lesbians are seen simply as unmarried women who have not yet found a man.[4] They may be able to follow the employment path of heterosexual single women for a few years but not forever, as their status as lesbians renders them incompatible with Japanese corporate expectations for career employees.

Second, it means that there is no place for lesbians in the Japanese family as traditionally conceived. As one lesbian noted, "In Japan there is a father and a mother and children, and no one can see family in any other way. Anything else isn't really family, but only a distortion, ..."[5]

There are potential tweaks to this scenario: for example, the man may also have a mistress and have illegitimate children by her, or his wife's family may have officially adopted him as a *mukoyōshi* to ensure a male heir. However, the basic template remains unchallenged and is provided official support via the *koseki* system of household registries (as discussed in a previous chapter).

In this scheme, a lesbian's existence is inherently incompatible with the idea of "family." As a woman, she cannot take on the role of household head traditionally reserved to men. As a woman who loves women, she cannot take on the role of wife to the (male) household head and bearer of her children.

So even though in theory, two lesbians could marry and have either or both of them give birth to children, many would not consider this a "family." Moreover, as discussed above, such a not-family (from the Japanese perspective) would also be financially nonviable since the idea of a lesbian as a long-term breadwinner in support of her wife and children runs up against lesbians' incompatibility with the conventional corporate employment narrative.

The approaches societies can take concerning those who don't conform to societal norms can range from singling out and condemning them to simply ignoring them. Many people in Japan seem to have taken the latter path, rendering Japanese lesbians invisible through what appears to be a willful refusal to recognize their existence as lesbians.

For example, Saori Kamano relates her encounters with Japanese graduate students in 1987 and at the turn of the century. In both cases, they confidently proclaimed, "There are no lesbians in Japan."[6] An example in *Sweet Blue Flowers* itself is the experience of Hinako after she tells her mother about her relationship with Orie: her mother still works with Hinako's aunt to try to arrange a meeting with a man (*SBF*, 4:209). Orie has a similar experience, with her parents refusing to discuss the issue (4:211).

Among other things, this imposed invisibility has in the past inhibited many Japanese lesbians from actually thinking of themselves as lesbians: it's hard to conceive of oneself as a member of a distinct group if you don't know of anyone else like you. In today's world, that knowledge might be just an Internet search away. (In fact, that might be where Maeda and her persecutors learned about lesbians.)

However, *Sweet Blue Flowers* was created in a world where the Internet was not as ubiquitous as it is now. And, in any case, it's more dramatically effective for Fumi to explore her identity in conversations with an actual adult lesbian, namely Hinako. The result is that although she doesn't yet apply the term *"rezubian"* to herself, she can come out to her friends and acknowledge that she's "that type of girl."

1. Friedman, "Is Yuri Queer?"
2. Daiki Hiramori and Saori Kamano, "Asking about Sexual Orientation and Gender Identity in Social Surveys in Japan: Findings from the Osaka City Residents' Survey and Related Preparatory Studies," *Journal of Population Problems* 76, no. 4 (December 2020), 443–66, http://www.ipss.go.jp/syoushika/bunken/data/pdf/20760402.pdf. This paper also has some interesting discussions regarding the difficulty of conducting surveys about sexual orientation and gender identity in a Japanese and Asian context.
3. Dentsu, "First time poll categorizes straight respondents; analyzes their knowledge, awareness of LGBTQ+ matters—Most 'knowledgeable but unconcerned'; do not think LGBTQ+ issues relate to them—," April 8, 2021, https://www.dentsu.co.jp/en/news/release/2021/0408-010371.html.
4. Sharon Chalmers, *Emerging Lesbian Voices from Japan* (London: RoutledgeCurzon, 2002), 81.
5. Chalmers, *Emerging Lesbian Voices from Japan*, 81, quoting interviewee Chiho.
6. Saori Kamano, "Entering the Lesbian World in Japan: Debut Stories," *Journal of Lesbian Studies* 9, no. 1/2 (2005), 12–13, https://doi.org/10.1300/J155v09n01_02.

Notes on Volume 4

This Way of Grief

In a previous chapter, I discussed the fate of Asako in the play *Rokumeikan* as a cautionary tale for Kyoko. But there is another cautionary tale for her much closer to hand, namely the life of her mother, Kayoko.

If we take the story of *Sweet Blue Flowers* as taking place in the early years of the twenty-first century, Kyoko would have been born soon after the beginning of the Heisei era in 1989. Kayako would then have married sometime in the late 1980s, in the waning years of the Shōwa era and Japan's economic boom.

Kayako's marriage was to some degree arranged. For many years she had been friends with her future husband, Akihiko. However, rather than confessing to her directly, Akihiko requested a marriage interview "behind her back," as it were, asking her parents (or other relatives—Kayoko's aunt is the only one mentioned). No one bothered to tell Kayako about this (*SBF*, 4:60–61).

Kayako's marriage, and her subsequent relationship with her husband, are presented as adhering to patriarchal norms. Unlike the other weddings pictured in the manga, Kayoko is shown not in a Western-style wedding dress but wearing a white wedding kimono (*shiromuku*). Her headdress (*tsunokakushi*) symbolizes the effacement of her selfishness and jealousy (covering its "horns") in favor of obedience and devotion to her husband (*SBF*, 4:62).

Before his marriage, Akihiko is portrayed as somewhat tentative and shy, but that is the last time we see his face: he appears obscured in Shimura's depiction of their wedding (*SBF*, 4:62).[1] Like the father of the Sugimoto sisters, Akihiko has disappeared into his role as familial patriarch, and traditional attitudes downplayed before his marriage now come to the fore: for example, he prizes the fact that Kayako was a virgin before her marriage (4:62–63).

These attitudes again become salient in the aftermath of Kyoko's losing her way in a forest as a young child. For Kyoko, this is a major event in her relationship with Ko, continually referenced throughout the manga.

Ko's rescue of Kyoko is a metaphor for their relationship: Ko sees in Kyoko someone he can love and protect, and Kyoko is alternately grateful for his coming to her aid and upset that she needed it.

But for Kayoko, that same event marks the beginning of the unraveling of her relationship with Akihiko, as he accuses her of failing to protect his child (*SBF*, 4:65). Kayako takes the blame on herself, and between Kyoko's crying and her husband's scolding, concludes that she is "truly an awful mother" (4:66).

Kayako speculates that her shortcomings are why Akihiko grows distant. But as she herself recognizes, it's more likely that he had simply grown tired of her and (as her sisters told her) preferred the company of younger women (*SBF*, 4:68–69).

Whatever the reason, it's strongly implied that Akihiko essentially abandoned his wife and daughter to their own devices. He presumably continues his monetary support of Kayako and Kyoko, including paying for Kyoko's education. But except for one possible instance, asking Kyoko about her drama club activities (*SBF*, 2:241–42), we do not encounter him elsewhere in the manga.

Akihiko is not alone in distancing himself from his family. Ko's (unnamed) father has also been absent for years (*SBF*, 2:50), and as noted previously, the father of the Sugimoto sisters shows up for Kazusa's wedding (2:94) but is otherwise unseen, unheard, and unmentioned.

His wife Chie Sugimoto appears to accept this with equanimity, as does Ko's mother. What distinguishes Kayako and makes her the object of criticism by others is not being a wife mostly abandoned by her husband—this is portrayed as a normal state of affairs, at least for the class to which these families belong—but rather her reaction to it.

Although this is not made explicit in the text, Kayako appears to have become severely depressed in the wake of her husband's leaving her. We do not see her face in the first three volumes but only hear her conversations with Kyoko and Ko. It is not until volume 4 that we first see her in the present day (*SBF*, 4:67–71). She appears haggard and disheveled—a far cry from the young woman depicted before her marriage, and when Kyoko got lost in the forest (4:64)—although at this point in the story, she would likely still have not yet turned forty.

Instructions

1. Each Click-N-Ship® label is unique. Labels are to be used as printed and used only once. DO NOT PHOTO COPY OR ALTER LABEL.

2. Place your label so it does not wrap around the edge of the package.

3. Adhere your label to the package. A self-adhesive label is recommended. If tape or glue is used, DO NOT TAPE OVER BARCODE. Be sure all edges are secure.

4. To mail your package with PC Postage®, you may schedule a Package Pickup online, hand to your letter carrier, take to a Post Office™, or drop in a USPS collection box.

5. Mail your package on the "Ship Date" you selected when creating this label.

Click-N-Ship® Label Record

USPS TRACKING # :

9405 5036 9930 0210 3189 49

		Priority Mail® Postage:	$9.90
		Total:	$9.90

Trans. #:   560277122
Print Date: 04/02/2022
Ship Date: 04/02/2022
Expected
Delivery Date: 04/04/2022

From: FRANKLIN W HECKER
3209 GREENWAY DR
ELLICOTT CITY MD 21042-2417

To: LIBRARY OF CONGRESS
COPYRIGHT OFFICE - TX
101 INDEPENDENCE AVE SE
WASHINGTON DC 20559-6222

* Retail Pricing Priority Mail rates apply. There is no fee for USPS Tracking® service on Priority Mail service with use of this electronic rate shipping label. Refunds for unused postage paid labels can be requested online 30 days from the print date.

UNITED STATES POSTAL SERVICE®   *Thank you for shipping with the United States Postal Service!*
Check the status of your shipment on the USPS Tracking® page at usps.com

Kayako's troubles, in turn, affected her relationship with her daughter, as Kyoko's emotions became a toxic stew of shame, guilt, pity, and anger: "I couldn't stop her from breaking. It was Dad's fault, but I couldn't stop him either. I hate both of them. ... My whole family is worthless" (*SBF*, 3:101, 3:103).

The situation was complicated by Kayako turning to religion in her despair. In volume 2, Kyoko thinks to herself, "Mom has her own special god. One just for her. ... Mom has her own special god ... because she needed one" (*SBF*, 2:301, 2:324). In volume 3, we learn that Kayako participates in a religious community of some sort. Kyoko again: "I learned that she and a lot of people I didn't know were praying to God. And her God is a little different than the one I know" (3:100).[2]

What this difference might be exactly is never explained, but it was different enough from Japan's traditional mix of Shinto and Buddhism, or the Catholicism of Fujigaya Women's Academy, to upset Kyoko: "But that embarrassed me. It was my father's fault ... but I was ashamed of my mother. I thought she was pitiful" (*SBF*, 2:324).

Kayoko's mental state becomes a topic of conversation for others as well. When Kyoko and her friends visit Ko's family's summer home, Akira overhears Ko's mother expressing her opinion about Kayako: "She's sick. And I don't like that sort of thing. ... Any sort of complication." In Ko's mother's mind, Kayako's troubles threaten to taint the previously-arranged union of Ko and Kyoko and the future of the Sawanoi line: "It looks bad for someone like that to join the family. I feel sorry for Kyoko, but ... But what if she has a child?" (*SBF*, 2:50–51).

Again, though this is not made explicit, the reasonable conclusion here is that Ko's mother (and others) think that Kayako is mentally ill and shun her because of it. If so, this is consistent with what appears to be relatively more severe stigmatization of mental illness in Japan versus other countries. "In the Japanese general population, few people think that people can recover from mental disorders. ... [The] majority of the general public in Japan keep a greater social distance from individuals with mental illness, especially in close personal relationships."[3]

In a different story, Kayako might have sought professional help. In *Sweet Blue Flowers*, Kayako's recovery, such as it is, begins when (after a long absence) Ko visits her, and then he and Kyoko reconcile (*SBF*, 4:69–72). After that, Kayoko throws herself into planning for their subsequent wedding, whatever objections Ko's family might have had presumably having been overcome. Even Ko's mother, who was previously so negative towards Kayako and (by extension) Kyoko, takes note of Kayako's work and looks forward to seeing Kyoko as a bride (4:333).

And in the context of her social milieu and the expectations placed on her, Kayako has every right to be satisfied and happy: whatever the state of her own marriage, she has achieved her long-time goal of seeing her daughter make a good match and can rest from her labors. However, whether Ko will be another Akihiko, and Kyoko another Kayako, is a question left hanging in the joy of their wedding—a wedding where both Akihiko and Kayako are presumably present but are nowhere to be seen.

1. This is reminiscent of the conclusion of Yasujirō Ozu's 1949 film *Late Spring*, in which Noriko defers to her father's wishes and marries a man recommended to her by her aunt. She is shown dressed in kimono and *tsunokakushi*, ready for her wedding, but the film never shows her husband's face. *Late Spring*, 1:38:12.
2. The difference in capitalization ("god" vs. "God") between the three quotes appears not to be significant. The Japanese text uses *kami-sama* in all three cases.
3. Shuntaro Ando, Sosei Yamaguchi, Yuta Aoki, and Graham Thornicroft, "Review of Mental-Health-Related Stigma in Japan," *Psychiatry and Clinical Neurosciences* 67, no. 7 (November 2013), 471, https://onlinelibrary.wiley.com/doi/10.1111/pcn.12086.

A Play of One's Own

One of the most effective aspects of *Sweet Blue Flowers* is how Takako Shimura uses the annual Fujigaya theater festival to move the plot forward and indirectly comment on the manga's themes. In volume 4, the Fujigaya drama club's annual production is a student adaptation of *The Three Musketeers* set at Fujigaya Women's Academy itself. It is joined by an initial effort by the heretofore-dormant drama club at Matsuoka Girls' High School, a student play based loosely on Fumi's experiences as a young lesbian (*SBF*, 4:167–68, 4:284–85).

In terms of themes, we see an overall progression from year to year towards more Japanese settings, more contemporary timeframes, and more stories centering female agency and authorship.

The first year's play was an adaptation of *Wuthering Heights*, a nineteenth-century novel set in late eighteenth-century England. As Akira's father remarked, even though it was not a musical, it had the general air of a Takarazuka Revue production, with Yasuko playing the *otokoyaku* role as Heathcliff (*SBF*, 1:236–46). The accompanying plot highlighted the limitations of the "girl prince" role, as the relationship between Fumi and Yasuko foundered on Yasuko's emotional immaturity and Fumi's jealousy.

The other plays that year were also adaptations of Western works: the nineteenth-century American novel *Little Women* and the twentieth-century French fantasy *The Little Prince* (*SBF*, 1:235).

Akira's second year at Fujigaya saw a slate of plays all rooted in Japanese literature and history: the tenth-century tale of Princess Kaguya, an adaptation of Yasunari Kawabata's short story "The Dancing Girl of Izu" (originally published in 1926), and Yukio Mishima's 1956 play *Rokumeikan*, set in the late nineteenth century (*SBF*, 3:70, 3:75, 3:80–87, 3:92–99, 3:102–3, 3:105–6).

All three of these feature women subject to the attention of or domination by men: Kaguya is beset by suitors, including the emperor himself, escaping them only by returning to the Moon. The young Izu dancer becomes the object of the fantasies of a male university student. Finally, and most tragically, the ex-geisha Asako loses both her ex-lover and her son by him due to the political schemes of her powerful and jealous husband.

Rokumeikan, in particular, featured the debut of Kyoko as Asako, with Asako's fate—bereft of her true love and trapped in a loveless marriage—implied to possibly be Kyoko's own in future, given the state of her relationship with Ko (*SBF*, 3:88–91). *Rokumeikan* also saw Akira take her turn on the stage as the ingénue Akiko (3:84–85, 3:92–95), and Fumi try and fail to audition for a part (2:279–86, 2:308–10, 2:313–16). Fumi's effort nonetheless directly led to her gaining the friendship of Haruka and indirectly to her confiding in Hinako, the partner of Haruka's sister Orie (2:328–31, 2:333-34, 3:48—50, 3:218, 3:224–27, 3:243–44).

Volume 4 sees Akira take over leadership of the Fujigaya drama club, with Kyoko as her second-in-command. They struggle with deciding what plays to put on for the high school, middle school, and elementary school productions. Initially, this seems like a replay of their first-year experience, as all the candidate plays are again based on Western works (*SBF*, 4:47–48).

They eventually decide to do *The Three Musketeers*, but Kyoko for one longs for them to do something original (*SBF*, 4:76–78, 4:88–89). As usual, their putative advisor, Mr. Kagami, is no help at all, not even showing up for meetings to discuss their plans. But Hinako attends in his place and makes the key suggestions: to break with the Takarazuka formula by having the main characters be women, rather than male characters played by women, and update the setting from seventeenth-century France to Fujigaya itself (4:165–67).

The resulting performance elicits the disapproval of the nuns who run Fujigaya and offends some audience members, including Akira's aunt Keiko (*SBF*, 4:167, 4:169). Why might this be? After all, *The Three Musketeers* is a universally popular work, beloved by young and old alike.

I speculate that the audience's discomfort arose because the play, though ostensibly based on a historical novel set in a different time and place, as adapted and modified per Hinako's advice could be seen as an indirect commentary on Fujigaya Women's Academy itself. By implication, the play promoted a vision of female agency and liberation from the constraints of gender that was at odds with the traditions of Fujigaya, as the action of the original novel—from spur-of-the-moment fighting to seducing women—was enacted by Fujigaya students playing a fantasy version of themselves.[1]

The girls of the Fujigaya drama club, inspired by a lesbian teacher,[2] thus took a fictional template of "masculine" adventure and made that story their own. It's likely not a coincidence that the other Fujigaya play mentioned in this volume, an adaptation of *The Diary of Anne Frank*, also features a girl writing her own story—and in the direst of circumstances.

That theme of girls writing their own stories continues with the performance of the Matsuoka drama club of a play, *Heavenly Creatures*, written by Fumi's friend Pon and loosely based on Fumi's life.[3] The roots of that performance lay in the junior high experiences of Pon, Mogi, and Yassan, in which they eagerly joined the drama club as first-year students and were warmly welcomed by the third-year students.

However, after the third-years graduated and the second-year students assumed their place at the top of the age-based hierarchy, they lorded it over the three friends and other drama club members. The resulting discord led to the eventual dissolution of the club (*SBF*, 4:191–98).

Yassan, in particular, was so discouraged by this experience that she accepted as fate Matsuoka's lack of a cultural festival and the fact that Matsuoka's drama club consisted only of herself, Mogi, and Pon (*SBF*, 4:199, 1:23). After Akira's attempt to lobby the Matsuoka faculty failed, Fumi did join the drama club, but it remained relatively moribund (3:271–73).

However, as the girls of the drama club entered their third year at Matsuoka, two separate events revived the club's fortunes. First, an enthusiastic first-year student, inspired by the acting manga *Glass Mask*, joined the drama club and persuaded her friend to do likewise (*SBF*, 4:15–18). Together they also lobbied the school's faculty and students to support a cultural festival at Matsuoka (4:187–90).

Second, rather than putting on an existing play, the girls of the drama club created a play of their own, inspired by one of their own. The previous Christmas, a conversation about boyfriends and a question from

Pon had led to Fumi coming out to her three friends (*SBF*, 3:304–11). That night Pon began writing a play about a girl like Fumi and (after asking Fumi's permission) presented the completed script as a proposed entry into the theater contest the club planned to participate in (4:102–5).

Though Pon wrote the play as a (presumed) heterosexual girl exercising her imagination on what she may have gleaned from observing and talking to Fumi, Fumi herself found the play to be relatively true to life ("I kept reading myself into it!") (*SBF*, 4:106). In fact, lines from the play ("That small, shy crybaby has died. What's inside me now is a strong will to be near the woman I love") are later echoed by Fumi herself as interior monologue (4:111–12, 4:185, 4:208, 4:279–80).

The play is an award-winning success, though it is performed only for the theater contest judges and other contest participants. This relatively small group of people echoes Fumi's own coming out, thus far limited only to her friends and Hinako. Nevertheless, the play finds its audience in the form of a girl who, mistaking Fumi for the playwright, tells her how moving she found the performance and script and how much it resonated with her feelings (*SBF*, 4:284–88).

It's worth noting here that the appearance of the girl in question does not conform to any of the traditional yuri types (types which *Sweet Blue Flowers* itself contains): the tall "*nadeshiko* beauty" with long black hair (represented in the manga by Fumi), the short lighter-haired "*genki* girl" (Akira), or the handsome "girl prince" (Yasuko).

She's just an ordinary girl, a bit plain, a bit plump. As such, she represents an intrusion of reality into the stereotypical yuri fantasy—almost a breaking of the fourth wall in which someone who could be a typical young Japanese lesbian takes her brief turn upon the stage. Perhaps she reads yuri manga like *Sweet Blue Flowers*, or even hopes to be like Takako Shimura and other yuri creators and one day write and draw them.

Although we as readers don't learn what Fumi might have told the girl about her own relationship to the play, it's clear that despite the girl's ordinariness, Fumi sees her as a kindred spirit and even a potential romantic partner had things worked out differently: "Wouldn't it have been nice if we had fallen in love with each other?" (*SBF*, 4:288).

But back in the reality of the story, Fumi is frustrated at the breakdown of her relationship with Akira, who is racked with doubts about her ability to return Fumi's love and satisfy her desires. These doubts apparently intensified as Akira read Pon's play and gained new insight into Fumi's feelings, and she felt compelled to voice them to Fumi. Fumi assured her that she'd be able to move on if they broke up, and Akira concluded that break up they must indeed (*SBF*, 4:201–7, 4:269).

And there things stand with Fumi and Akira as we enter the concluding chapters of *Sweet Blue Flowers*.

1. Although it's not anti-clerical per se, *The Three Musketeers* also pokes gentle fun at the Church (for example, in the chapter "The Thesis of Aramis" addressing Aramis's vacillation between being a musketeer and becoming a priest), another possible reason for the Fujigaya nuns' disapproval if any of that humor made its way into the play. Alexandre Dumas, *The Three Musketeers*, trans. Richard Pevear (New York: Penguin Books, 2007), chapter 26, Kindle.

2. They were also rescued from a potential disaster by another lesbian, as Orie took off work at Hinako's request to retrieve costumes that Haruka had accidentally left at home (*SBF*, 4:152–56, 4:161).

3. "Heavenly Creatures" is also the title of chapter 46 of the manga, which tells the story of the play's genesis (*SBF*, 4:186). However, in the Japanese edition, both the play and chapter title are *Otome no inori*, which can be literally translated as *A Maiden's Prayer*. Shimura, *Aoi hana*, 8:6, 8:25, 8:104.

Men, What Are They Good For?

Throughout the first three volumes of *Sweet Blue Flowers*, we encounter adult men and male university students, but not until we reach volume 4 do we meet a high-school boy. One of Fumi's fellow cram-school students, Atsushi Tanaka, confesses to her (4:270–77).[1] His sudden appearance and swift rejection by Fumi form a parallel with her relationship with Akira (in a chapter titled "Unrequited Love") and highlight the limited role men play in the manga and how it characterizes men in general.

If we look back to *Maria Watches Over Us*, the most likely immediate inspiration for *Sweet Blue Flowers*, we find male characters who, though peripheral to the main action at Lillian Girls' Academy, nevertheless have some role in the story and exercise a fair degree of agency. There was even a ten-volume spinoff series of light novels featuring Yuki Fukazawa, brother of the main character Yumi Fukazawa, and his classmates at an all-boys school.

It's hard to imagine any male character in *Sweet Blue Flower* meriting such treatment. Instead, the men of the manga are—with some key exceptions—generally portrayed as ineffectual and passive, acted upon rather than acting on their own. Atsushi Tanaka, Fumi's would-be boyfriend, is a partial exception: he does muster up the courage to confess to her, something Fumi is not unmindful of. However, he hasn't even bothered to learn her actual name ("It's Makime! Or maybe not..."), much less tried to converse with her and strike up a friendship before confessing.

Ko is another exception, but only partially. He doggedly continues his pursuit of Kyoko, but how much of that is genuine initiative rather than just following a track laid down for both of them in childhood? Indeed, as a university student, he would have had plenty of opportunities to meet other women. His continued attachment to Kyoko seems at times as implausible and even off-putting as Mamoru's to Usagi in *Sailor Moon*.

Our next two examples, Akira's brother Shinobu and Mr. Kagami, can't even muster that level of initiative, at least as portrayed in their stories. Like his fellow university student Ko, Shinobu seems to have no interest in or relationships with women his age. He acquires a girlfriend (and potential future wife) in Fumi's friend Mogi only through a plot contrivance seemingly introduced only to close out the subplot involving his siscon tendencies.

Likewise, Mr. Kagami is pursued by three different Sugimoto sisters (with Kazusa winning out), even though his appeal to women remains mysterious: "We must have a genetic weakness for guys like you," speculates Yasuko (*SBF*, 2:88). His work persona is no better: it's a long-running joke that he can't be bothered to attend meetings of the Fujigaya drama club of which he's ostensibly the faculty advisor. The situation is so bad that Hinako has to step in to help the club decide on a production for Akira and Kyoko's third year (4:165–66). As one of the drama club presidents tells him, "It doesn't matter if you're there or not" (1:111).

Mr. Kagami does have one accomplishment to his name, though, namely siring a child (*SBF*, 4:18–20). In this, he joins other fathers portrayed in the manga. Akira's father seems to exist in a state of perpetual bewilderment, while Fumi's father appears only briefly. Hinako's father can't be bothered to stop reading baseball news long enough to talk seriously about his daughter's relationship with Orie (4:210).

Presumably, all these men work to support their families, although this topic never comes up in the manga. (Even Mr. Kagami is never shown in the classroom, let alone teaching.) The overall effect is that most men in *Sweet Blue Flowers* are portrayed as aliens in a world they don't belong to.

As an outsider, I can't speak from personal experience. Still, from my reading and general impressions, it seems as if within the middle- to upper-middle-class milieu in which *Sweet Blue Flowers* is set, the worlds of Japanese men and women are largely separate and intersect only in a few times and places.

The world of men is the world of work, the stereotypical salaryman and his corporate employer, long workdays followed by long nights socializing with coworkers, and business trips and remote assignments away from family. The world of women is the world of home, managing a household, and caring for children and aging parents.

Will these two worlds ever grow closer together? Beyond objective economic measures such as gender wage gaps and labor force participation, we can look to changes in culture, particularly those occurring in the postbubble timeframe (the 1990s to the present). Here two suggestive phenomena present themselves.

The first is a change in the language used by male protagonists in that most stereotypical masculine of media, anime adapted from manga published in the magazine *Shōnen Jump* and targeted at the *shōnen* demographic of teenaged boys. During the height of Japan's postwar economic boom, *shōnen* heroes almost exclusively used the first-person pronoun *ore*, associated with "the 'hot-blooded hero,' an aggressive, no-nonsense character." But since the middle of the 1990s, many *shōnen* protagonists have begun using *boku* instead, a more neutral pronoun. The hypothesis is that "expectations for protagonists in *shōnen* works changed as the power of masculinity structures that were dominant during the 1980s began to weaken."[2]

Another example, which came into prominence while Shimura was writing *Sweet Blue Flowers*, is Japanese media obsession with so-called "herbivore men": "young men who are heterosexual but are not assertive ... in trying to pursue women," and who engage in stereotypical feminine behaviors like using makeup and having an interest in fashion.[3]

The "herbivore men" were accused of violating traditional Japanese ideals of masculinity and contributing to the nation's decline in fertility while at the same time being hailed as blurring gender boundaries and providing a potential new model for Japanese men.[4]

The reality is perhaps more prosaic. Displaying male vanity through an interest in makeup and fashion no more implies a revolution in male opinions regarding gender, much less a dismantling of patriarchal structures, than did the adoption of long hair and earrings by American men in the 1960s and 70s. Or, to express it in more academic language, "the mere reconfiguration of conventional hegemonic masculinity to 'softer,' seemingly more egalitarian forms does not necessarily result in equalizing the relationship between masculinity and femininity."[5]

As for disinterest in sex and marriage, the economic explanation is more parsimonious: in Japanese government surveys, "those who reported no interest in heterosexual romantic relationships had lower income and educational levels and were more likely have no regular employment." Japan's relatively stagnant economy and the decline in traditional corporate employment meant that more men did not feel economically secure enough to enter into a marriage, especially given societal expectations that men will be the primary breadwinners for their families. And because Japanese norms discourage sexual activities outside marriage, such men had less interest in finding sexual partners.[6]

It's worth noting that this feeling of financial insecurity appears *not* to apply to the two leading male characters of *Sweet Blue Flowers*, Ko and Shinobu. Although Ko does express some concern to Kyoko's mother about finding a job (*SBF*, 4:70), he apparently feels financially secure enough to marry Kyoko. Shinobu is in the same situation: both Akira and Yassan expect that he'll marry Mogi relatively soon, and Mogi appears to agree (4:95, 4:353). So for Ko and Shinobu, at least, the salaryman ideal is still alive and active as the "hegemonic masculinity."

Finally, two men are *not* portrayed as passive and ineffectual: the father of the Sugimoto sisters, and Count Kageyama, the antagonist of *Rokumeikan*. Instead, they are men who exercise power over others: Sugimoto within his company and over his family, Kageyama within the Japanese state and over his wife, her lover, and her son. They appear only fleetingly—the first seen but not heard, the second only spoken to—presumably because their presence is incompatible with the feminine world that is the manga's focus. However, we as readers cannot ignore their existence and that of the patriarchal society within which *Sweet Blue Flowers* is situated.

1. The Ishide cram school Fumi and Atsushi attend is presumably named after Den Ishide, Shimura's friend and sometime assistant (*SBF*, 3:175, 4:270).
2. Hannah Dahlberg-Dodd, "Talking like a *Shōnen* Hero: Masculinity in Post-Bubble Era Japan through the Lens of *Boku* and *Ore*," *Buckeye East Asian Linguistics* 3 (October 2018), 31–42, https://kb.osu.edu/bitstream/handle/1811/86767/BEAL_v3_2018_Dahlberg-Dodd_31.pdf.
3. Chris Deacon, "All the World's a Stage: Herbivore Boys and the Performance of Masculinity in Contemporary Japan," in *Manga Girl Seeks Herbivore Boy: Studying Japanese Gender at Cambridge*, ed. Brigitte Steger and Angelika Koch (Berlin: LIT Verlag, 2013),

https://www.academia.edu/34610378/All_the_Worlds_a_Stage_Herbivore_Boys_and _the_Performance_of_Masculinity_in_Contemporary_Japan_in_Brigitte_Steger_and _Angelika_Koch_eds_Manga_Girl_Seeks_Herbivore_Boy_Studying_Japanese_Gender_at _Cambridge_LIT_Verlag_2013

4. Deacon, "All the World's a Stage," 135, 159–66.

5. Justin Charlebois, "Herbivore Masculinity as an Oppositional Form of Masculinity," *Culture, Society & Masculinities* 5, no. 1 (Spring 2013), 100.

6. Cyrus Ghaznavi, Haruka Sakamoto, Shuhei Nomura, Anna Kubota, Daisuke Yoneoka, Kenji Shibuya, and Peter Ueda, "The Herbivore's Dilemma: Trends in and Factors Associated with Heterosexual Relationship Status and Interest in Romantic Relationships among Young Adults in Japan—Analysis of National Surveys, 1987–2015," PLoS ONE 15(11): e0241571, https://journals.plos.org/plosone/article?id=10.1371/journal .pone.0241571, 13.

Emotional Incontinence

In my first reading of *Sweet Blue Flowers*, I couldn't make sense of Fumi's strange dream in chapter 50, in which young Akira urinates down her legs and young Fumi laps it up (*SBF*, 4:289–92).

But then I thought, what is incontinence? It's an involuntary release of bodily fluids due to a lack of control over one's own body. In a social context, this lack of control translates into public shame and embarrassment—embarrassment because one has broken social norms about proper social behavior (i.e., confining urination to appropriate spaces and times), and shame because others judge one for that transgression.

Tears are another example of an involuntary release of bodily fluids, in this case, due to a lack of control over one's own emotions. Crying is a much milder social transgression than public incontinence. However, in a society focused on social harmony and maintaining a public "face" that is different and more restrained than one's private "face," openly crying in public could presumably be considered a transgression as well. If so, it too could occasion shame and embarrassment.

This brings us to Fumi and Akira. After Akira meets her childhood friend Fumi on the train without knowing who she is, and their two mothers arrange a reunion, Akira's mother asks her, "Do you remember Fumi?" (*SBF*, 1:28). In the subsequent flashback, young Fumi can't make it to the bathroom in time, and her classmates call Akira in from another elementary school class to help out (1:29–30). (Note the implication that this is not the first time that Fumi has done this.) Akira takes control of the situation and gets Fumi to the school nurse to get cleaned up and changed (1:31).

In a nutshell, young Fumi is a person who cannot control herself and, in particular, cannot control her own body. Since elementary school, Fumi has presumably overcome her childhood incontinence. Still, her continued and frequent crying is another indicator of her lack of self-control, this time of her emotions.

Akira, secure in her control of her own body and emotions, can then step in and help Fumi regain both her physical and emotional equilibrium. Just as she takes control when young Fumi urinates on herself, she urges young Fumi to stop crying (*SBF*, 3:318). As a teenager, she continues to be the level-headed person in their relationship, drying Fumi's tears just as she once helped her dry her underpants.

But Akira's self-control is accompanied by her seeming inability to feel certain emotions herself. In particular, she does not (cannot?) feel a strong romantic or sexual attraction towards anyone, including Fumi. She also does not (cannot?) cry openly. It's not that Akira is unemotional in general: throughout the manga, we see her be alternately happy, angry, embarrassed, nervous, puzzled, and distraught. But through most of the manga, we never see her cry in the presence of someone else.[1]

Being in love and crying are connected in Akira's mind. Thinking to herself, she wonders, "Will I ever like someone ... and end up in tears like Fumi? ... Fumi is *always* crying ..." (*SBF*, 2:66). Given her frequent admonitions to Fumi to not be a "crybaby," it's no surprise that Akira might have at least an unconscious bias against romance as well.

This is, of course, very frustrating to Fumi. She has a powerful romantic and sexual attraction to Akira, an attraction Akira does not (and cannot?) feel toward her. From this perspective, I see Fumi's dream of Akira's incontinence as a manifestation of her desire that Akira not let self-control hold her back from a relationship. Fumi unconsciously wants Akira to lose control of herself in love, just as Fumi succumbs to her own emotions (*SBF*, 4:290).

Unlike young Akira, the dreaming Fumi does not see Akira's incontinence as an opportunity for her to step in and restore Akira's self-control and emotional equilibrium, as Akira had once done for her. Instead, she responds to Akira's loss of control in a manner that seems to welcome it and reads as intensely sexual (*SBF*, 4:291). No wonder Fumi dreams of Akira (or their teacher?) shouting "Stop that, Fumi!" and then covers her face in embarrassment upon waking (4:292).

Beyond Fumi's dream, the manga has an ongoing theme of Akira and urination, depicting Akira needing to rush to the bathroom (*SBF*, 1:265, 1:281, 1:374, 2:35, 2:139–40). This occurs so often that it's hard to avoid the conclusion that Shimura consciously intended these scenes to be read metaphorically, perhaps as representing the pressure of emotions within Akira that she has resisted letting herself express.

This is capped off by a dream in which Akira imagines herself visiting Yasuko and Kawasaki in England and urgently needing to use their bathroom (*SBF*, 4:224–25). This (almost) loss of bladder control has a parallel loss of emotional control on Akira's actual trip to England, as we see Akira's eyes fill with tears as she talks to Yasuko about Fumi and their relationship (4:254).[2]

The final scene of *Sweet Blue Flowers* touches on the topic of tears once more. As Fumi and Akira lie in Fumi's bedroom sometime after Akira's confession, one of them muses to herself about wanting to stay awake and talk all night and concludes, "And I felt like crying" (*SBF*, 4:365). Shimura does not make explicit whose thoughts these are, an ambiguity that may be deliberate: as the story ends, perhaps Akira, as well as Fumi, is willing and able to lose herself in tears, finally giving in to her overflowing emotions.

1. Akira does cry once while dreaming of young Fumi and herself (*SBF*, 3:319). But those are private tears and not shed while awake.
2. Akira's body betrays her again on the flight from England back to Japan, as she becomes violently ill (*SBF*, 4:262).

The Halting Problem

Why does *Sweet Blue Flowers* end where it does? To answer that, let's look at a different question, or rather multiple questions: How long should a manga run? How long can it run? Will it ever end?

In western comics, this last question is unanswerable: corporate ownership of copyrights and trademarks means that a popular comic can exist in perpetuity, like a corporation itself. It's impossible to predict which comics will ever halt publication and which will not.

On the other hand, there's an expectation that manga will not survive the artist's death—that one day we will see an end to long-running works. But that day may not be soon.[1]

Even with other manga that are not so long-lived, commercial success can lead to extended runs as the story gets stretched out to satisfy readers' desires for more entertainment and publishers' desires for more profit. Other series are canceled well before the end of their natural life, with the story left hanging or rushed to a conclusion.

Where does *Sweet Blue Flowers* fit in this picture? It is relatively short by Japanese standards at only eight volumes (in the original Japanese edition). For example, *Wandering Son* went to fifteen volumes, and it's not unusual for manga to go to thirty or forty.

I've seen occasional speculation that *Sweet Blue Flowers* was brought to a close prematurely. Indeed, the last chapters seem somewhat rushed. For example, in chapter 51, Shimura resorts to the shortcut of having an omniscient narrator herald Akira's change of heart (*SBF*, 4:225), as opposed to showing this happening through more gradual plot developments and internal monologues.

On the other hand, a case can be made that Shimura ended the manga where she wanted to end it and that it had come to a natural stopping point.

First, why end it at fifty-two chapters? Shimura may have done this in homage to Nobuko Yoshiya's *Hana monogatari*, which contained fifty-two stories. The title of the last chapter is "Sweet Blue Flowers" ("*Aoi* hana" in the Japanese edition), repeating the title of the manga itself, just as the title of the first chapter, "Flower Story" ("*Hana monogatari*") namechecked the title of Yoshiya's series.

Assuming that this is intentional, I see this as Shimura concluding the series by subtly highlighting its status as her response to Yoshiya, the ideals of Class S relationships, and the Class S literary genre.

Second, why end the manga at this point in the plot? Arguably, once Fumi and Akira graduated from high school, it was time to wrap things up. The manga as a whole, like many manga about the lives of Japanese schoolgirls, is structured around the rhythm of the school year, particularly the summer breaks and the Fujigaya theater festival.

Once that rhythm is absent, the framework underlying the plot is broken, and the manga moves toward its conclusion. It lasts only long enough to take the characters into adulthood, bring Kyoko's story to a conclusion with her marriage to Ko, and see Fumi and Akira enter into a new phase of their relationship.

I think Shimura did rush things a bit to bring the story to an end at a possibly symbolic fifty-two chapters. However, plotwise, I believe she intended to end *Sweet Blue Flowers* exactly where she did, with the reader left to imagine the continuation of Fumi and Akira's life together.

1. There are at least twenty-five manga series with a hundred or more volumes in print, most of them written and illustrated by a single person. "List of Manga Series by Volume Count," Wikipedia, last modified January 31, 2022, https://en.wikipedia.org/wiki/List_of _manga_series_by_volume_count.

Equally Jealous

In the previous chapter, I wondered why Takako Shimura ended *Sweet Blue Flowers* where she did and concluded that the story had come to a natural stopping point, but the ending was somewhat rushed. One unfortunate consequence of that rush is the somewhat muddled resolution of Akira's relationship with Fumi.

After their graduation from high school, Fumi and Akira had come to a point where Akira felt she could no longer continue their relationship (*SBF*, 4:318–20, 4:323). At that point, the story could go in several directions: Akira and Fumi could remain apart, going their separate ways through life without further contact; they could reach an accommodation in which Fumi found someone else to be her partner, and Akira continued as Fumi's close friend; or they could get back together and try to restart their relationship as a couple.

If we perceive Fumi as the main protagonist of *Sweet Blue Flowers* and the manga itself as a realistic fiction, then either of the first two scenarios makes the most sense. After her conversation with Hinako and Pon's writing a play based on her experiences, Fumi is coming into her own as a self-identified lesbian. The logical next step would be to begin a new relationship with another woman equally self-identified. In particular, Fumi could meet someone else while attending university—and, in fact, the manga nods in that direction by introducing her new friend Hanae Mori (*SBF*, 4:324–26).

As it turns out, though, Fumi's friendship with Hanae is simply a friendship and not a prelude to a relationship, as Hanae has a boyfriend (*SBF*, 4:333). But before we as readers find that out, we watch with Akira as Fumi and Hanae talk and laugh together, and Akira grows jealous that Fumi has seemingly found someone else (4:326–27).

Akira's jealousy drives the final section of the plot. But why jealousy? It seems somewhat of a *deus ex machina*, a rather clichéd and clumsy way to motivate Akira to overcome her indecisiveness and hesitation regarding Fumi's love of her—and to do so in as low a page count as possible.

However clumsy though it might be, I think one can make a case for why this development makes sense in the context of the story and themes of *Sweet Blue Flowers*. Earlier plot points have also partially foreshadowed Akira's jealousy and its role in bringing her and Fumi together.

Start with the assumption that one of the core themes of the manga is the valorization of equality in relationships, as I've argued in previous chapters. Now consider that the relationship between Fumi and Akira as it's developed over the course of the manga is manifestly unequal. Fumi has strong feelings of romantic love and sexual attraction towards Akira that Akira herself does not and—from her perspective—cannot reciprocate: "My brain and my body just aren't in sync" (*SBF*, 4:319).

How might Fumi's and Akira's relationship—and in particular, the emotions they bring to it—become more equal? Here it's worth noting two points, one about Akira and one about Fumi. Although Akira is not strongly romantically or (especially) sexually attracted to Fumi, she is by no means emotionless. As discussed in a previous chapter, Akira is perfectly able to experience feelings of happiness and friendship and also experience strong negative emotions like anger and irritation.

As for Fumi, she's also capable of experiencing strong negative emotions, with the most notable being jealousy. Her anger at Chizu's marriage seems clearly connected to her jealousy towards Chizu's husband, for whom Chizu abandoned her (at least in Fumi's view). And, of course, Fumi's jealousy regarding Yasuko's feelings toward Mr. Kogami was a major factor, perhaps *the* major factor, in their breaking up. Even as she (rightly) dismisses the idea that Akira and Ko might be dating, she gives herself a headache thinking about it: "When I get jealous, my temples hurt" (*SBF*, 2:156).

It's therefore thematically appropriate, if not fully motivated by the manga, that Akira should be provoked into jealousy herself at the sight of Fumi's apparent ease and friendliness with another woman—a woman who (unlike Fumi's high school friends) is unknown to Akira and thus (in Akira's mind) might be Fumi's new lover.

While at this point in the story Akira's emotions may not fully match Fumi's in all respects, in her jealousy she feels an emotion that in its nature and intensity equals any that Fumi has displayed. In a sense,

Fumi's dream (discussed in a previous chapter) has been fulfilled: Akira has moved beyond her previous confusion and hesitation regarding Fumi and let her emotions out. And now that jealousy has so overwhelmed her, Akira looks into her heart to explore what this implies about her evolving feelings toward Fumi.

Four Weddings (No Funeral)

For a manga set in high school, *Sweet Blue Flowers* sure has a lot of weddings (and talk of more). Chizu's marriage and Fumi's anger at it help (re)start Fumi's friendship with Akira. Kazusa's wedding to Mr. Kagami (re)surfaces emotions that Yasuko had suppressed, which indirectly leads to her break-up with Fumi. As the story heads to its conclusion, Kyoko weds Ko and Hinako and Orie envision what their wedding might be like, should it ever be possible.

The earliest wedding depicted in *Sweet Blue Flowers* is that of Kayako to Akihiko Ikumi. Unlike the other wedding pictures, which show the couples in Western attire, theirs features them in traditional Japanese outfits. Or perhaps I should write "traditional" in quotes since what seems to be a time-honored style is in many ways a product of the modern era, "a 'cultural product' ... invented in order to further the business interests of the purveyors of this product ... [and] a purveyor of a sense of cultural identity."[1]

That "cultural identity" is a product of the Meiji-era project to forge Japan into a unified modern nation. That nation-building project touched all areas of Japanese life, including weddings. The state formalized Shinto as a set of rituals binding the Japanese with each other and with the emperor. Those rituals then became the heart of the wedding ceremony. Formerly held at home, weddings became a public display in 1900, when the future Taishō emperor married his bride in a Shinto ceremony held at a shrine. It was a reaction against the perceived dangers of Westernization, "a public statement about Japanese identity in contrast to others through the wedding ceremony."[2]

In contrast to this state ceremony, weddings for the general populace continued to be held at home in the Taishō and early Shōwa periods, including weddings of those descended from the samurai class. The bride's outfit was typically "a white under kimono (*shiromuku*) under a formal black adult's kimono," with "hair oiled and pulled up into a Japanese hair style (*nihonga*) which was not much more elaborate than the way most of them wore their hair on any given day."[3]

However, bridal outfits became more elaborate over time, especially after World War II. Bombing had destroyed the large homes previously used for weddings, so new "wedding palaces" catered to postwar brides. (The palaces included their own Shinto shrines in which to hold ceremonies.) As the economy grew in the postwar period, this wedding industry (for such it was) made available to the broad Japanese middle class bridal clothing and accessories previously confined to the samurai class. Those items combined with a style of makeup otherwise associated with geisha and Kabuki theater to create the image of the "Japanese bride" we know today.[4]

That image is often paired with images of modernity—a bullet train, a computer chip, or the Tokyo skyline—to portray Japan as a nation racing into the future while remaining respectful of and rooted in the past. It is part and parcel of the process of "samuraization," "the configuring of Japanese identity according to a perception of samurai lifestyle from the Tokugawa Period."[5]

This process includes imagining modern Japanese men, especially salarymen, as torch-bearers of the samurai spirit. Akihiko Ikumi was presumably one such man. His marriage to Kayako occurred at the high point of Japanese economic power and self-confidence, the late 1980s and the end of the Shōwa era. (In retrospect, it may also have marked the high point of the Japanese patriarchal system.)

However, Japan soon slid into its "lost decades" of economic stagnation and diminished prospects. All the other weddings depicted in *Sweet Blue Flowers* feature Western wedding gowns and other Western attire, a turning away from the (partly invented and imagined) Japanese marriage traditions.

This carries over to other aspects of *Sweet Blue Flowers*. Unlike other manga set in high schools, there are no visits to Shinto shrines or Buddhist temples. And when the students go on class trips in volume 4, they go not to Kyoto (a traditional destination for Japanese high-school classes), but England and Nagasaki, famous as the site where European goods and ideas first entered Japan.

Kazusa and Mr. Kagami's wedding, the next one pictured in the chronology of *Sweet Blue Flowers,* is held in the Catholic chapel of Fujigaya Women's Academy, complete with an organist, stained glass windows, and a cross on the building's exterior (*SBF,* 2:93, 2:96). Its setting represents the other significant development of the Meiji era, the influx of Western ideas and, in particular, Western religion. That religion was influential not so much as a religion per se, but as a source of images (including the white lily) and traditions (such as the celebration of Christmas) divorced from their religious roots and incorporated into Japanese popular culture.

In Kyoko and Ko's wedding, the religious symbolism is gone: although their wedding was presumably also held at Fujigaya (note the transition into the scene showing the woods surrounding the school), the exterior of the building in which they are married, and the interior rooms at the reception, betray no hint of Christianity (*SBF,* 4:335–37, 4:339–40, 4:348).

Unlike the wedding of Kazusa and Mr. Kagami, the symbols of the patriarchy are absent as well, as there is no sign of Kyoko's father (or Ko's). (We hear mention of Kyoko's and Ko's mothers only in the run-up to the event.) Instead, Kyoko and Ko walk down the aisle by themselves, surrounded by their friends (4:332–33, 4:349).

The fourth and final wedding shown in *Sweet Blue Flowers* is imagined only, as Hinako and Orie respond to Haruka's query, "Hina, do you and Orie want a wedding too?" They picture themselves in wedding gowns even more Western and "fashion-forward" than Kyoko's and Kazusa's (*SBF,* 4:350–51).

However, they have ambiguous feelings about marriage itself ("Actually, an official ceremony isn't that important ...") and are passive regarding anything they might do to make such a wedding possible ("But if no one would mind...") (*SBF,* 4:350). Like the characters in many other yuri manga who imagine weddings and wedding dresses for themselves, they do not (yet?) identify themselves as members of a community that has shared interests and can work to achieve shared political goals.

We find an unlikely exception to this omission in the manga *Love Me for Who I Am,* superficially a story notable mainly for fluffy art and *moe* characters. In volume 3, a lesbian joins her nonbinary friend and their co-worker, a trans girl, as they leave the community they've created with each other at "Café Question" and join the larger LGBTQ community at "Rainbow Festa." As they wander among the people, events, and booths, her companions stop to sign a petition for marriage equality.[6]

It is at once the simplest and potentially most consequential of political acts. Their quickly-written signatures mark a personal crossing of the Rubicon, a transition from inner thoughts and private conversations to public support of a cause near to their hearts and those of their friends. As their futures unfold, they may progress from signing petitions to soliciting signatures for them, from watching parades to marching in them, perhaps even to organizing, leading, or inspiring them.

Who among the characters of *Sweet Blue Flowers* might one day make that journey? One candidate is Haruka: bold, outgoing, able to make friends easily, her concern for her sister might motivate her to become an activist—though she still seems to be coming to terms with Orie's relationship with Hinako.

Another is Akira. Her presidency of the drama club shows she has a talent for organizing. Her behavior throughout the series shows fearlessness and a strong sense of justice, at least where other people are concerned. And now that she's acknowledged her love for Fumi, who knows what actions that love might spur her to?

But I must put such speculation on hold, as I turn to the final scenes of *Sweet Blue Flowers*.

1. Ofra Goldstein-Gidoni, *Packaged Japaneseness: Weddings, Business, and Brides* (Honolulu: University of Hawai'i Press, 1997), 3–4.
2. Teresa A. Hiener, "Shinto Wedding, Samurai Bride: Inventing Tradition and Fashioning Identity in the Rituals of Bridal Dress in Japan," PhD diss., University of Pittsburgh, 1997, 3, 12–13, 144–55.
3. Hiener, "Shinto Wedding, Samurai Bride," 56–57.
4. Goldstein-Gidoni, *Packaged Japaneseness*, 34–39. Hiener, "Shinto Wedding, Samurai Bride," 139–41.
5. Hiener, "Shinto Wedding, Samurai Bride," 17.
6. Kata Konayama, *Love Me for Who I Am*, vol. 3, trans. Amber Tamosaitis (Los Angeles: Seven Seas Entertainment, 2021), 97–101.

Two Women Together

two women together is a work
nothing in civilization has made simple

Adrienne Rich[1]

After the excitement of Kyoko's wedding and the shock of Akira's confession to Fumi, we now come to the final pages of *Sweet Blue Flowers*. Akira's "rude awakening" from sleep at the beginning of chapter 1 of the manga is replaced by morning greetings between Akira and Fumi, after a night in which they reenact as adults the conversation-filled sleepovers they enjoyed as children and teenagers.

If *Sweet Blue Flowers* were a Class S story of spiritual love between two girls, it would have ended in a tearful parting once they graduated high school. If it were like many yuri stories, the confession would have been followed with a kiss, and the "Story A" formula would have been fulfilled: two girls like each other, the end. If it were like other modern schoolgirl yuri stories, it might have ended with lovemaking, as do, for example, Milk Morinaga's *Girl Friends*[2] and *Hana & Hina After School*.[3]

But in *Sweet Blue Flowers* Akira and Fumi do not part.[4] Instead, Fumi's interior monologue strongly implies that their lives will be intertwined for the next ten or twenty years (*SBF*, 4:360–61). Though the manga echoes the "Story A" structure and concludes with Akira's confession, previous chapters already showed their first kiss. There is but the hint of one here. Finally, they've already spent a night together experiencing physical intimacy (4:141–46), but here they wake up in separate beds. If they've made love to each other, it was through their words, not their bodies.

Why does *Sweet Blue Flowers* end this way? If, as I've hypothesized, a primary theme of the manga is the valorization of equality in relationships, the final scene shows how that might play out in practice. Akira has acknowledged that she is romantically attracted to Fumi and has traveled a fair distance in bridging the gap between their separate conceptions of what their relationship is and should be.

As for Fumi, the manga leaves ambiguous when or even whether she will have the physical relationship with Akira that she so clearly craves. Just as Akira came around to Fumi's view of their relationship as a romance and not simply friendship, Fumi may have to accept that Akira's nature means that the romantic aspect of their relationship may always far outweigh the sexual.

But what matters is that they can (re)start their relationship on equal grounds, negotiating the contours of that relationship as partners, and as partners facing the outside world together—including coming out to the rest of their friends, to their families, and perhaps also to their future co-workers and other associates.

To echo Adrienne Rich, nothing in contemporary Japan will make their life together simple. They live in a country where social attitudes toward LGBTQ people are slowly evolving, but where such evolution is impeded by a conservative government thus far unwilling to reform the patriarchal character of Japanese laws relating to marriage and the family.

Though such social and political concerns form the background to the lives of the women of *Sweet Blue Flowers*, at its heart is the story of two people struggling to discover whom they love and how they can mutually express that love in their lives with each other. Adrienne Rich also wrote, "two people together is a work / heroic in its ordinariness."[5] The last page of *Sweet Blue Flowers* takes a final look back at Fumi and Akira's friendship as children, but the chapter as a whole looks forward to the "work" that will be Fumi and Akira's relationship in the years to come.

1. Adrienne Rich, "Twenty-One Love Poems," in *The Dream of a Common Language: Poems 1974–1977* (New York: W. W. Norton, 1978), 35, https://archive.org/details/dreamof commonlan0000rich.

2. Milk Morinaga, *Girl Friends*, vol. 5, trans. Anastasia Moreno (Los Angeles: Seven Seas Entertainment, 2017), 129–36.

3. Milk Morinaga, *Hana & Hina After School*, vol. 3, trans. Jennifer McKeon (Los Angeles: Seven Seas Entertainment, 2017), 149–52.

4. Among other things, we can see this as Shimura's final homage to Nobuko Yoshiya, here to the ending of *Yaneura no nishojo*.

5. Rich, "Twenty-One Love Poems," 35.

After Reading

Gourd Tale

> If a woman in an office is a willow,
> A poetess a violet,
> And a teacher an orchid,
> Then a factory woman is a vegetable gourd.
> > *Sung by workers in the textile mills of Meiji Japan.*[1]

Fans celebrated 2019 as the one-hundredth anniversary of the yuri genre.[2] In this penultimate chapter, I take a final look back at the world that gave rise to that genre before concluding with a look at the present and future of yuri in the next.

Sweet Blue Flowers contains many elements that reflect and indirectly comment on contemporary Japan, but one aspect of Japanese society is almost totally absent from its pages: class. It is not alone in this respect. Class S literature, early (proto-)yuri works like *Dear Brother*, the light novel series *Maria Watches Over Us*, and the various yuri works influenced by *Marimite* all feature relatively affluent students in all-girls schools. Often a younger middle-class girl enters into an S-like relationship with an older girl born to great wealth, as Yumi does with Sachiko in *Maria Watches Over Us*.

In *Maria Watches Over Us*, in particular, the upper-class half of the pair is depicted as a victim, oppressed by a patriarchal system just as much as any other girl. Their relationship with a representative of the middle class is presented as the cure to heal their ills. This serves to flatter the (presumed middle-class) reader regarding the value and importance of the middle class while artfully distracting that same reader from the power that the truly wealthy exercise over them.[3]

This trope is present in *Sweet Blue Flowers* as well, in the relationship between Fumi and Yasuko. Yasuko's family is shown to be on another level entirely when it comes to their wealth—as Fumi herself marvels when she visits the Sugimoto estate: "Her family's rich..." (*SBF*, 1:303). If *Sweet Blue Flowers* used the trope as did *Maria Watches Over Us* then Fumi's love would likely be the key to healing Yasuko's emotional immaturity.

Sweet Blue Flowers subverts this trope by having Fumi break up with Yasuko and redirect her attentions to Akira, someone of a similar station in life. In the meantime, Yasuko matures on her own, helped perhaps by her getting out of Japan.

But although Fumi and Akira both have middle-class backgrounds, they are arguably nearer the upper end of the middle-class spectrum. Their families live in single-family detached houses, and both families own at least one car. More tellingly, both families can send their children to private schools—in the case of Akira, what appears in all respects to be a very expensive and exclusive school. Kyoko's family is even more likely to be wealthy; she attended Fujigaya from elementary school on.[4]

Thus *Sweet Blue Flowers*, like other yuri manga and Class S stories, portrays a world in which the poor and even the lower-middle class are absent, their stories untold.

Where then can we find them? Let's turn back the clock to the late Meiji era in which *shōjo* culture and Class S literature were born, and consider a hypothetical girl born on the same day as Nobuko Yoshiya in 1896, but to a poor peasant family eking out a miserable living in the hinterlands of Japan. What might her tale have been?

One option for her family, and a very common one at the time, would have been to sell her to a brothel. But in the Meiji era, another possibility opened up: sending her to work in a mill producing silk or cotton thread. In 1907, when our young girl (like Nobuko Yoshiya) would have been eleven years old, there were over two hundred thousand girls and women working in such mills, with ages ranging from the twenties down to the early teens or even younger.[5] While Yoshiya was reading the newly-established magazines for girls and looking forward to attending high school, our girl's parents would likely have been contemplating sending her off to work as a "factory girl" (*kōjo*).

In earlier times, she might have stayed at home to help with farming or in-home production of goods. But in the Meiji era, families like hers needed cash to pay new government taxes and were at the same time in economic distress due to cheap imports displacing domestic household production. In turn, the Meiji government needed cash to meet foreign exchange needs and economic growth to forestall popular rebellions but saw export opportunities handicapped by free trade agreements forced on Japan by Western countries. These prevented Japan from raising tariffs on imports, including textiles.[6]

The government found an answer in the large-scale production of silk and (later) cotton thread, products that could compete on the international market and drive export growth. After an initial period of government-run mills that trained the daughters of low-rank samurai in new professions, the industry became dominated by private mill owners employing a workforce of poor urban dwellers and poor migrants from rural areas. The vast majority of these were girls or young women.[7] Our hypothetical young girl might have been one of them.

What might have been our girl's experience if she went to work in the mills? She would likely have been recruited by an independent agent working on commission from a mill owner. The recruiter would spin stories of good pay for girls who worked hard, hearty and nutritious meals for the workers, after-work life in comfortable dormitories where she could learn to read or take other classes, and days off work when she could join other girls in sightseeing expeditions. If her parents were swayed by such stories (and who might not be, knowing nothing to the contrary?), her father would sign a contract committing her to work for several years, look forward to the extra money she would bring the family, and commit her to the care of the recruiter.[8]

Assuming that she arrived at her destination safely (as some did not, sold into brothels or to rival mills), she would have found the reality of the mills to be much different than the promises. The productivity of Japanese factory workers was still significantly lower than that of foreign mills, and to successfully compete on price with foreign silk mills, Japanese mills chose not to try to make workers more productive but rather to reduce costs (and thus improve profits) by any means possible.

They did this by lowering wages, forcing workers to work longer hours, running second shifts, and practicing various forms of wage theft: for example, fining workers for relatively trivial infractions, or holding back wages for a year or more—all measures outlined in the contract, the language of which the typical poor farmer (like our girl's father) would be incapable of reading.[9]

Thus from the time our young girl entered the mill, she would have found herself paying back debts (including the expenses of transporting her to the factory), incurring fines, and having her already-meager wages reduced in various ways. She would have found herself competing with other workers, with the most productive workers receiving the highest wages, and production quotas increasing but wages remaining the same. If she were of relatively plain appearance (like Nobuko Yoshiya), she would likely have found her wages to be lower than others of fairer face more favored by the mill owner.[10]

After work hours, she would have been locked in a dormitory to prevent her escaping, surrounded by high fences topped with barbed wire or sharpened bamboo stakes. She would have been fed a meager diet of rice mixed with barley, with the costs of the meals deducted from her wages. At night she would have slept in a room where each girl had a single *tatami* mat's worth of space and might have shared her sleeping garments with a girl on another shift.[11]

As for the promised education, some mill owners offered rudimentary classes in Japanese and arithmetic to their workers, but many workers found themselves too tired to attend such classes after a twelve-hour shift.[12] Our young girl would likely have been left semi-literate at best. She might have had access to shared copies of the girls' magazines in which Nobuko Yoshiya's stories appeared (20 to 40 percent of factory workers read magazines[13]) but might have found it challenging to understand Yoshiya's ornate prose.

More typical "educational" fare were lectures intended to persuade workers to show devotion to their employers, as a loyal retainer might serve his lord. Like the eighteen-year-old Kikue Yamakawa—later to become famous as a socialist and feminist activist—our factory girl might have found herself attending a sermon, in which visiting Christian missionaries would encourage the girls and women to work hard like Jesus the carpenter, be obedient and submissive to their employers, and be grateful for what was given to them. (Yamakawa, who attended one such sermon as a guest of the missionaries, left the mill vowing never to work with them again.)[14]

What if she had been a lesbian, like Yoshiya? Watched over like a hawk by supervisors both on the factory floor and in the dormitory, crammed into a room at night with twenty or more other girls, allowed to leave the factory grounds only at long intervals, how could she have sustained a relationship with another factory girl? It's more likely that she would have been sexually harassed or even raped by a male coworker, a male supervisor, or the mill owner—who had keys to the dormitory rooms.[15]

If she were lucky, she would complete her contract and return to her village to live out her life—a life perhaps even harder than that in the mill if her family were still in poverty. If she were unlucky, she might have become sick, be pressed to continue to work while ill, and then (if she took a turn for the worse) be sent home to die. The mills were breeding grounds for disease, including epidemics of cholera and dysentery and chronic cases of tuberculosis and beriberi, to which the girls and young women were made vulnerable by long work hours and inadequate nutrition. Teenaged factory girls were particularly affected: their death rate was over twice that of girls in the general population.[16]

What connects our hypothetical factory girl and her real-life counterparts to Nobuko Yoshiya, to the world of Class S literature of which Yoshiya herself was the preeminent practitioner, and to the world of *shōjo* culture of which that literature was a key element?

The life of a factory girl, the life of a schoolgirl, and indeed the life of Nobuko Yoshiya herself were made possible because Meiji Japan lacked one of the prime characteristics of other patriarchal societies. Although fathers in Japan typically exercised strict control over whom their daughters could marry, they did not seek to isolate them entirely from the outside world.

In this respect, Japan differed from patrilineal societies in the Middle East and—more germane in this context—on the Indian subcontinent. In Japan, there was a long tradition of peasant boys *and* girls "going out to work" (*dekasegi*), that is, leaving the family home to seek employment elsewhere. Poor families were willing to send their daughters off to work in the mills, accepting the risk that they would be raped, seduced, or otherwise bring "dishonor" to the family in return for the economic benefits that they could provide. In other words, "South Asia had a stronger preference for female seclusion, and East Asia a stronger preference for female exploitation."[17]

There were several notable women active in the nascent Japanese labor movement, including Kikue Yamakawa. However, the fact that the vast majority of mill workers were girls and women likely made the Japanese factory workforce easier to control than the male factory workers on the Indian subcontinent, where teenaged girls and adult women were isolated and kept out of the labor market. This improved the ability of Japanese factory owners to repress worker unrest, which helped drive the rapid and profitable growth of the Japanese manufacturing sector.[18]

Just as poor families were willing to risk sending their daughters to the mills, so more affluent families were willing to risk sending their daughters to schools, even to relatively distant schools where the girls lived beyond the immediate reach of parental control. If the Japanese patriarchal system had been more strict, then the very premise of Yoshiya's *Yaneura no nishojo* would have been absurd: the virgins of the title would have had their virginity assured by their fathers never allowing them to leave the family home.

In the end, the girls and women in the mills helped make the lives of both the readers and writers of Class S fiction possible. Japan's rapid industrialization and its rise as an exporting nation led to strong economic growth, urbanization, and the emergence of a thriving middle class. Middle-class families became affluent enough to educate their girls through middle and high school, and allow the girls themselves to afford subscriptions to the girls' magazines in which the Class S genre began.

A growing Japanese economy also drove the creation of an urban service sector in which women could find employment as office workers. The *shōjo* who read girls' magazines during her teen years gave rise to the stereotypical "modern girl" (*moga*) who set fashion trends and read women's magazines in her twenties. Behind the *shōjo* and the *moga* stood the *kōjo*, so that when Nobuko Yoshiya's writings in those magazines made her one of the richest women in Japan, she stood at the top of an economic pyramid built in large part by the anonymous, ill-compensated, and often back-breaking labor of hundreds of thousands of Japanese factory girls.

If the lives of Japanese factory girls found scant representation in the Class S stories of the *shōjo* magazines, where if anywhere can we find their voices, their dreams, their hopes and fears?

Mill owners themselves commissioned reading materials for the workers, short textbooks glossed with *furigana* for those girls who were at least semi-literate. They celebrated the factory girl as the backbone of Japan, who through her hard work would make Japan a great nation and fulfill her filial duty to her parents, her employer (who supposedly treasured her more than his own child), and the emperor.[19]

Mill owners also commissioned songs for the workers to sing while at their work: "Thread is the treasure of the empire! / More than a hundred million yen worth of exports, / What can be better than silk thread!"[20] But the factory girls preferred their own songs. If our young girl were as gifted with words as Nobuko Yoshiya, she might have been one of the many anonymous creators of the workers' songs that have come down to us.

Sometimes they sang of the hardships of life in the mill: "Factory work is prison work, / All it lacks are iron chains." Sometimes they sang of how they were viewed by others, as in the song with which this chapter begins, or defended themselves against those who looked down on them: "Don't sneer at us / Calling us 'Factory girls, factory girls'! / Factory girls are / Treasure chests for the company." And sometimes they looked to the future, to a time when they would be free of the mill: "Looking out at the growing darkness / I recall the evening bell at Takayama Temple. / When my term expires I'll cross the Nomugi Pass / And they'll say, 'Our daughter is home!'"[21]

I am far in time and space from the lives of the factory girls who sang these songs. But in writing about the Class S stories of yesteryear and the yuri manga of today and tomorrow, I would be remiss if I did not take the opportunity to honor the memory of the girls and women whose work helped make that literature possible, but who rarely if ever grace its pages.

1. E. Patricia Tsurumi, "Yet to Be Heard: The Voices of Meiji Factory Women," *Bulletin of Concerned Asian Scholars* 26, no. 4, 27, https://doi.org/10.1080/14672715.1994.10416166.
2. Erica Friedman, "Yuri, 1919–2019, from Then to Now," Anime Herald, February 6, 2019, https://www.animeherald.com/2019/02/06/yuri-1919-2019-from-then-to-now.

3. Similar relationships are also present in non-yuri manga. For example, the romantic comedy *Kaguya-sama: Love Is War* features a boy from a formerly upper-class family, now reduced to middle-class status, and his relationship with the titular Kaguya, whose family is reputed to be among the wealthiest in Japan. Aka Akasaka, *Kaguya-sama: Love Is War*, trans. Emi Louie-Nishikawa, 21 vols. (San Francisco: VIZ Media, 2018–).

4. According to Japanese government statistics, educating a child in private schools from nursery school through high school is about three times as expensive as educating a child in public schools, with an average cost of ¥17.7 million (about $160,000 at current exchange rates). "Private School Costs Triple Public Education Level through High School," Nippon.com, October 4, 2018, https://www.nippon.com/en/features/h00299.

5. E. Patricia Tsurumi, *Factory Girls: Women in the Thread Mills of Meiji Japan* (Princeton, NJ: Princeton University Press, 1990), 10, Table 1.1, and 87, Table 4.7.

6. Tsurumi, *Factory Girls*, 19–24.

7. Tsurumi, *Factory Girls*, 25–26, 34–38, 41–42.

8. Tsurumi, *Factory Girls*, 59–60.

9. Tsurumi, *Factory Girls*, 63–67.

10. Tsurumi, *Factory Girls*, 75–85.

11. Tsurumi, *Factory Girls*, 67–70.

12. Tsurumi, *Factory Girls*, 68–69.

13. Sarah Frederick, *Turning Pages: Reading and Writing Women's Magazines in Interwar Japan* (Honolulu: University of Hawai'i Press, 2006), 16.

14. Tsurumi, *Factory Girls*, 139–40. Yamakawa: "I felt my whole body shake with shame and rage. What blessings from God came into the lives of these pale young girls with the lifeblood sucked out of them, who had worked all night without sleep next to roaring machines? What blessings deserved thankfulness? Should their slave labor be treated as holy?"

15. Tsurumi, *Factory Girls*, 135–36.

16. Tsurumi, *Factory Girls*, 168–71.

17. Alice Evans, "How Did East Asia Overtake South Asia?," *The Great Gender Divergence* (blog), March 13, 2021, https://www.draliceevans.com/post/how-did-east-asia-overtake-south-asia.

18. Pseudoerasmus [pseud.], "Labour Repression and the Indo-Japanese Divergence," *Pseudoerasmus* (blog), October 2, 2017, https://pseudoerasmus.com/2017/10/02/ijd.

19. Tsurumi, *Factory Girls*, 93–96. A later example of such propaganda is Akira Kurosawa's 1944 film *The Most Beautiful*. In the film, we get glimpses of the lives of the girls who work in an optics factory: the work they do, the reverses they suffer, the friendships they enter into, and the support they provide each other. But in the end, the film focuses on how the girls gladly work their fingers to the bone and ruin their health in service to the imperial ambitions of the Japanese state. *The Most Beautiful*, directed by Akira Kurosawa, in *Eclipse Series 23: The First Films of Akira Kurosawa (Sanshiro Sugata / The Most Beautiful / Sanshiro Sugata, Part Two / The Men Who Tread on the Tiger's Tail)* (1944; New York: Criterion Collection, 2010), 1 hr., 25 min., DVD.

20. Tsurumi, *Factory Girls*, 93.

21. Tsurumi, *Factory Girls*, 98, 97, 101.

Yuri After *Sweet Blue Flowers*

It's now been eighteen years since Takako Shimura first began serialization of *Aoi hana* in *Manga Erotics F* in 2004, ten years since its first volume was released in English as *Sweet Blue Flowers* in 2012, and nine years since Shimura completed its serialization in 2013. In this chapter I look at how the yuri genre has evolved since that time and pronounce my final judgment on *Sweet Blue Flowers*.

The yuri genre is still relatively insignificant in the grand scheme of things, with yuri manga series making up a tiny percentage of the overall manga market. In comparison, the BL genre featuring relationships between men has several times more titles.[1] However, the years since *Aoi hana* ended serialization have seen a significant expansion of the yuri genre. More than nine out of ten yuri series began publication after the year *Aoi hana* began serialization, and more than half of them began publication after *Aoi hana* concluded.[2]

More and more of these yuri manga are being officially released in English translation. Anime-focused streaming services like Crunchyroll have expanded the audience for anime in the US and other countries outside Japan. That has driven up Western readership for manga, the source material for most anime, as the Western market for manga has rebounded from a sales crash in the late 2000s. Yuri manga, in particular, have also benefited from the increased visibility and acceptance of LGBTQ individuals in popular culture and the increased popularity of e-books, which makes publishing manga with niche appeal a more attractive business proposition than traditional print publication.

At the time of writing, almost the entire spectrum of manga publishers is releasing yuri works in English. Such publishers include mainstream Japanese-owned companies like VIZ Media (publisher of *Sweet Blue Flowers*), independent US publishers like Seven Seas Entertainment for whom LGBTQ-themed works form a significant part of their output, and niche yuri-only imprints like Lilyka (part of Digital Manga) that specialize in self-published works (*dōjinshi*) that in the past would never have had an official English release.

Rather than attempt to provide a comprehensive overview of the current yuri scene, I instead briefly discuss some representative works that illustrate various themes in the evolution of yuri.

First up is *Kiss and White Lily for My Dearest Girl*, which carries on the tradition of classic yuri tropes.[3] Like many other works in this vein, it is set in a "yuritopia," an all-girls school in a world where men are absent and every girl finds another girl (or, in one case, more than one) to pair up with.

Yuri is My Job! (the first yuri manga from mainstream publisher Kodansha USA) parodies yuri tropes while still following time-honored conventions.[4] Its characters spend their time after school working in a yuri-themed café featuring the fictional Liebes Girls Academy, in which, as in *Maria Watches Over Us*, older girls pick younger girls to be their "schwestern" (the equivalent of *Maria*'s *sœurs*). In keeping with the works that it's parodying, *Yuri is My Job!* teases the possibility of romantic relationships developing between the girls while they're "off the clock," without (as of the time of writing) committing to that being the case.

Next are two series that have broken out of the pack, achieved widespread popularity, and had well-regarded anime adaptations.

Bloom Into You, which began publication in Japan (as *Yagate kimi ni naru*) two years after *Aoi hana* ended its run, is in many ways a successor work to *Sweet Blue Flowers*.[5] It shares with the earlier work common yuri tropes, including a pairing between a tall beauty with long black hair and a shorter girl with shorter and lighter-colored hair, who feels unable at first to experience love. *Bloom Into You* also features elements more unique to *Sweet Blue Flowers*, including a play used to shed light on the characters and their emotions and a lesbian teacher and her partner who mentor the main characters.

However, *Bloom Into You* perpetuates the hierarchical *senpai-kōhai* dynamic that (to my mind) *Sweet Blue Flowers* rejects as the basis for a relationship between women. It also relegates the one unequivocally lesbian girl (the closest equivalent to Fumi) to the role of a side character whose love for her classmate, one of the two main characters, goes unrequited. (Fortunately, that side character is given her due as the lead character in a spinoff series of light novels.)[6]

The two main characters in the *Kase-san* series (five volumes, beginning with *Kase-san and Morning Glories*[7]) differ in appearance and temperament, like Fumi and Akira, but also like Fumi and Akira, they meet each other as classmates and equals. The follow-on series *Kase-san and Yamada* goes beyond *Sweet Blue Flowers* to explore the main characters' relationship beyond high school in more depth.[8]

All of the works discussed above are primarily focused on girls in high school, as the vast majority of yuri works have been. However, in recent years there have been a growing number of works featuring adult couples as the central characters. Many of these are now seeing official releases in English. One work worth noting is *The Conditions of Paradise*, a story collection originally published in 2006 by long-time yuri manga artist Akiko Morishima.[9] It and its follow-up volumes contain stories from *Comic Yuri Hime*, the most prominent Japanese magazine devoted to the yuri genre.

Though they may focus on adults and not on teenagers, many adult yuri manga follow *Bloom Into You*, *Kase-san*, and other schoolgirl yuri manga in perpetuating the idea of yuri as "lesbian content without lesbian identity."[10] They feature women who have emotional and physical relationships with other women but do not apply the term "lesbian" to themselves. (In *Sweet Blue Flowers* Fumi never goes beyond describing herself circumspectly as "that type of girl," but the word "lesbian" *is* used in conversation, albeit only by side characters (*SBF*, 1:307, 1:309, 3:357, 3:359).)

That is not true of the next two works I discuss, both of which escape the boundaries of the yuri genre entirely. *My Lesbian Experience with Loneliness* puts the issue of identity front and center in its title. However, the "lesbian experience" as such forms just a part of the work, most of which focuses on the author's struggles with her mental and physical health.[11] In their honest and often emotionally raw portrayal of the author's life, the manga and its sequels resemble the autobiographical and semi-autobiographical comics created by women cartoonists in the West (some lesbian, some not), including works by Alison Bechdel, Julie Doucet, and Phoebe Gloeckner.

In contrast, issues of gender and sexual orientation are front and center in *Our Dreams at Dusk: Shimanami Tasogare*, whose characters are variously gay, lesbian, transgender, nonbinary (or "X-gender," to use the roughly equivalent Japanese term), asexual, aromantic, or unsure of their identity. *Shimanami Tasogare* also foregrounds the importance of finding and creating an LGBTQ community, something rare to nonexistent in yuri works.[12]

This lack is especially felt in many adult yuri works. They either recreate the unrealistic school-based "yuritopia" in work settings populated almost solely by lesbians, as in the *Saturday* series of *dōjinshi*,[13] or find improbable ways to bring characters together in a relationship, as in *I Married My Best Friend to Shut My Parents Up*.[14]

Having found an audience in the West and publishers to serve that audience, what's next for the yuri genre? I have no power of prophecy, so my best guess is a continuation of past and present trends relating to (sub)genre, audience, format, and creators.

I do not doubt that fluffy tales of schoolgirls in love will continue to be produced. But they will coexist with a growing number of adult yuri works (including "office yuri" featuring workplace romances), as well as yuri-flavored takes on *isekai* stories of fantasy worlds, science fiction stories, mysteries, thrillers, horror tales, and so on. They will likely be joined over time by more works based squarely in the LGBTQ experience, works which may not be yuri as such but will appeal to many readers in the all-genders audience driving yuri's growing popularity.

Here *Sweet Blue Flowers* proved prophetic, not so much in its subject matter but in its publication in a magazine (*Manga Erotics F*) that explicitly targeted such an all-genders adult audience. It was an early indication that (as Nicki Bauman claims), "yuri is for everyone," and that the present audience for yuri, both in Japan and elsewhere, contains people of all age groups, gender identities, and sexual orientations.[15]

In this regard, the example of *Comic Yuri Hime* is instructive. The magazine's publisher attempted to split its audience in two by spinning off a separate magazine *Comic Yuri Hime S* targeted at men, only to end the experiment and fold it back into the main magazine three years later. However, this was not simply a reversion to the previous state. Instead, the language used to address readers of the "new" *Comic Yuri Hime* signified a more inclusionary approach by the editors, even when the nature of the content itself did not change.[16]

In terms of format, I doubt we will see many actual yuri anime, as opposed to anime in which yuri relationships are present only as subtext. Even with the low pay of animators, anime production is too expensive for works for which the potential audience is still relatively small. Instead, the action will be in formats for which both the costs of creation and the costs of distribution are relatively low: besides digital versions of manga, we are seeing yuri—and will see more—in the form of light novels, "super light" novels (designed to be easily read on smartphones), webcomics, and visual novels.

Finally, just as manga aesthetics and themes have influenced non-Japanese comic artists around the world, there is a growing body of yuri-influenced works—including webcomics, in particular—created outside Japan and marketed using the "GL" label. This is especially true in East Asia, with popular works created in South Korea, Thailand, China, and the Philippines.[17]

What is the place of *Sweet Blue Flowers* in all this? As I wrote in the introduction, I think it, like its characters, tries to span the past, present, and future of yuri in a single work. Straddling like this can be awkward, and sometimes *Sweet Blue Flowers* wobbles more than a bit.

For example, I think that the Class S-like environment of Fujigaya coexists uneasily with the more modern sensibility exemplified by Fumi and some other characters. I also believe the resolution of the relationship between Fumi and Akira (and the implication that since childhood they were fated to be together) works better as a symbolic reconciliation of two modes of yuri than it does as a picture of real-life individuals.

However, to me the virtues of *Sweet Blue Flowers* greatly outweigh its flaws. These virtues include the sensitive portrayal of its three main characters (not forgetting Kyoko here), the deftly-handled narrative of Fumi coming out as a lesbian, and the rejection of hierarchy and emphasis on equality in relationships that I see running as a thread throughout the entire series.

In the end, I'll agree with Erica Friedman that *Sweet Blue Flowers* was "an important stepping stone to where we are now" and that "it's time to move forward into a genre that has matured."[18] My journey with *Sweet Blue Flowers* ends here. But Takako Shimura is taking her next step (at least as far as readers in the West are concerned) with the release in English of her adult yuri manga *Even Though We're Adults*. It marks a welcome return by Shimura to the genre that she helped bring into the twenty-first century.

1. "Browse manga," Anime Planet, accessed February 2, 2022, https://www.anime-planet .com/manga/all. A search for manga in general returns 1,336 pages of results after excluding works tagged as *manwha* and *manhua* (Korean and Chinese comics respectively), "OEL" (Western comics drawn in a manga style), webtoons, light novels, and web novels. Adding a search filter for works tagged "GL" returns 45 pages of results, about 3 percent of the total. (Anime Planet uses an older scheme devised by Western fans in which works are categorized as "yuri" only if they feature sexually explicit content.) Filtering for works tagged "BL" returns 269 pages of results, about 20 percent of the total and six times the number of "GL" results.
2. "Browse manga," Anime Planet. As of February 2, 2022, there were 1,564 manga series tagged as "GL" with a year of first publication listed. Of these, 1,432, or 92 percent, began publication in 2005 or later, and 875, or 56 percent, began publication in 2014 or later.
3. Canno, *Kiss and White Lily for My Dearest Girl*, trans. Jocelyne Allen, 10 vols. (New York: Yen Press, 2013–19).
4. Miman, *Yuri is My Job!*, trans. Diana Taylor, 8 vols. (New York: Kodansha, 2016–).
5. Nio Nakatani, *Bloom Into You*, trans. Jenni McKeon, 8 vols. (Los Angeles: Seven Seas Entertainment, 2017–20).
6. Hitoma Iruma, *Bloom Into You: Regarding Saeki Sayaka*, trans. Jan Cash and Vincent Castenada, 3 vols. (Los Angeles: Seven Seas Entertainment, 2019–20).
7. Hiromi Takashima, *Kase-san and Morning Glories*, trans. Jocelyne Allen (Los Angeles: Seven Seas Entertainment, 2017).
8. Hiromi Takashima, *Kase-san and Yamada*, trans. Jocelyne Allen, 2 vols. (Los Angeles: Seven Seas Entertainment, 2020–).
9. Akiko Morishima, *The Conditions of Paradise*, trans. Elina Ishikawa-Curran (Los Angeles: Seven Seas Entertainment, 2020).
10. Erica Friedman, "Overthinking Things 04032011."
11. Kabi Nagata, *My Lesbian Experience with Loneliness*, trans. Jocelyne Allen (Los Angeles, Seven Seas Entertainment, 2017).
12. Yuhki Kamatani, *Our Dreams at Dusk: Shimanami Tasogare*, trans. Jocelyne Allen, 4 vols. (Los Angeles: Seven Seas Entertainment, 2019).
13. Ruri Hazuki, *Saturday: Introduction* (Gardena CA: Lilyka, 2019).
14. Naoko Kodama, *I Married My Best Friend to Shut My Parents Up*, trans. Amber Tamosaitis (Los Angeles: Seven Seas Entertainment, 2019).
15. Nicki Bauman, "Yuri Is for Everyone: An Analysis of Yuri Demographics and Readership,"

Anime Feminist, February 12, 2020, https://www.animefeminist.com/yuri-is-for
-everyone-an-analysis-of-yuri-demographics-and-readership.

16. Hannah E. Dahlberg-Dodd, "Script Variation as Audience Design: Imagining Readership
and Community in Japanese Yuri Comics," *Language in Society* 49, no. 3 (2020), 365–66,
372–74, https://doi.org/10.1017/S0047404519000794.

17. For example, an Anime Planet search using the tags "GL" and "webtoons" returns well
over two hundred works, almost all created in the last six years and nearly all created and
published outside Japan. "Browse manga," Anime Planet.

18. Erica Friedman, review of *Sweet Blue Flowers* vol. 4, by Takako Shimura, *Okazu* (blog), July
9, 2018, http://okazu.yuricon.com/2018/07/09/yuri-manga-sweet-blue-flower-volume
-4-english.

Suggestions for Further Reading

Below I've highlighted a selection of works that I consider particularly significant and well worth seeking out for anyone interested in the topics discussed in this book. I've also included a final section of works in Japanese that I'd like to see released in official English translations.

See the full bibliography for more information on these works, along with a complete list of all the other works I consulted in writing this book and have referenced in its pages.

Class S Culture and Literature

Alice Mabel Bacon, *Japanese Girls and Women*. Bacon provides a contemporary perspective on the lives of Japanese girls and women in the Meiji era. She grew up with Sutematsu Yamakawa, a Japanese girl studying in the US, and was also close friends with Yamakawa's fellow US students, Ume Tsuda and Shige Nagai. (See the chapter "Setting the Stage.") Bacon visited and taught in Japan in 1889–1890 and 1900–2. She wrote this book afterward with assistance from Tsuda (who wanted her participation to remain anonymous).

Edward Carpenter, *The Intermediate Sex: A Study of Some Transitional Types of Men and Women*. This collection of essays is an early example of what we'd refer to today as LGBTQ advocacy. Carpenter's ideas influenced Nobuko Yoshiya's thinking on Class S relationships, as discussed in the chapter "Homage to Yoshiya." See, in particular, the 1899 essay "Affections in Education," reprinted in this volume and translated into Japanese in 1920 by the feminist socialist Kikue Yamakawa.

Hiromi Tsuchiya Dollase, *Age of Shōjo: The Emergence, Evolution, and Power of Japanese Girls' Magazine Fiction*. *Age of Shōjo* is a book-length treatment of Class S culture and literature, including how it was influenced by Western literature in translation.

Sarah Frederick, "Not That Innocent: Nobuko Yoshiya's Good Girls."

Frederick provides an overview of Yoshiya's life and work, with a particular focus on her novel *Yaneura no nishojo* (*Two Virgins in the Attic*), for which Frederick provides a detailed plot description and translates several passages. (Frederick is also working on a book project focusing on Yoshiya's work in the context of twentieth-century Japanese literature and history.)

Gregory M. Pflugfelder, "'S' is for Sister: School Girl Intimacy and 'Same-Sex Love' in Early Twentieth-Century Japan." Pflugfelder provides a good overview of Class S culture from the late nineteenth century to World War II, emphasizing how it was perceived by sexologists, journalists, and feminists. The paper also references interviews with several women who had first-hand experience of Class S relationships while schoolgirls. Unfortunately, Pflugfelder does not quote the women at length—ironic since the last line of the paper laments that Japanese schoolgirls were "more often spoken to than listened to."

Deborah Shamoon, *Passionate Friendship: The Aesthetics of Girls' Culture in Japan*. This is another book-length treatment of Class S culture and literature, including a discussion of its postwar fate.

Nobuko Yoshiya, *Yellow Rose*. The only work by Nobuko Yoshiya available in an official English translation (by Sarah Frederick), this story from *Hana monogatari* gives a taste of Yoshiya's sentimental themes and ornate prose.

Yuri Literature and Criticism

Nicki Bauman, *The Holy Mother of Yuri*. This regularly-updated blog covers yuri-related news stories and reviews yuri works, including *dōjinshi* and visual novels released in English. Bauman has also published on the demographics of the yuri readership (see the bibliography).

Erica Friedman (ed.), *Okazu*. Written by Friedman with occasional guest posts, this is the most well-known and authoritative blog covering the yuri genre and related topics. It features regular reviews of yuri manga and light novels (in both Japanese and English editions) and news reports on yuri-related events.

Erica Friedman, *By Your Side: The First 100 Years of Yuri Manga & Anime*. This forthcoming work promises to be the most comprehensive history of the yuri genre yet, ranging from Nobuko Yoshiya and Class S literature to current yuri works and related topics.

Verena Maser, "Beautiful and Innocent: Female Same-Sex Intimacy in the Japanese Yuri Genre." To my knowledge, Maser's 2015 PhD dissertation is the most extensive academic treatment of the yuri genre in English. It discusses the disputed boundaries of the genre, its history, how yuri manga and related works are produced and distributed, and the results of a survey of yuri fans.

Yuricon, "Essays." Part of the Yuricon website that hosts the *Okazu* blog, this web page contains a comprehensive collection of links to yuri-related resources in English. It is a recommended starting point for anyone interested in exploring the history of the yuri genre.

Lesbianism and Feminism in Japan

Sharon Chalmers, *Emerging Lesbian Voices from Japan*. This 2002 book is a pioneering treatment in English of the lives of Japanese lesbians, marred in places by excessive academic jargon. It includes extensive quotes from women interviewed by Chalmers.

Hiroko Kakefuda, *On Being a "Lesbian"* (*"Rezubian" de aru to iu koto*). Far from being a dry academic work of theory, Kakefuda's 1992 book is eminently readable, a combination of personal memoir and exploration of various topics around being a lesbian in Japan.

Mark McClelland, Katsuhiko Suganuma, and James Welker, eds., *Queer Voices from Japan: First-Person Narratives from Japan's Sexual Minorities*. *Queer Voices from Japan* is a collection of interviews and first-person articles discussing the lives of LGBTQ individuals in postwar Japan. Several chapters provide glimpses into the lives of Japanese lesbians from the 1950s to the 1990s. The book also includes insider accounts of the early years of the Japanese lesbian feminist movement, for anyone wanting more detail than is found in James Welker's paper (referenced below).

James Welker, "From Women's Liberation to Lesbian Feminism in Japan:

Rezubian Feminizumu within and beyond the *Ūman Ribu* Movement in the 1970s and 1980s." This is a good overview of the early history of the lesbian feminist movement in Japan, including a discussion of how it was influenced by the contemporary lesbian feminist movement in the US.

Other Works of Interest

David Chapman and Karl Jakob Krogness, eds., *Japan's Household Registration System and Citizenship: Koseki, Identification, and Documentation*. Reading detailed discussions of the history and application of Japanese laws and regulations relating to personal identity and household registration can be a tough slog. However, this volume is invaluable as an inside look into how the Japanese state regulates the lives of individuals and their families, especially those in marginalized groups.

Marius B. Jansen, *The Making of Modern Japan*. It's difficult to make sense of twentieth and twenty-first-century Japanese social and literary movements without some knowledge of Japanese history. You can skip the portion of the book covering the Tokugawa shogunate if you're impatient, but the discussion of the Meiji, Taishō, and Shōwa eras provides helpful background for the Class S and yuri genres and Japanese popular culture in general.

kyuuketsukirui, "Don't Want to Know What I'll Be without You." Unfortunately, there's not a lot of *Sweet Blue Flowers* fan fiction; other yuri works like *Bloom Into You* and the *Kase-San* series have an order of magnitude more fan-written stories. Of the fan fiction that does exist, this is my favorite: almost four hundred words that provide an intimate picture of Akira and the nature of her love for Fumi.

Yoshio Sugimoto, *An Introduction to Japanese Society*. A comprehensive overview of various aspects of Japanese society, including social classes, the educational system, gender and the family, politics, ethnicities, religion, and culture. It's written from the viewpoint that Japan is not "uniquely monocultural" but rather is "fraught with cultural diversity and class competition" (from the preface). The book was intended to be a university textbook; this latest edition adds a concise history of Japan, links to online sources and videos, and suggestions for student research projects.

Works in Japanese

Eureka, November 2017. This special issue of a literary magazine focuses on the work of Takako Shimura. It includes a nineteen-page interview with Shimura and what appears to be a complete bibliography of her works.

Takako Shimura, *Awashima hyakkei*. Set at a girls' school associated with a Takarazuka-like musical theater troupe, this manga (initially published online) looks to be Shimura going all-out in her fascination with the stage. Begun in 2011, it was on hiatus for a few years but recently resumed publication.

Nobuko Yoshiya, *Hana monogatari*. This is Yoshiya's famous collection of Class S stories published from 1916 to 1924.

―――. *Yaneura no nishojo*. Erica Friedman and others have hailed this 1919 novel as the first yuri (or proto-yuri) work.

Appendices

Appendix 1: Character Index

This index is for readers trying to keep track of the characters in *Sweet Blue Flowers*, many of whom are unnamed or not given full names upon their first appearance in the manga. It lists characters under both their given names and family names where known, and where appropriate also by their roles in relation to other characters (e.g., "Yasuko's mother").[1]

The index lists pages on which a particular character is depicted or (for minor characters) mentioned, omitting incidental appearances by major characters.[2] The index also lists significant events in the characters' lives, for example, for readers wishing to consult the parts of the manga dealing with Fumi's relationship with Yasuko. Events are listed in chronological order (as best I can determine such order) rather than by their location in the manga.

Characters with names in boldface are those included in the profiles at the beginnings of the original Japanese volumes. Page numbers in italics refer to depictions of characters on cover pages, tables of contents, or chapter title pages, or in character profiles or afterwords.

growing distance between herself and her husband and daughter, 4:66–68; asks Kyoko if she's lonely, 3:100; tries and fails to get Kyoko to go out with her, 3:101; is complimented by Ko on her appearance, 1:94; claims that it's her fault that Ko doesn't visit anymore, 4:48–50; is visited by Ko after a long absence, 4:69–72

Ikumi, Kyoko (friend of Akira), *1:3, 1:117, 1:198, 1:282, 2:38, 2:181, 2:183, 2:229, 3:4, 3:182, 4:4, 4:27, 4:99, 4:147, 4:182*

childhood: is praised for her looks, 4:28–29; gets lost in the woods and is found by Ko, 2:37, 2:67–68, 4:24–25, 4:64–66; tells Ko that she's glad that they'll get to marry, 4:30–32; tells Ko again how much she likes him, 4:33–35; is lonely as a child, and discovers her mother and others pray to a different God, 3:100;

junior high: thinks to herself that she hates her mother and father and that everyone in her family is worthless, 3:101, 3:103; deals with her mother's illness, 4:35–38; has sex with Ko and calls herself "ugly," 4:39–44; joins the Fujigaya art club and meets Yasuko, 4:45; imitates Yasuko by cutting her hair and contemplating joining the Fujigaya drama club, 2:115–16

high school, year 1: introduces herself to Akira, 1:26; is asked by Akira to join the Fujigaya drama club, 1:55; gets a love letter from a junior high girl, 1:78–79;

meets Yasuko again and is seen crying by Fumi afterward, 1:83–84, 1:87; refuses an offer of a lift from Ko, 1:95–96; invites Akira to a singles party and tells her that "the person I like rejected me," 1:97–98; introduces Akira to Ko, and tells her that Ko took a liking to her, 1:103, 1:129–31; meets Mr. Kagami and asks about Yasuko, 1:132–34, 1:136–37; talks to Akira about liking girls, 1:145–46; asks Fumi if she likes Yasuko, 1:170–72; breaks down in front of Akira while talking about Fumi and Yasuko, 1:174–75; is comforted by Akira regarding other girls' interest in Yasuko, and tells herself that she's different from them, 1:208–12; talks with Yasuko about their non-relationship, 1:212–15; talks with Yasuko backstage at *Wuthering Heights*, 1:244–45; tells Ko (and Akira) that she thinks of him like a big brother, 1:261–62; learns about Yasuko's breakdown on seeing Mr. Kagami, 1:263–64; meets Akira's family, 1:265; teases Akira about her having to go to the bathroom and getting scolded by a nun, 1:282, 1:284; tells Akira about her time at Fujigaya and studying with Kazusa, 1:285–90; accuses Mr. Kagami of lying about not knowing Yasuko, 1:336–40; invites Akira to visit Ko's family with Fumi and Fumi's friends, 1:357–58; after learning that Fumi and Yasuko have broken up, approaches

groper, 1:17; enters Fujigaya Women's Academy, 1:19–20; meets Kyoko and describes her as "kinda sexy," 1:26–27; has a reunion with Fumi, 1:28, 1:34–37; renews her friendship with Fumi, 1:42–43, 1:46–49, 1:51–53, 1:66–67; decides to join the Fujigaya drama club, 1:54–55; consoles Fumi after Chizu and her husband visit, 1:59–64; tells Fumi about the Fujigaya Theater Festival and her joining the drama club, 1:72–75; marvels at Kyoko receiving a love letter, and wonders whether Fumi had feelings toward Chizu, 1:78–80; meets Yasuko and sees how Fumi reacts to her, 1:82, 1:85, 1:88, 1:91–92; attends Ko's singles party, 1:97–99, 1:102–3; yells at Shinobu for following her to the singles party, and tells him that he'll never have a girlfriend, 1:109–10; meets Yasuko while going to school with Fumi, 1:124–26; hears from Kyoko that Ko wants to see her again, 1:129–31; learns about Fumi dating Yasuko, 1:135–40; wonders about liking a girl, and asks Kyoko about it, 1:141, 1:143–46; asks Fumi how she can support her, 1:151–54; talks with Fumi about Yasuko and Kyoko, 1:169, 1:182–83; talks with Kyoko about Yasuko, 1:174–75; tries to reassure Kyoko regarding Yasuko, 1:203–5, 1:209–11; advises Fumi to tell Yasuko "not to be so popular," 1:218–19; helps with *Wuthering Heights* production, 1:222–24, 1:229, does Yasuko's hair and thinks she's a "lady-killer," 1:232–34; meets Ko Sawanoi, 1:257–62; rides home with Kyoko and Ko, but rushes to the bathroom before introducing them to her family, 1:265–66; visits Aunt Keiko with Fumi, 1:268–73; tries to comfort Fumi about her relationship with Yasuko, 1:275–81; rushes back to class after going to the bathroom and is scolded by a nun, 1:281, 1:283–84; talks to Kyoko about Fujigaya and the Sugimoto sisters, 1:285–90; goes with Fumi to see a movie and learns about Fumi's breakup, 1:321; 1:323–25, 1:332–35; confronts Yasuko regarding her behavior toward Fumi, 1:341–49; consoles Fumi about her breakup with Yasuko, 1:350–52; is invited by Kyoko to visit Ko's family's summer home, 1:357–58; tells Kyoko that Fumi and Yasuko broke up, 1:358–59, 1:364; invites Fumi on the trip to Ko's family's summer home, 1:370–75; goes with Fumi and her other friends on a trip to Ko's family's summer home, 2:6–7, 2:9–10, 2:13, 2:16, 2:18, 2:20, 2:25–33, 2:61–63; wakes up to go the bathroom and asks Fumi to accompany her, then stays up late with Fumi and catches a cold, 2:34–36; protests Shinobu hanging around her and Fumi while they're sick, and tells Fumi that he's "super creepy," 2:39, 2:41, 2:43–44; eavesdrops on Ko's mother's comments about Kyoko, 2:51–56; talks with Ko about Kyoko's family situation and Kyoko's feelings towards him, 2:57–60, 2:64–65; wonders if she'll ever like someone like Fumi does Yasuko, 2:66–67; attends the wedding of Kazusa and Mr. Kagami, 2:71–72, 2:82, 2:92–94; fights with Shinobu during her trip to Enoshima with Fumi, 2:105–7, 2:118–21; witnesses Fumi's breakup with Yasuko, 2:108, 2:123; has all her friends over for a sleepover, 2:130–32, tells Fumi that she's never experienced a first love, 2:135–38; helps Ko shop for a Christmas present for Kyoko, 2:149–52; recalls a conversation with Fumi about sex, 3:35–9

high school, year 2: begins her second year at Fujigaya and encounters Haruka, 2:193–97; meets Ueda, 2:201–3; is upset by student gossip about Hinako and her girlfriend, 2:205–8; starts to ask Ueda about her situation with Fumi, but doesn't, 2:217–20; meets Haruka again at the Fujigaya drama club, 2:221–24; thinks about asking Fumi about whether Fumi has a crush on her, but doesn't, 2:228; reads *Rokumeikan* and imagines a scene from it, 2:230–35; is encouraged by Ueda to audition for *Rokumeikan*, 2:265–68; auditions for a part in *Rokumeikan*, 2:281; reads *Rokumeikan*, 2:317, 2:332–33; is confessed to by Fumi, and learns about Fumi wanting to have sex

with her, 2:335–36, 2:338, 2:341; talks to Fumi about Fumi's liking her, and is frightened by talk of sex, 3:35–37; wonders what "stuff" Fumi wants to do with her, 3:8–9; meets Fumi for the first time since Fumi confessed to her, 3:28–30; is reassured by Fumi before Akira's performance in *Rokumeikan*, 3:64–70, 3:76; plays Akiko in *Rokumeikan*, 3:31, 3:84–85, 3:87, 3:92–95; invites Fumi on the trip to Haruka's grandfather's inn, 3:149–50; thinks to herself that she and Fumi no longer have sleepovers, 3:151; is embarrassed after staring at Fumi naked in the bath, 3:203–6, 3:210; thinks about the fact that a girl likes her, 3:229; has a sleepover at Fumi's house and overhears Fumi saying that she likes her, 3:240–41, 3:248–49, 3:251; tells Fumi that she doesn't feel the same way toward her, 3:252–54; suggests to Fumi that they date, 3:255–56, 3:259; tells Kyoko about her relationship with Fumi, and is overheard by Ueda and others, 3:267–70; is the (unnamed) subject of gossip in the Fujigaya newspaper, 3:270–71; asks Fumi out on a date, 3:277–78; goes on a date with Fumi, 3:280–82, 3:289–93, 3:297–300; kisses Fumi, 3:302, 3:320–21; wakes up crying after a dream about her and Fumi as children, and remembers their kiss, 3:318–21; visits Fumi on Christmas day,

1. One ambiguous case is regarding Fumi's cousin Chizu. Since Chizu's family name is not given until volume 3, well after she is married early in volume 1, I have assumed that Hanashiro is her husband's family name and that Chizu took it upon marrying him.
2. The book's source repository (see the colophon) contains an unabridged character index that lists all appearances by all characters.

Appendix 2: Character Relationships

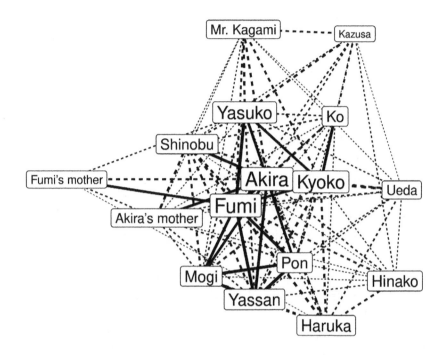

In addition to serving as a guide to the characters who appear in *Sweet Blue Flowers*, the character index also provides data helpful in analyzing other aspects of the manga. Examples of such analyses include determining how prominently a given character is featured in the manga, how that character relates to other characters, and how prominently such relationships are featured. The character index included in Appendix 1 is abridged for readability, but I've used a complete and unabridged character index to do an initial analysis of these questions.[1]

The first question that might come to mind is: how prominently is each character featured in *Sweet Blue Flowers*? For example, does Fumi appear more often than Akira, or vice versa? And what about Kyoko? How frequently does she appear relative to Fumi and Akira? We can answer these questions by counting the number of pages on which each character appears and then seeing which are featured on the most pages.[2]

Such an analysis shows that Fumi and Akira are almost equally prominent in the manga, with Fumi having a slight edge. Each of the two girls appears on around half of the manga's pages. Kyoko is the next most prominent character, appearing on about a quarter of all pages, half as many as Fumi or Akira. Yasuko appears on about one sixth of all pages. All other characters appear on no more than one in ten pages. (A few characters appear only on one or two pages.)[3]

We can also use the character index to analyze relationships between characters. In particular, if two characters appear on the same page, I consider them to have a connection to each other.

This criterion is not foolproof—for example, a given page may have one or two panels with one group of characters and then transition to other panels with other characters. However, if those instances are relatively few (and I believe they are), then the "relationships" discovered using this method will map relatively closely to the actual relationships in the manga.

There are eighty-two "characters" in the character index. (Some entries correspond to groups of people, such as Fujigaya elementary-school students.) If each character appeared on at least one page with every other character, there would be over three thousand "relationships" depicted in the manga. In actuality, most characters in the manga appear together on a page with only a few other characters. There are less than four hundred unique instances of pairs of characters appearing together on one or more pages, so only about one in ten of the possible relationships is depicted.[4]

In addition to knowing which characters have a relationship with others, I would also like to know how prominently those relationships are featured in the manga. I use the number of pages on which two characters appear together as a proxy measure of the prominence of their relationship.

As one would expect, the relationship between Fumi and Akira is the most prominent one. They appear together on almost a third of the manga's pages. No other relationship is featured on more than a tenth of the manga's pages, with the relationships between Akira and Kyoko and

Fumi and Yasuko being the next most prominent.[5]

Finally, the relationships between characters in Sweet Blue Flowers can be represented graphically, again using joint appearances on a page as a proxy for characters having some connection to each other. There are many possible ways of constructing such a graph. The graph above shows one such way.[6]

The complete "social graph" of *Sweet Blue Flowers* is too cluttered to be readable, even without all possible relationships being represented in the manga. Therefore, the graph above shows only the relationships between the top sixteen characters ranked by their prominence in the manga (i.e., the number of pages on which they appear). The size of the label for each character is related to each character's prominence, with Akira and Fumi appearing most prominently, as expected.[7]

The links between each pair of characters reflect the prominence of their relationship, with character pairs with more prominently-featured relationships positioned more closely together. Since Fumi and Akira's relationship is featured most prominently, they are shown close together on the graph.

Solid lines between characters represent the top twenty percent of relationships ranked by prominence, dashed lines the other eighty percent. Lines corresponding to more prominently-featured relationships are also thicker.

In addition to Akira and Fumi, there are also clusters of other people whose relationships with each other are more prominently featured. These clusters include Akira and her mother and brother; Fumi and her mother; Kyoko and Ko; Mogi, Pon, and Yassan; and Yasuko, Kyoko, Fumi, and Akira. There's also a less prominently-featured set of relationships among Yasuko, Kazusa, and Mr. Kagami.

These clusters could be intuited by anyone reading the manga, but it's helpful to have them confirmed by a more formal analysis. Such an analysis could also uncover other clusters of characters not necessarily apparent at first glance and discover other things relating to *Sweet Blue Flowers*—for example, the chains of relationships connecting characters not directly connected. However, I leave further analyses to others who can reuse or adapt the code I used to do this one.

1. Frank Hecker, "Relative Prominence of Characters and Their Relationships in Takako Shimura's *Sweet Blue Flowers*," RPubs.com, March 7, 2022, https://rpubs.com/frankhecker /874648. The unabridged character index is available in this book's public source repository; see the colophon for more information.

2. The analysis omits the cover pages for each volume and the two parts of each volume, and the pages at or near the front of each chapter used for character portraits not related to the narrative. The analysis also omits pages in the character profiles and afterwords included in each volume.

3. Hecker, "Relative Prominence of Characters." Fumi appears on 52.1 percent of the manga's pages, Akira on 49.4 percent, Kyoko on 23.1 percent, and Yasuko on 16.5 percent. The "median character" appears on only seven pages or about 0.5 percent of the manga.

4. Hecker, "Relative Prominence of Characters." In theory, each of the eighty-two characters in the character index could appear on a page with any of the other eighty-one characters. The product of these two numbers is 6,642. However, we must divide this number by two to avoid double counting, giving 3,321 possible "relationships." According to the character index, there are 350 unique instances of characters appearing together on at least one page. Thus only 11 percent of all possible character relationships are realized in the manga.

5. Hecker, "Relative Prominence of Characters." Fumi and Akira appear together on 30.3 percent of all pages, Akira and Kyoko on 9.7 percent, and Fumi and Yasuko on 8.8 percent.

6. Hecker, "Relative Prominence of Characters." This particular graph was laid out using the the force-directed algorithm of Fruchterman and Reingold, with the prominence values for nodes and edges calculated using the logarithms of the page counts for the characters and character pairs respectively. Thomas M. J. Fruchterman and Edward M. Reingold, "Graph Drawing by Force-Directed Placement," *Software: Practice and Experience* 21, no. 11 (November 1991), 1129–64, https://doi.org/10.1002/spe.4380211102.

7. The difference in prominence between characters is even more pronounced than the sizes of the labels imply since the code that created the graph forces labels to be larger than a specific minimum size to improve readability.

Appendix 3: Errata

I noticed only a few errors or other issues with the VIZ Media edition of *Sweet Blue Flowers*. Leaving aside matters of hyphenation (where sometimes the available space forces an incorrect hyphenation), here's what I believe to be the complete list of errata and related issues with the text.

Volume 1

SBF, 1:206, panel 1: "But you're a principle character!" "Principle" should be "principal."

SBF, 1:288, panel 1: "Lots of families have attended Matsuoka since the Meiji period." Given the context, it's clear that the reference to Matsuoka should instead be to Fujigaya.

SBF, 1:337, panel 3: "Interview with Kyoko Sugimoto." "Kyoko" should be "Yasuko."

Volume 2

SBF, 2:358: Ryoko Ueda's character description (2:183) says that "Her name reminds me of a place name. ... or I am just imagining that?" and advises the reader, "Try googling my name!" The endnotes then state, "There is a bus stop in Gifu Prefecture that uses the same kanji as Ryoko Ueda but is pronounced differently" (2:358).

In my opinion, it's much more likely that Shimura was referring to the city of Ueda in Nagano Prefecture, the very first result if you use the Japanese version of Google to search for the kanji for "Ueda."

Volume 3

There appear to be no typographical errors or other issues in volume 3.

Volume 4

SBF, 4:234–36: These pages repeat the dialogue and action from a scene in volume 2 when Hinako assumes her role as Akira's homeroom teacher

(2:204–5). Presumably, the pages in volume 4 were intended to be a flashback to the events of volume 2. However, the style used for dialogue text in volume 4 is not that normally used in the manga for flashbacks (italicized text in a lighter typeface), making it appear to the unwary reader that the events of 4:234–36 are occurring in the present.

This appears to be an error carried over from the Japanese edition of *Aoi hana*. That edition also uses a lighter typeface for dialogue in flashbacks (see, e.g., *Aoi hana*, 8:51) but does not do so on pages 8:54–56, the pages corresponding to 4:234–36 in the English edition.

SBF, 4:262, panel 1: "I'll be in the bathrrom." "Bathrrom" should be "bathroom."

SBF, 4:336, panel 6: "Your friend is in the hospital, right? For appendicitis? How unfortunate ..." 4:337, panel 1: "How mean! She left her friend and came back alone!" "No, I didn't! We came back together!" This sequence doesn't make sense when interpreted according to the most straightforward reading.

The reference to "your friend" (*SBF*, 4:336) is clearly to Kawasaki, according to information conveyed by Ueda (4:338). The straightforward reading is that the reference to "her friend" (4:337) is also to Kawasaki and that Yasuko is being accused (by Shinako?) of leaving Kawasaki alone in England while sick.

Yasuko's subsequent statement apparently refutes that accusation, implying that Kawasaki had also returned to Japan. But this is refuted in turn by Ueda's comment that Kawasaki is still in England being cared for by others (*SBF*, 4:338).

The original Japanese text of the accusation against Yasuko contains the word "kōhai" ("junior"), which may refer to Ueda (*Aoi hana*, 8:157). So perhaps the charge is that Yasuko left Ueda alone in Japan (i.e., to care for Kawasaki), an accusation that (as Yasuko asserts) is, in fact, not true. This may be a case where the English translation doesn't quite capture the meaning of the Japanese.

Appendix 4: Reviews

Now that I've finished my comments on *Sweet Blue Flowers*, let's take a look at what other people thought of it. This appendix contains a not-quite-comprehensive list of reviews of volumes 1 through 4 of the VIZ Media edition, omitting video reviews and reader reviews posted to online bookstores and book review websites.

Volume 1

Rose Bridges at Anime News Network. ANN is the most prominent anime news and review site; they also do a fair number of manga reviews. Bridges gave *Sweet Blue Flowers* an overall B+ grade, with a B for story and an A for art. "Overall, this release is an excellent way to dive into a yuri manga that's a cut above the rest. *Sweet Blue Flowers* still has plenty of its genre's trappings, but also enough bite for those seeking something more realistic."[1]

Ash Brown at *Experiments in Manga*. A generally favorable review that highlights Shimura's artwork and its relation to theatrical performance, as well as the realism of character actions and interactions. "*Sweet Blue Flowers* is a wonderful series. The manga is emotionally resonate, with a realistic portrayal of the experiences of young women who love other young women."[2]

Alex Cline at Adventures in Poor Taste. A generally favorable review on a website focusing on popular culture. Cline liked the characters and how they were handled, and thought the artwork stood out. One criticism he voiced was regarding a lack of clarity in some scenes regarding who was talking and where the scenes fit in the overall timeline. "Overall, *Sweet Blue Flowers* Vol. 1 is a solid start for the series. The characters are likable and well introduced, and the artwork throughout is beautiful. With that said, none of the volume's more emotional moments are very memorably so. This is a volume that shows promise and generates enough interest to warrant giving the next installment a look, but it doesn't quite reach greatness as is. I would recommend it, but not enthusiastically so."[3]

Amelia Cook at *Otaku USA*. *Otaku USA* is a print and online magazine covering anime and manga; Cook is also the founder of the Anime Feminist website. Her review is favorable. She particularly calls out the depiction of the four main characters (Akira, Fumi, Yasuko, and Kyoko) as realistic and nuanced. She rated *Sweet Blue Flowers* as "recommended." "*Sweet Blue Flowers* [paints] a picture of everyday life with complicated young women going through important formative experiences. You'll end the 400-page volume rooting for them all to have a happy ending."[4]

Leroy Douresseaux at The Comic Book Bin. A favorable review (score 8 out of 10) on a general comics site. "Fans of yuri and shojo romance will want to smell the *Sweet Blue Flowers*."[5]

EyeSpyeAlex [Alexandra Nutting] at The Geekly Grind. A favorable review on a website focused on anime, manga, and video games. "At the end of the day, I really enjoy *Sweet Blue Flowers*. The characters feel real and have a depth and complexity to their lives. While the visuals could be a little more striking, it fits the down to earth tone of the manga."[6]

Erica Friedman at *Okazu*. Friedman is one of the most well-known promoters and reviewers of yuri manga and anime, and hers is the single most authoritative site in English for yuri-related news. She also did previous reviews of the Japanese edition of *Aoi hana*. In this review she rated volume 1 as 8 out of 10 overall, with art and characters at 8 and story and "yuri" at 7. "Although the opening and the ending are—in my opinion—very weak, the rest of the story is excellent. It's got surprising depth and breadth. Characters that surround Fumi and Akira are as well-developed as they and as interesting."[7]

Sean Gaffney at *A Case Suitable for Treatment*. A favorable review from a manga-focused site. Gaffney acknowledges that the long delay in bringing out a complete official translation of *Sweet Blue Flowers* makes it seem less distinctive compared to more recent works like *Bloom Into You* or *Kiss and White Lily for My Dearest Girl*. "*Sweet Blue Flowers* is absolutely worth reading and checking out, both if you like yuri and if you like Takako Shimura. It's also only four volumes, so shouldn't devastate your bookshelf too much."[8]

Helen at TheOASG. A generally favorable review at a group anime and manga blog, albeit with some concerns expressed about the use of yuri tropes, possible queer-baiting, and the reaction by Yasuko's family to her and Fumi's relationship being unrealistic. Helen rated *Sweet Blue Flowers* at 3 out of 5. "*Sweet Blue Flowers* ... treats its characters as people, not characters created for the reader's gaze but real teenaged girls dealing with the always overly-complicated world of high school. But it still remains to be seen just how many times these girls have their hearts broken and mended by the time they graduate."[9]

Chuck Hodgin at *School Library Journal*. A very favorable review that was highlighted on the web pages for *Sweet Blue Flowers* on two online bookstores. "These collected first volumes of Shimura's manga tell an honest, poignant story about the joys, pains, and loves of gay and bisexual young women. ... A no-brainer for yuri (manga focusing on lesbian romance) fans, but strong enough to recommend to romance readers and general manga enthusiasts."[10]

livresdechevet at *More Bedside Books*. A generally favorable review that focuses in particular on translation issues and changes from previous digital releases of volume 1. "All in all *Sweet Blue Flowers* is an enduring series about maturing and girls in love with other girls finally receiving print treatment in English. ... Whether someone is familiar with the genre and history or not it's a story with characters that can reach out to teenagers as well as older readers."[11]

Terry Hong at *BookDragon*. A favorable review on a blog hosted by the Smithsonian Asian Pacific American Center. "For impatient readers, an 11-part anime adaptation debuted in 2009. For manga purists who appreciate the gorgeous art on the page, Shimura has never disappointed."[12]

Volume 2

Melina Dargis at The Fandom Post. A lukewarm to favorable review. She gave it a grade B for content, B for art, A for packaging, and A for text/translation. "While reading the second volume of this manga, I kept feeling lost in the story. There seemed to be a lot of jumping around and some reading in between the lines that perhaps I was just not good at it. The main story does come through, but with such a large cast of characters, it's was hard to follow what was in everyone's heart. That distraction is why I gave the content a lower grade. ... Yet, beyond everything that could have been better, this story is a story that is desperately needed for not only manga, but mainstream reading in general."[13]

Leroy Douresseaux at The Comic Book Bin. A favorable review: grade A, score 8 out of 10.[14]

EyeSpyeAlex [Alexandra Nutting] at The Geekly Grind. A very favorable review, with volume 2 rated 9 out of 10 overall, 8.6 for story, 9.5 for art, and 9 for character. "Despite having an unclear storyline at times, I really enjoy *Sweet Blue Flowers*. Each volume is longer than your typical manga volume, which is nice as it means the story doesn't need to rely on cliff hangers. The soft art style and simple dialogue gives this manga a calming effect. *Sweet Blue Flowers* is by no means a page turning thriller, and I appreciate that. It's nice to have a manga to read that I can enjoy for its' [sic] relaxing story."[15]

Erica Friedman at *Okazu*. Friedman rated volume 2 as 8 out of 10 overall (same as volume 1), with art and characters at 8, story at 7, and "lesbian" at 4. (Friedman usually assigns works a "yuri" score, as she did for volume 1. I presume she switched it to "lesbian" here because she thought *Sweet Blue Flowers* is not a typical yuri work.) "This is an excellent English release and I think we can expect it to maintain this high quality. ... If you haven't already picked up this 'new classic' of Yuri, I definitely recommend it, for having a depth of early 20th century literary history and still being grounded in the present."[16]

Sean Gaffney at *A Case Suitable for Treatment*. A generally favorable review, though not as favorable as for volume 1. "*Sweet Blue Flowers* is a good series. That said, it's exhausting as well, and I suspect that it's best enjoyed either in one gulp—waiting till the other two omnibuses are out—or in smaller quantities, such as reading only half and then coming back. There is such a thing as too much Fumi. (And too [sic] be fair, too much Akira, though that's slightly less pressure-heated.)"[17]

Volume 3

Melina Dargis at The Fandom Post. Dargis gave volume 3 a grade B for content, B- for art, A- for packaging, and A for text/translation. "From a reviewer's point of view, this story is difficult to summarize its content. In one chapter, it easily has up to five several short scenes that are only a few pages in length. This is very different from most manga where a chapter usually focuses on a specific character or situation. This is nice for reading, however. What is also nice about this style of storytelling is that it feels like it's more like watching a story versus reading one. It also keeps the story interesting, moving and more in depth, but for some it might be distracting and confusing."[18]

EyeSpyeAlex [Alexandra Nutting] at The Geekly Grind. A very favorable review: rated 9.1 out of 10 overall, 8.8 for story, 9.2 for art, and 9.3 for characters. "Funny, endearing, and a little sexy. Those are the words I would use to describe the latest volume of *Sweet Blue Flowers*."[19]

Erica Friedman at *Okazu*. Friedman rated volume 3 as 8 out of 10 overall (the same score as volumes 1 and 2), with art and characters at 8, story at 7, "lesbian" at 6, and "service" at 1. "This volume is, in my opinion the strongest of what Viz will release as four volumes. We can see the progress the young women make as people, before the story turns back into itself to fulfill the requirements of a romance series."[20]

Sean Gaffney at *A Case Suitable for Treatment*. A generally favorable review, with qualifications. "*Sweet Blue Flowers*, of course, also has the same issues that it's had before. ... That said, this is still a very good volume, and since I believe it ends with the fourth book, there's no reason for you not to get it so that you can wallow in pangs of young love once more."[21]

Volume 4

EyeSpyeAlex [Alexandra Nutting] at The Geekly Grind. A very favorable review: rated 9.5 out of 10 overall, 9.0 for story, 9.5 for art, and 9.0 for characters. "As far as finales go, *Sweet Blue Flowers* nailed theirs. This latest volume had the perfect balance of drama and resolution. The pacing was great and held my attention the entire time."[22]

Erica Friedman at *Okazu*. Friedman rated volume 4 as 9 out of 10 overall (a slightly higher score than previous volumes), with art, characters, and story at 9, "service" at 3, and "LGBTQ" at 10. "Here's the the [sic] thing that's amazing about *Sweet Blue Flowers*—it started serialization in 2005.

It's 13 years old. More than a decade ago it was a beacon of Yuri. In 2018, it's an important stepping stone to where we are now, and now that we have a definitive edition for this in English, it's time to move forward into a genre that has matured."[23]

Sean Gaffney at *A Case Suitable for Treatment*. A generally favorable review, with some qualifications. "The final volume of *Sweet Blue Flowers* shows off all the strengths and weaknesses of this particular series. ... I do think this series ended at just the right length—it would have been exhausting to carry on for 3–4 more volumes. In the end, *Sweet Blue Flowers* had its bittersweet moments, but the end showed that sweetness can win out."[24]

Jaime at *Yuri Stargirl*. A favorable review with qualifications regarding the translation and localization. She rates volume 4 as 8 out of 10 ("Highly Recommended") and the series overall as 9 out of 10 ("Essential"). "Not only is [*Sweet Blue Flowers*] one of my all-time favorite anime but it is also one of my all-time favorite mangas and so to finally have the story complete made my week. ... The story, naturally, is wonderful ... ."[25]

1. Rose Bridges, review of *Sweet Blue Flowers*, vol. 1, by Takako Shimura, Anime News Network, October 20, 2017, https://www.animenewsnetwork.com/review/sweet-blue -flowers-2-in-1-edition/gn-1/.122727.

2. Ash Brown, review of *Sweet Blue Flowers*, vol. 1, by Takako Shimura, *Experiments in Manga* (blog), October 27, 2017, http://experimentsinmanga.mangabookshelf.com/2017/10 /sweet-blue-flowers-omnibus-1.

3. Alex Cline, review of *Sweet Blue Flowers*, vol. 1.

4. Amelia Cook, review of *Sweet Blue Flowers*, vol. 1, by Takako Shimura, *Otaku USA*, December 9, 2017, http://www.otakuusamagazine.com/sweet-blue-flowers-review.

5. Leroy Douresseaux, review of *Sweet Blue Flowers*, vol. 1, by Takako Shimura, The Comic Book Bin, October 3, 2017, http://www.comicbookbin.com/sweetblueflowers001.html.

6. EyeSpyeAlex [Alexandra Nutting], review of *Sweet Blue Flowers*, vol. 1, by Takako Shimura, The Geekly Grind, October 7, 2017, http://www.thegeeklygrind.com/sweet-blue-flowers -part-one.

7. Erica Friedman, review of *Sweet Blue Flowers*, vol. 1.

8. Sean Gaffney, review of *Sweet Blue Flowers*, vol. 1, by Takako Shimura, *A Case Suitable for Treatment* (blog), September 30, 2017, http://suitablefortreatment.mangabookshelf.com /2017/09/30/sweet-blue-flowers-omnibus-1.

9. Helen, review of *Sweet Blue Flowers*, vol. 1, by Takako Shimura, TheOASG, December 7, 2017, https://www.theoasg.com/reviews/manga/sweet-blue-flowers-volume-1-review.

10. Chuck Hodgin, review of *Sweet Blue Flowers*, vol. 1, by Takako Shimura, in Kent Turner, "25

LGBTQAI+ Titles for Pride Month—and Onward," *School Library Journal*, June 12, 2018, https://www.slj.com/?detailStory=25-lgbtqai-titles-celebrate-pride.

11. livresdechevet [pseud.], review of *Sweet Blue Flowers*, vol. 1, by Takako Shimura, *More Bedside Books* (blog), accessed February 12, 2022, https://morebedsidebooks.tumblr.com /post/166815771350/sweet-blue-flowers-1-english-viz.

12. Terry Hong, review of *Sweet Blue Flowers*, vol. 1, by Takako Shimura, *BookDragon* (blog), December 22, 2017, http://smithsonianapa.org/bookdragon/sweet-blue-flowers-vol-1 -takako-shimura-translated-adapted-john-werry.

13. Melina Dargis, review of *Sweet Blue Flowers*, vol. 2, by Takako Shimura, The Fandom Post, April 11, 2018, https://www.fandompost.com/2018/04/11/sweet-blue-flowers-vol-02 -manga-review.

14. Leroy Douresseaux, review of *Sweet Blue Flowers*, vol. 2, by Takako Shimura, The Comic Book Bin, January 8, 2018, http://www.comicbookbin.com/sweetblueflowers002.html.

15. EyeSpyeAlex [Alexandra Nutting], review of *Sweet Blue Flowers*, vol. 2, by Takako Shimura, The Geekly Grind, January 5, 2018, http://www.thegeeklygrind.com/sweet-blue-flowers -part-two.

16. Erica Friedman, review of *Sweet Blue Flowers*, vol. 2, by Takako Shimura, *Okazu* (blog), January 8, 2018, http://okazu.yuricon.com/2018/01/08/yuri-manga-sweet-blue-flowers -volume-2-english.

17. Sean Gaffney, review of *Sweet Blue Flowers*, vol. 2, by Takako Shimura, *A Case Suitable for Treatment* (blog), December 22, 2017, http://suitablefortreatment.mangabookshelf.com /2017/12/22/sweet-blue-flowers-omnibus-2.

18. Melina Dargis, review of *Sweet Blue Flowers*, vol. 3, by Takako Shimura, The Fandom Post, April 11, 2018, https://www.fandompost.com/2018/12/08/sweet-blue-flowers-vol -03-manga-review.

19. EyeSpyeAlex [Alexandra Nutting], review of *Sweet Blue Flowers*, vol. 3, by Takako Shimura, The Geekly Grind, March 25, 2018, http://www.thegeeklygrind.com/sweet-blue-flowers -volume-4-review [sic].

20. Erica Friedman, review of *Sweet Blue Flowers*, vol. 3, by Takako Shimura, *Okazu* (blog), April 11, 2018, http://okazu.yuricon.com/2018/04/11/yuri-manga-sweet-blue-flowers -volume-3-english.

21. Sean Gaffney, review of *Sweet Blue Flowers*, vol. 3, by Takako Shimura, *A Case Suitable for Treatment* (blog), March 20, 2018, http://suitablefortreatment.mangabookshelf.com /2018/03/20/sweet-blue-flowers-omnibus-3.

22. EyeSpyeAlex [Alexandra Nutting], review of *Sweet Blue Flowers*, vol. 4, by Takako Shimura, The Geekly Grind, July 2, 2018, http://www.thegeeklygrind.com/sweet-blue-flowers -volume-4-review-2.

23. Erica Friedman, review of *Sweet Blue Flowers*, vol. 4.

24. Sean Gaffney, review of *Sweet Blue Flowers*, vol. 4, by Takako Shimura, *A Case Suitable for Treatment* (blog), July 3, 2018, http://suitablefortreatment.mangabookshelf.com/2018 /07/03/sweet-blue-flowers-omnibus-4.

25. Jaime, review of *Sweet Blue Flowers*, vol. 4, by Takako Shimura, *Yuri Stargirl* (blog), June 22, 2018, https://www.yuristargirl.com/2018/06/sweet-blue-flowers-aoi-hana-vol-4.html.

Bibliography

For the convenience of those without access to university libraries, I have included URLs to directly download public domain and open access books and papers, as well as other books and papers for which complete versions have been made legally available online with no paywall. For other papers, I have included DOI URLs.

Akasaka, Aka. *Kaguya-sama: Love Is War*. Translated by Emi Louie-Nishikawa. 21 vols. San Francisco: VIZ Media, 2018–.

Ando, Shuntaro, Sosei Yamaguchi, Yuta Aoki, and Graham Thornicroft. "Review of Mental-Health-Related Stigma in Japan." *Psychiatry and Clinical Neurosciences* 67, no. 7 (November 2013), 471–82. https://onlinelibrary.wiley.com/doi/10.1111/pcn.12086.

Anime Feminist. "About Us." https://www.animefeminist.com/about.

Anonymous. "What is a Plot Summary of 'The Izu dancer'?" Answers.com. Accessed November 28, 2019. https://www.answers.com/Q/What_is_a_plot_summary_of_The_Izu_dancer.

Aoki, Ei, dir. *Wandering Son*. Aniplex, 2011. https://www.crunchyroll.com/hourou-musuko-wandering-son.

Austen, Jane. *Mansfield Park*. London: 1814; Project Gutenberg, 1994. https://gutenberg.org/ebooks/141.

———. *Pride and Prejudice*. London: 1813; Project Gutenberg, 2013. https://gutenberg.org/ebooks/42671.

Bacon, Alice Mabel. *Japanese Girls and Women*. Rev. ed. Boston: Houghton Mifflin, 1919. https://archive.org/details/japanesegirlswom00baco_2.

Bauman, Nicki. *The Holy Mother of Yuri* (blog). https://yurimother.com.

———. "Yuri Is for Everyone: An Analysis of Yuri Demographics and Readership." Anime Feminist, February 12, 2020. https://www.animefeminist.com/yuri-is-for-everyone-an-analysis-of-yuri-demographics-and-readership.

Borker, Gorija. "Safety First: Perceived Risk of Street Harassment and

Educational Choices of Women." Job market paper, Department of Economics, Brown University, 2018. https://data2x.org/wp-content /uploads/2019/11/PerceivedRiskStreetHarassmentandEdChoicesof Women_Borker.pdf.

Bowers, Faubion. "Politics and Love in Japan." *New York Times*, April 14, 1963. https://archive.nytimes.com/www.nytimes.com/books/98/10 /25/specials/mishima-banquet.html.

Bridges, Rose. Review of *Sweet Blue Flowers*, vol. 1, by Takako Shimura. Anime News Network. October 20, 2017. https://www .animenewsnetwork.com/review/sweet-blue-flowers-2-in-1 -edition/gn-1/.122727.

Brown, Ash. Review of *Sweet Blue Flowers*, vol. 1. *Experiments in Manga* (blog). October 27, 2017. http://experimentsinmanga .mangabookshelf.com/2017/10/sweet-blue-flowers-omnibus-1.

Burton, Margaret E. *The Education of Women in Japan.* New York: Fleming H. Revell, 1914. https://archive.org/details/educationwomenja00 burtuoft.

Butler, Shane. "A Problem in Greek Ethics, 1867–2019: A History." John Addington Symonds Project. Accessed February 13, 2022. https:// symondsproject.org/greek-ethics-history.

Canno. *Kiss and White Lily for My Dearest Girl.* Translated by Jocelyne Allen. 10 vols. New York: Yen Press, 2013–19.

Cao, Caroline. "The Patriarchal Pains of Womanhood in the Films of Studio Ghibli's Isao Takahata." Anime Feminist. January 25, 2019. https://www.animefeminist.com/feature-the-patriarchal-pains-of -womanhood-in-the-films-of-studio-ghiblis-isao-takahata.

Carpenter, Edward. *The Intermediate Sex: A Study of Some Transitional Types of Men and Women.* London: Swan Sonnenschein, 1908. https:// archive.org/details/B20442178.

Chalmers, Sharon. *Emerging Lesbian Voices from Japan.* London: RoutledgeCurzon, 2002.

Chapman, David. "Geographies of Self and Other: Mapping Japan through the *Koseki.*" *Asia-Pacific Journal: Japan Focus* 9, no. 29 (July 19, 2011). https://apjjf.org/-David-Chapman/3565/article.pdf.

Chapman, David, and Karl Jakob Krogness, ed. *Japan's Household*

Registration System and Citizenship: Koseki, Identification, and Documentation. London: Routledge, 2014.

Charlebois, Justin. "Herbivore Masculinity as an Oppositional Form of Masculinity." *Culture, Society & Masculinities* 5, no. 1 (Spring 2013), 89–104.

Cline, Alex. Review of *Sweet Blue Flowers*, vol. 1, by Takako Shimura. Adventures in Poor Taste. October 19, 2017. http://www .adventuresinpoortaste.com/2017/10/19/sweet-blue-flowers-vol-1 -review.

Cook, Amelia. Review of *Sweet Blue Flowers*, vol. 1, by Takako Shimura. *Otaku USA*. December 9, 2017. http://www.otakuusamagazine.com /sweet-blue-flowers-review.

Dahlberg-Dodd, Hannah E. "Script Variation as Audience Design: Imagining Readership and Community in Japanese Yuri Comics." *Language in Society* 49, no. 3 (2020), 357–78. https://doi.org/10.1017 /S0047404519000794.

————. "Talking like a *Shōnen* Hero: Masculinity in Post-Bubble Era Japan through the Lens of *Boku* and *Ore*." *Buckeye East Asian Linguistics* 3 (October 2018), 31–42. https://kb.osu.edu/bitstream /handle/1811/86767/BEAL_v3_2018_Dahlberg-Dodd_31.pdf.

Dargis, Melina. Review of *Sweet Blue Flowers*, vol. 2, by Takako Shimura. The Fandom Post. April 11, 2018. https://www.fandompost.com /2018/04/11/sweet-blue-flowers-vol-02-manga-review

————. Review of *Sweet Blue Flowers*, vol. 3, by Takako Shimura. The Fandom Post. April 11, 2018. https://www.fandompost.com/2018/12 /08/sweet-blue-flowers-vol-03-manga-review.

Deacon, Chris. "All the World's a Stage: Herbivore Boys and the Performance of Masculinity in Contemporary Japan." In *Manga Girl Seeks Herbivore Boy: Studying Japanese Gender at Cambridge*, edited by Brigitte Steger and Angelika Koch, 129–76. Berlin: LIT Verlag, 2013. https://www.academia.edu/34610378/All_the_Worlds_a_Stage _Herbivore_Boys_and_the_Performance_of_Masculinity_in _Contemporary_Japan_in_Brigitte_Steger_and_Angelika_Koch_eds _Manga_Girl_Seeks_Herbivore_Boy_Studying_Japanese_Gender_at _Cambridge_LIT_Verlag_2013.

Dentsu. "First time poll categorizes straight respondents; analyzes their knowledge, awareness of LGBTQ+ matters—Most 'knowledgeable but unconcerned'; do not think LGBTQ+ issues relate to them—." April 8, 2021. https://www.dentsu.co.jp/en/news/release/2021/0408-010371.html.

Dezaki, Osamu, dir. *Dear Brother*. 1991–92; Altamonte Springs, FL: Discotek Media, 2021. Blu-ray Disc, 1080p HD.

Dollase, Hiromi Tsuchiya. *Age of Shōjo: The Emergence, Evolution, and Power of Japanese Girls' Magazine Fiction*. Albany: SUNY Press, 2019.

———. "Yoshiya Nobuko's 'Yaneura no nishojo': In Search of Literary Possibilities in 'Shōjo' Narratives." *U.S.-Japan Women's Journal*, English supplement, no. 20/21 (2001), 151–178. https://www.jstor.org/stable/42772176.

Douresseaux, Leroy. Review of *Sweet Blue Flowers*, vol. 1, by Takako Shimura. The Comic Book Bin. October 3, 2017. http://www.comicbookbin.com/sweetblueflowers001.html.

———. Review of *Sweet Blue Flowers*, vol. 2, by Takako Shimura. The Comic Book Bin. January 8, 2018. http://www.comicbookbin.com/sweetblueflowers002.html.

Duke, Benjamin. *The History of Japanese Education: Constructing the National School System, 1872–1890*. New Brunswick, NJ: Rutgers University Press, 2009.

Dumas, Alexandre. *The Three Musketeers*. Translated by Richard Pevear. New York: Penguin Books, 2007. Kindle.

Eureka, November 2017. Tokyo: Seidosha, 2017.

"Essays." Yuricon. Accessed February 14, 2022. https://www.yuricon.com/essays.

Evans, Alice. "How Did East Asia Overtake South Asia?" *The Great Gender Divergence* (blog). March 13, 2021. https://www.draliceevans.com/post/how-did-east-asia-overtake-south-asia.

EyeSpyeAlex [Alexandra Nutting]. Review of *Sweet Blue Flowers*, vol. 1, by Takako Shimura. The Geekly Grind. October 7, 2017. http://www.thegeeklygrind.com/sweet-blue-flowers-part-one.

———. Review of *Sweet Blue Flowers*, vol. 2, by Takako Shimura. The Geekly Grind. January 5, 2018. http://www.thegeeklygrind.com

/sweet-blue-flowers-part-two.

———. Review of *Sweet Blue Flowers*, vol. 3, by Takako Shimura. The Geekly Grind. March 25, 2018. http://www.thegeeklygrind.com /sweet-blue-flowers-volume-4-review [sic].

———. Review of *Sweet Blue Flowers*, vol. 4, by Takako Shimura. The Geekly Grind. July 2, 2018. http://www.thegeeklygrind.com/sweet -blue-flowers-volume-4-review-2.

Frederick, Sarah. "Not That Innocent: Nobuko Yoshiya's Good Girls." In *Bad Girls of Japan*, edited by Laura Miller and Jan Bardsley, 65–79. New York: Palgrave Macmillan, 2005.

———. Review of *Passionate Friendship: The Aesthetics of Girls' Culture in Japan*, by Deborah Shamoon. *Mechademia*, October 7, 2013. https:// www.mechademia.net/2013/10/07/book-review-passionate -friendship.

———. Translator's introduction to *Yellow Rose*, by Nokuko Yoshiya.

———. *Turning Pages: Reading and Writing Women's Magazines in Interwar Japan*. Honolulu: University of Hawai'i Press, 2006.

Freedman, Alisa. "Commuting Gazes: Schoolgirls, Salarymen, and Electric Trains in Tokyo." *Journal of Transport History* 23, no. 1 (March 2002), 23–36. https://doi.org/10.7227/TJTH.23.1.4.

Friedman, Erica. *By Your Side: The First 100 Years of Yuri Manga & Anime*. Vista, CA: Journey Press, forthcoming.

———. "Is Yuri Queer?" Anime Feminist. June 7, 2019. https://www .animefeminist.com/feature-is-yuri-queer.

———. "*Maria-sama ga miteru*: 20 Years of Watching Mary Watching Us." *Okazu* (blog). January 28, 2018. https://okazu.yuricon.com/2018/01 /28/maria-sama-ga-miteru-20-years-of-watching-mary-watching -us.

———, ed. *Okazu* (blog). https://okazu.yuricon.com.

———. "On Defining Yuri." *Transformative Works and Cultures* 24 (2017). https://journal.transformativeworks.org/index.php/twc/article /view/831/835.

———. "Overthinking Things 03/02/2011." The Hooded Utilitarian. March 2, 2011. https://www.hoodedutilitarian.com/2011/03 /overthinking-things-03022011.

———. "Overthinking Things 04/03/2011: 40 Years of the Same Damn Story, Pt. 1." The Hooded Utilitarian. April 3, 2011. https://www.hoodedutilitarian.com/2011/04/overthinking-things-04032011.

———. "Overthinking Things 05/03/2011: 40 Years of the Same Damn Story, Part 2." The Hooded Utilitarian. May 2, 2011. http://www.hoodedutilitarian.com/2011/05/21840.

———. Review of *Passionate Friendship: The Aesthetics of Girls' Culture in Japan*, by Deborah Shamoon. *Okazu* (blog). February 6, 2014. http://okazu.yuricon.com/2014/02/06/passionate-friendship-the-aesthetics-of-girls-culture-in-japan.

———. Review of *Shiroi heya no futari*, by Ryoko Yamagishi. *Okazu* (blog). June 3, 2004. https://okazu.yuricon.com/2004/06/03/yuri-manga-shiroi-heya-no-futari.

———. Review of *Sweet Blue Flowers*, disc 1. *Okazu* (blog). May 6, 2013. https://okazu.yuricon.com/2013/05/06/yuri-anime-sweet-blue-flowers-aoi-hana-disk-1-english.

———. Review of *Sweet Blue Flowers*, vol. 1, by Takako Shimura. *Okazu* (blog). October 4, 2017. http://okazu.yuricon.com/2017/10/04/yuri-manga-sweet-blue-flowers-volume-1-english.

———. Review of *Sweet Blue Flowers*, vol. 2, by Takako Shimura. *Okazu* (blog). January 8, 2018. http://okazu.yuricon.com/2018/01/08/yuri-manga-sweet-blue-flowers-volume-2-english.

———. Review of *Sweet Blue Flowers*, vol. 3, by Takako Shimura. *Okazu* (blog). April 11, 2018. http://okazu.yuricon.com/2018/04/11/yuri-manga-sweet-blue-flowers-volume-3-english.

———. Review of *Sweet Blue Flowers*, vol. 4, by Takako Shimura. *Okazu* (blog). July 9, 2018. http://okazu.yuricon.com/2018/07/09/yuri-manga-sweet-blue-flower-volume-4-english.

———. Review of *Yagate kimi ni naru*, vol. 3, by Nio Nakatani. *Okazu* (blog). January 26, 2017. https://okazu.yuricon.com/2017/01/26/yuri-manga-yagate-kimi-ni-naru-volume-3-%e3%82%84%e3%81%8c%e3%81%a6%e5%90%9b%e3%81%ab%e3%81%aa%e3%82%8b.

———. Review of *Yaneura no nishojo*, by Nobuko Yoshiya. *Okazu* (blog). May 10, 2010. https://okazu.yuricon.com/2010/05/09/yuri-novel-yaneura-no-nishojo.

———. "Why We Call It 'Yuri.'" Anime Feminist. August 9, 2017. https://www.animefeminist.com/history-why-call-yuri.

———. "Yuri, 1919–2019, from Then to Now." Anime Herald. February 6, 2019. https://www.animeherald.com/2019/02/06/yuri-1919-2019-from-then-to-now.

Fruchterman, Thomas M. J., and Edward M. Reingold. "Graph Drawing by Force-Directed Placement." *Software: Practice and Experience* 21, no. 11 (November 1991), 1129–64. https://doi.org/10.1002/spe.4380211102.

Fujimoto, Yukari. "Where Is My Place in the World? Early Shōjo Manga Portrayals of Lesbianism." Translated by Lucy Frazier. *Mechademia* 9 (2014), 25–42. https://doi.org/10.5749/mech.9.2014.0025.

Gaffney, Sean. Review of *Sweet Blue Flowers*, vol. 1, by Takako Shimura. *A Case Suitable for Treatment* (blog). September 30, 2017. http://suitablefortreatment.mangabookshelf.com/2017/09/30/sweet-blue-flowers-omnibus-1.

———. Review of *Sweet Blue Flowers*, vol. 2, by Takako Shimura. *A Case Suitable for Treatment* (blog). December 22, 2017. http://suitablefortreatment.mangabookshelf.com/2017/12/22/sweet-blue-flowers-omnibus-2.

———. Review of *Sweet Blue Flowers*, vol. 3, by Takako Shimura. *A Case Suitable for Treatment* (blog). March 20, 2018. http://suitablefortreatment.mangabookshelf.com/2018/03/20/sweet-blue-flowers-omnibus-3.

———. Review of *Sweet Blue Flowers*, vol. 4, by Takako Shimura. *A Case Suitable for Treatment* (blog). July 3, 2018. http://suitablefortreatment.mangabookshelf.com/2018/07/03/sweet-blue-flowers-omnibus-4.

Ghaznavi, Cyrus, Haruka Sakamoto, Shuhei Nomura, Anna Kubota, Daisuke Yoneoka, Kenji Shibuya, and Peter Ueda. "The Herbivore's Dilemma: Trends in and Factors Associated with Heterosexual Relationship Status and Interest in Romantic Relationships among Young Adults in Japan—Analysis of National Surveys, 1987–2015." *PLoS ONE* 15(11): e0241571. https://journals.plos.org/plosone/article?id=10.1371/journal.pone.0241571.

Goldstein-Gidoni, Ofra. *Packaged Japaneseness: Weddings, Business, and*

Brides. Honolulu: University of Hawaiʻi Press, 1997.

Gosho, Heinosuke, dir. *The Dancing Girl of Izu*. Shochiku, 1933. 1 hr., 32 min. https://www.youtube.com/watch?v=yd36RJ0nzdM.

Hagio, Moto. *The Heart of Thomas*. Translated by Rachel Thorn. Seattle: Fantagraphics Books, 2012.

Harano, Mami. "Anatomy of Mishima's Most Successful Play *Rokumeikan*." Master's thesis, Portland State University, 2010. https://pdxscholar.library.pdx.edu/cgi/viewcontent.cgi?article =1386&context=open_access_etds.

Hazuki, Ruri. *Saturday: Introduction*. Gardena, CA: Lilyka, 2019.

Hecker, Frank. "Relative Prominence of Characters and Their Relationships in Takako Shimura's *Sweet Blue Flowers*." RPubs.com. March 7, 2022. https://rpubs.com/frankhecker/874648.

Helen. Review of *Sweet Blue Flowers*, vol. 1, by Takako Shimura. TheOASG. December 7, 2017. https://www.theoasg.com/reviews/manga/sweet -blue-flowers-volume-1-review.

Hiener, Teresa A. "Shinto Wedding, Samurai Bride: Inventing Tradition and Fashioning Identity in the Rituals of Bridal Dress in Japan." PhD diss., University of Pittsburgh, 1997.

Hiramori, Daiki, and Saori Kamano. "Asking about Sexual Orientation and Gender Identity in Social Surveys in Japan: Findings from the Osaka City Residents' Survey and Related Preparatory Studies." *Journal of Population Problems* 76, no. 4 (December 2020), 443–66. http://www .ipss.go.jp/syoushika/bunken/data/pdf/20760402.pdf.

Hodgin, Chuck. Review of *Sweet Blue Flowers*, vol. 1, by Takako Shimura. In "25 LGBTQAI+ Titles for Pride Month—and Onward," by Kent Turner. *School Library Journal*. June 12, 2018. https://www.slj.com/ ?detailStory=25-lgbtqai-titles-celebrate-pride.

Hong, Terry. Review of *Sweet Blue Flowers*, vol. 1, by Takako Shimura. *BookDragon* (blog). December 22, 2017. http://smithsonianapa.org /bookdragon/sweet-blue-flowers-vol-1-takako-shimura-translated -adapted-john-werry.

Horii, Mitsutoshi and Adam Burgess. "Constructing Sexual Risk: 'Chikan,' Collapsing Male Authority and the Emergence of Women-Only Train Carriages in Japan." *Health, Risk & Society* 14, no. 1 (2012), 41–55.

https://doi.org/10.1080/13698575.2011.641523.

Ikeda, Riyoko. *Rose of Versailles*. Translated by Mori Morimoto. 5 vols. Richmond Hill, ON: Udon Entertainment, 2019–21.

Ikuhara, Kunihiko, dir. *Revolutionary Girl Utena*. 1997; Grimes, IA: Nozomi Entertainment, 2017. Blu-ray Disc, 1080p HD.

Iruma, Hitoma. *Bloom Into You: Regarding Saeki Sayaka*. Translated by Jan Cash and Vincent Castenada. 3 vols. Los Angeles: Seven Seas Entertainment, 2019–20.

Jaime. Review of *Sweet Blue Flowers*, vol. 4, by Takako Shimura. *Yuri Stargirl* (blog). June 22, 2018. https://www.yuristargirl.com/2018/06/sweet -blue-flowers-aoi-hana-vol-4.html.

Jansen, Marius B. *The Making of Modern Japan*. Cambridge, MA: Belknap Press, 2002.

Kakefuda, Hiroko. *On Being a "Lesbian" ("Rezubian" de aru to iu koto)*. Translated by Indiana Scarlet Brown. In "A Translation and Analysis of Japan's Seminal Lesbian Studies Work," 45–202. Masters thesis, University at Albany, State University of New York, 2018. https:// scholarsarchive.library.albany.edu/honorscollege_eas/3.

Kálovics, Dalma. "The Missing Link of Shōjo Manga History: The Changes in 60s Shōjo Manga as Seen Through the Magazine *Shūkan Margaret*." *Journal of Kyoto Seika University* 49 (2016), 3–22. https:// www.academia.edu/36310321/The_missing_link_of_sh%C5%8Djo _manga_history_the_changes_in_60s_sh%C5%8Djo_manga_as _seen_through_the_magazine_Sh%C5%ABkan_Margaret.

Kamano, Saori. "Entering the Lesbian World in Japan: Debut Stories." *Journal of Lesbian Studies* 9, no. 1/2 (2005), 11–30. https://doi.org/10 .1300/J155v09n01_02.

Kamatani, Yuhki. *Our Dreams at Dusk: Shimanami Tasogare*. Translated by Jocelyne Allen. 4 vols. Los Angeles: Seven Seas Entertainment, 2019.

Karlin, Jason G. *Gender and Nation in Meiji Japan: Modernity, Loss, and the Doing of History*. Honolulu: University of Hawai'i Press, 2014. https:// www.academia.edu/42197271/Gender_and_Nation_in_Meiji_Japan _Modernity_Loss_and_the_Doing_of_History.

Kasai, Kenichi, dir. *Sweet Blue Flowers*. 2009; Grimes, IA: Lucky Penny Entertainment, 2013. DVD.

Katai, Tayama. "The Girl Watcher." In *The Quilt and Other Stories by Tayama Katai*. Translated by Kenneth G. Henshall. Tokyo: University of Tokyo Press, 1981.

Kawabata, Yasunari. "The Dancing Girl of Izu." In *The Dancing Girl of Izu, and Other Stories*, 3–33. Translated by J. Martin Holman. Washington, DC: Counterpoint, 1998.

———. "The Izu Dancer." Translated by Edward Seidensticker. In *The Izu Dancer, and Other Stories*. Yasunari Kawabata and Yasushi Inoue. Translated by Edward Seidensticker and Leon Picon. Tokyo: Tuttle, 2011. Kindle.

Kawahara, Kazune. *My Love Story!!*. Vol. 1. Translated by Ysabet Reinhardt MacFarlane and JN Productions. San Francisco: Viz Media, 2014.

Kawai, Michi. *My Lantern*. 3rd ed. Tokyo: privately published, 1949.

Kimino, Sakurako. *Strawberry Panic*. Translated by Michelle Kobayashi and Anastasia Moreno. 3 vols. Los Angeles: Seven Seas Entertainment, 2008.

Kodama, Naoko. *I Married My Best Friend to Shut My Parents Up*. Translated by Amber Tamosaitis. Los Angeles: Seven Seas Entertainment, 2019.

Komori, Yuri. "Trends in Japanese First Names in the Twentieth Century: A Comparative Study." *International Christian University Publications 3-A, Asian Cultural Studies* 28 (2002), 67–82. https://icu.repo.nii.ac .jp/?action=repository_action_common_download&item_id=1637 &item_no=1&attribute_id=18&file_no=1.

Konayama, Kata. *Love Me for Who I Am*. Vol. 3. Translated by Amber Tamosaitis. Los Angeles: Seven Seas Entertainment, 2021.

Kuni, Akiko. *Unexpected Destinations: The Poignant Story of Japan's First Vassar Graduate*. Translated by Kirsten McIvor. Tokyo: Kodansha International, 1993.

Kurosawa, Akira, dir. *The Most Beautiful*. 1944; in *Eclipse Series 23: The First Films of Akira Kurosawa (Sanshiro Sugata / The Most Beautiful / Sanshiro Sugata, Part Two / The Men Who Tread on the Tiger's Tail)*; New York: Criterion Collection, 2010. 1 hr., 25 min. DVD.

kyuuketsukirui [pseud.]. "Don't Want to Know What I'll Be without You." Archive of Our Own. April 29, 2011. https://archiveofourown.org /works/202164.

"List of Manga Series by Volume Count." Wikipedia. Last modified January 31, 2022. https://en.wikipedia.org/wiki/List_of_manga _series_by_volume_count.

livresdechevet [pseud.]. Review of *Sweet Blue Flowers*, vol. 1, by Takako Shimura. *More Bedside Books* (blog). Accessed February 12, 2022. https://morebedsidebooks.tumblr.com/post/166815771350/sweet -blue-flowers-1-english-viz.

McLelland, Mark. *Love, Sex, and Democracy in Japan during the American Occupation*. New York: Palgrave Macmillan, 2012. Kindle.

———. *Queer Japan from the Pacific War to the Internet Age*. Lanham, MD: Rowman & Littlefield, 2005. Kindle.

McClelland, Mark, Katsuhiko Suganuma, and James Welker, eds. *Queer Voices from Japan: First-Person Narratives from Japan's Sexual Minorities*. Lanham, MD: Lexington Books, 2007.

Mackie, Vera. "Birth Registration and the Right to Have Rights: The Changing Family and the Unchanging *Koseki*." In Chapman and Krogness, *Japan's Household Registration System and Citizenship*, 203–17.

Maree, Claire. "Sexual Citizenship at the Intersections of Patriarchy and Heteronormativity: Same-Sex Partnerships and the *Koseki*." In Chapman and Krogness, *Japan's Household Registration System and Citizenship*, 187–202.

Mars-Jones, Adam. *Noriko Smiling*. London: Notting Hill Editions, 2011.

Maser, Verena. "Beautiful and Innocent: Female Same-Sex Intimacy in the Japanese Yuri Genre." PhD diss., Universität Trier, 2015. https://ubt .opus.hbz-nrw.de/frontdoor/index/index/docId/695.

Matsushita, Yukihiro and Toshiyuki Kato, dir. *Maria Watches Over Us*. 2004–9; Houston: Sentai Filmworks, 2020. Blu-ray Disc, 1080p HD.

Miman. *Yuri Is My Job!*. Translated by Diana Taylor. 8 vols. New York: Kodansha, 2016–.

Ministry of Education, Culture, Sports, Science, and Technology. "Overview." MEXT website. Accessed January 2, 2022. https://www .mext.go.jp/en/policy/education/overview/index.htm.

Mishima, Yukio. "The Rokumeikan: A Tragedy in Four Acts." In *My Friend Hitler, and Other Plays of Yukio Mishima*, 4–54. Translated by Hiroaki

Sato. New York: Columbia University Press, 2002.

Morinaga, Milk. *Girl Friends*. Vol. 5. Translated by Anastasia Moreno. Los Angeles: Seven Seas Entertainment, 2017.

———. *Hana & Hina After School*. Vol. 3. Translated by Jennifer McKeon. Los Angeles: Seven Seas Entertainment, 2017.

Morishima, Akiko. *The Conditions of Paradise*. Translated by Elina Ishikawa-Curran. Los Angeles: Seven Seas Entertainment, 2020.

Morris, Mark. "Orphans." Review of *The Dancing Girl of Izu, and Other Stories*, by Yasunari Kawabata. *New York Times*, October 12, 1997. https://archive.nytimes.com/www.nytimes.com/books/97/10/12 /reviews/971012.12morrist.html.

Nagata, Kabi. *My Lesbian Experience with Loneliness*. Translated by Jocelyne Allen. Los Angeles, Seven Seas Entertainment, 2017.

Nakatani, Nio. *Bloom Into You*. Translated by Jenni McKeon. 8 vols. Los Angeles: Seven Seas Entertainment, 2017–20.

National Institute of Population and Social Security Research. "Marriage Process and Fertility of Japanese Married Couples / Attitudes toward Marriage and Family among Japanese Singles: Highlights of the Survey Results on Married Couples/ Singles." Tokyo: National Institute of Population and Social Security Research, 2017. http:// www.ipss.go.jp/ps-doukou/e/doukou15/Nfs15R_points_eng.pdf.

Nimura, Janice P. *Daughters of the Samurai: A Journey from East to West and Back*. New York: W. W. Norton, 2015. Kindle.

Ninomiya, Shūhei. "The *Koseki* and Legal Gender Change." Translated by Karl Jakob Krogness. In Chapman and Krogness, *Japan's Household Registration System and Citizenship*, 169–86.

Novalis. *Henry of Ofterdingen: A Romance*. Translated by John Owen. Cambridge, MA: Cambridge Press, 1842; Project Gutenberg, 2013. https://gutenberg.org/ebooks/31873.

Ozu, Yasujirō, dir. *Equinox Flower*. 1958; in *Eclipse Series 3: Late Ozu (Early Spring / Tokyo Twilight / Equinox Flower / Late Autumn / The End of Summer)*; New York: Criterion Collection, 2007. 1 hr., 58 min. DVD.

———. dir. *Late Autumn*. 1958; in *Eclipse Series 3: Late Ozu (Early Spring / Tokyo Twilight / Equinox Flower / Late Autumn / The End of Summer)*; New York: Criterion Collection, 2007. 2 hr., 8 min. DVD.

————. dir. *Late Spring*. 1949; New York: Criterion Collection, 2012. 1 hr., 48 min. Blu-ray Disc, 1080p HD.

Pflugfelder, Gregory M. "'S' Is for Sister: School Girl Intimacy and 'Same-Sex Love' in Early Twentieth-Century Japan." In *Gendering Modern Japanese History*, edited by Barbara Monoly and Kathleen Uno, 133–90. Cambridge, MA: Harvard University Asia Center, 2005. https://doi.org/10.1163/9781684174171_006.

Prang, Margaret. *A Heart at Leisure from Itself: Caroline Macdonald of Japan*. Vancouver: UBC Press, 1995.

"Private School Costs Triple Public Education Level through High School." Nippon.com. October 4, 2018. https://www.nippon.com/en/features/h00299.

Prough, Jennifer S. *Straight from the Heart: Gender, Intimacy, and the Cultural Production of Shōjo Manga*. Honolulu: University of Hawai'i Press, 2011.

Pseudoerasmus [pseud.]. "Labour Repression and the Indo-Japanese Divergence." *Pseudoerasmus* (blog). October 2, 2017. https://pseudoerasmus.com/2017/10/02/ijd.

Quinn, Josephine Crawley and Christopher Brooke. "'Affection in Education': Edward Carpenter, John Addington Symonds, and the Politics of Greek Love." In *Ideas of Education: Philosophy and Politics from Plato to Dewey*, edited by Christopher Brooke and Elizabeth Frazer, 252–66. London: Routledge, 2013.

Rich, Adrienne. "Twenty-One Love Poems." In *The Dream of a Common Language: Poems 1974–1977*. New York: W. W. Norton, 1978. https://archive.org/details/dreamofcommonlan0000rich.

Robertson, Jennifer. "The Politics of Androgyny in Japan: Sexuality and Subversion in the Theater and Beyond." *American Ethnologist* 19, no. 3 (August 1992), 419–42. https://doi.org/10.1525/ae.1992.19.3.02a00010.

————. "Yoshiya Nobuko: Out and Outspoken in Practice and Prose." In *Same-Sex Cultures and Sexualities: An Anthropological Reader*, edited by Jennifer Robertson, 196–211. Malden, MA: Blackwell Publishing, 2005. https://doi.org/10.1002/9780470775981.ch11.

Satō, Takuya, dir. *Happy-Go-Lucky Days*. 2020; Houston: Sentai

Filmworks, 2021. 55 min. Blu-ray Disc, 1080p HD.

Shamoon, Deborah. "Class S: Appropriation of 'Lesbian' Subculture in Modern Japanese Literature and New Wave Cinema." *Cultural Studies* 35, no. 1, 27–43. https://doi.org/10.2307/2527277.

———. *Passionate Friendship: The Aesthetics of Girls' Culture in Japan.* Honolulu: University of Hawai'i Press, 2012.

Shimura, Takako. *Aoi hana.* 8 vols. Tokyo: Ohta Books, 2006–13.

———. *Awashima hyakkei.* 3 vols. Tokyo: Ōta Shuppan, 2015–.

———. *Even Though We're Adults.* Translated by Jocelyne Allen. 3 vols. Los Angeles: Seven Seas Entertainment, 2021–.

———. *Fleurs bleues.* Translated by Satoko Inaba and Margot Maillac. 8 vols. Paris: Kazé, 2009–15.

———. *Flores azules.* Translated by Ayako Koike. 8 vols. Colombres, Spain: Milky Way Ediciones, 2015–16.

———. *Happy-Go-Lucky Days.* Translated by RReese. 2 vols. Gardena, CA: Digital Manga Guild, 2013. Kindle.

———. *Sweet Blue Flowers.* Translated by John Werry. 4 vols. San Francisco: VIZ Media, 2017–18.

———. *Sweet Blue Flowers.* Translated by Jeffrey Steven LeCroy. Vol. 1. Gardena, CA: Digital Manga, 2014. Kindle.

———. *Wandering Son.* Translated by Rachel Thorn. 8 vols. Seattle: Fantagraphics Books, 2011–.

Sugimoto, Yoshio. *An Introduction to Japanese Society.* 5th ed. Cambridge: Cambridge University Press, 2020.

Suzuki, Michiko. *Becoming Modern Women: Love and Female Identity in Prewar Japanese Literature and Culture.* Palo Alto: Stanford University Press, 2009.

———. "The Translation of Edward Carpenter's *Intermediate Sex* in Early Twentieth-Century Japan." In *Sexology and Translation: Cultural and Scientific Encounters Across the Modern World,* edited by Heike Bauer, 197–215. Philadelphia: Temple University Press, 2015.

Symonds, John Addington. *A Problem in Greek Ethics, being an Inquiry into the Phenomenon of Sexual Inversion, addressed especially to medical psychologists and jurists.* London: privately published, 1901. https://archive.org/details/cu31924021844950.

————. *Letters of John Addington Symonds.* Vol. 3, *1885–1893.* Edited by Herbert M. Schueller and Robert L. Peters. Detroit: Wayne State University Press, 1969. https://archive.org/details/lettersofjohnadd 0003symo.

Takeuchi, Naoko. *Pretty Guardian: Sailor Moon.* Translated by William Flanagan. 12 vols. New York: Kodansha, 2011–13.

Takashima, Hiromi. *Kase-san and Morning Glories.* Translated by Jocelyne Allen. Los Angeles: Seven Seas Entertainment, 2017.

————. *Kase-san and Yamada.* Translated by Jocelyne Allen. 2 vols. Los Angeles: Seven Seas Entertainment, 2020–.

Takashima, Rica. *Tokyo Love ~ Rica 'tte Kan ji!?* Translated by Erin Subramanian and Erica Friedman. ALC Publishing, 2013. Kindle.

Thorn, Rachel. "Snips and Snails, Sugar and Spice: A Guide to Japanese Honorifics as Used in *Wandering Son.*" In Shimura, *Wandering Son,* 1:ii–iv.

Trainor, Joseph C. *Educational Reform in Occupied Japan: Trainor's Memoir.* Tokyo: Meisei University Press, 1983.

Tsubaki, Izumi. *Monthly Girls' Nozaki-kun.* Translated by Leighann Harvey. 12 vols. New York: Yen Press, 2015–.

Tsurumi, E. Patricia. *Factory Girls: Women in the Thread Mills of Meiji Japan.* Princeton, NJ: Princeton University Press, 1990.

————. "Yet to Be Heard: The Voices of Meiji Factory Women." *Bulletin of Concerned Asian Scholars* 26, no. 4, 18–27. https://doi.org/10.1080 /14672715.1994.10416166.

Van Hecken, Joseph L. *The Catholic Church in Japan Since 1859.* Translated by John Van Hoydonck. Tokyo: Herder Agency, 1960. https://archive .org/details/catholicchurchin0000heck.

Welker, James. "From Women's Liberation to Lesbian Feminism in Japan: *Rezubian Feminizumu* within and beyond the *Ūman Ribu* Movement in the 1970s and 1980s." In *Rethinking Japanese Feminisms,* edited by Julia C. Bullock, Ayako Kano, and James Welker, 50–67. Honolulu: University of Hawai'i Press, 2018. https://www.jstor.org/stable/j .ctv3zp07j.

White, Linda E. "Challenging the Heteronormative Family in the *Koseki:* Surname, Legitimacy, and Unmarried Mothers." In Chapman and

Krogness, *Japan's Household Registration System and Citizenship*, 239–56.

Wikimedia Foundation. "Category:Literature Museum of Kamakura." Wikimedia Commons. Updated June 23, 2018. https://commons .wikimedia.org/wiki/Category:Literature_Museum,_Kamakura.

Yamada, Kana. "Now with a Legal Father, Saitama Man, 36, Ready to Start Own Life." *Asahi Shimbun*, February 21, 2018. https://web.archive.org /web/20180222034739/http://www.asahi.com/ajw/articles /AJ201802210043.html.

Yoshiya, Nobuko. *Hana monogatari.* 2 vols. Tokyo: Kawade Shobō Shinsha, 2009.

———. *Yaneura no nishojo.* Tokyo: Kokusho Kankōkai, 2003.

———. *Yellow Rose.* 2nd ed. Translated by Sarah Frederick. Los Angeles: Expanded Editions, 2016. Kindle.

About the Author

The author's interest in things Japanese was sparked by a business trip he took to Japan many years ago—a trip that coincidentally saw him spend two weeks near the future settings of *Sweet Blue Flowers*. His interest in manga and anime is much more recent.

He has not written, nor does he plan to write, any other books about manga, anime, or Japanese popular culture in general. You can find his articles on other topics at frankhecker.com or follow him on Twitter at @hecker. You can contact him via email at frank@frankhecker.com.

Colophon

This book was created using the Electric Book workflow[1] operating on a set of plain text source files written in the kramdown variant of the Markdown formatting language.[2]

The text for the PDF and print versions is set in a combination of CrimsonPro[3] for body text and Source Sans Pro[4] for display text. The text for the cover is set in Sorts Mill Goudy[5] and Libre Franklin.[6]

The cover image was created from an original illustration by Ola Tarakanova,[7] using the Pixelmator Pro image processing software.[8]

The Markdown files for the book's text are available in the public repository https://gitlab.com/frankhecker/that-type-of-girl, along with instructions and other files needed to create the book's PDF and EPUB output files. Please submit suggested corrections as issues against the repository or via email to the author.

1. "The Electric Book workflow," Electric Book Works, accessed March 21, 2020, https://electricbookworks.github.io/electric-book/index.html.
2. "kramdown," Thomas Leitner, updated January 2019, https://kramdown.gettalong.org.
3. "CrimsonPro," Jacques Le Bailly, Sebastian Kosch, et al., accessed May 19, 2020, https://github.com/Fonthausen/CrimsonPro.
4. "Source Sans Pro," Adobe, accessed April 25, 2020, https://github.com/adobe-fonts/source-sans-pro.
5. Barry Schwarz, "Sorts Mill Goudy," Google Fonts, accessed December 7, 2021, https://fonts.google.com/specimen/Sorts+Mill+Goudy.
6. Impallari Type, "Libre Franklin," Google Fonts, accessed December 7, 2021, https://fonts.google.com/specimen/Libre+Franklin.
7. Ola Tarakanova, "Watercolor Blue Flowers Stock Illustration," iStock by Getty Images, accessed December 24, 2021, https://www.istockphoto.com/vector/watercolor-blue-flowers-gm1148509305-310182255.
8. "Pixelmator Pro," Pixelmator Team, accessed December 7, 2021, https://www.pixelmator.com/pro.